Kitted Out

Kitted Out

STYLE AND YOUTH CULTURE
IN THE SECOND WORLD WAR

CAROLINE YOUNG

First published 2020

The History Press
97 St George's Place, Cheltenham,
Gloucestershire, GL50 3QB
www.thehistorypress.co.uk

British Library Cataloguing in Publication Data.
A catalogue record for this book is available from the British Library.

ISBN 978 0 7509 9217 6

Typesetting and origination by The History Press
Printed and bound in Great Britain by TJ International Ltd.

Contents

1

Debutantes, Blackshirts and Life Before the War

When Britain declared war on Germany on 3 September 1939, *The Wizard of Oz* had just been released in the United States, and the Bette Davis melodrama *Dark Victory* had brought audiences to tears in the UK over the summer. British youths in the 1930s dressed as if they were in an American gangster movie or a Hollywood romance, smoked cigarettes and bought make-up, waltzed at town hall dances, sang 'Run Rabbit Run' in unison in the cinema or on buses, and played Judy Garland's 'Somewhere Over the Rainbow' on the gramophone, the most popular song of that year.

Young people born during or just after the First World War were the ones who were expected to put on a uniform for a new global conflict. They resented the older generation who were taking them on this path, yet they knew that when the time came, they would do their duty and take up arms with the clear goal of defeating Hitler. By the end of the decade, towns across Britain were awash in a sea of khaki and blue serge as men and women enlisted in the armed forces, and difference of dress had become eclipsed by uniformity.

The 1930s was a decade marked by tribalism; whether one was a blackshirt or a communist, a pacifist or a patriot. When war broke out, uniforms, and a love of jazz and movies, became an equaliser; but still, even in wartime, hierarchies were forged, and young people continued to express their individuality despite the army regulations.

In some respects, the thirties were optimistic times, as towns were transformed by the bright lights of entertainment venues, households bought radios and motor cars, and new suburbs sprung up in the countryside to ease the pressures of overcrowding in cities. There were also increased rights for workers, resulting in more leisure time. However, tensions grew across Europe during this decade as fascism and populist movements seemed to offer alternative answers to the problems caused by the Great Depression.

During the period between the two world wars, from 1918 to 1939, huge economic and social changes directly impacted on youth culture. The twenties was a decade famed as the 'Jazz Age', a time when women found new freedoms of expression; where they could drink, smoke and go on unchaperoned dates to the cinema or in a motor car. The end of the Great War brought a mini-boom of low unemployment and high wages, and those who had fought, known as the 'lost generation', lived to forget the trauma. However, their shocking and debilitating injuries were all too evident.

The Wall Street Crash of 1929 triggered a global recession, and in the UK in January 1930 over 1.5 million people were out of work. By December of that year, unemployment figures had risen to 2.5 million. Britain did not suffer as greatly as Germany, but the slump was still evident, particularly in areas that were reliant on heavy industry, such as northern England and Wales.

The motivation of the twenties had been pleasure, with elite young people like the 'Bright Young Things' behaving outrageously with their fancy-dress parties. But by the 1930s, the focus had fallen onto the disadvantages of youth. A sociologist, W.F. Lestrange, travelled across England and Wales to demonstrate how the state was squandering the lives of millions of youngsters, and he published his findings in his book, *Wasted Lives*.

In 1935, 80 per cent of boys and 81 per cent of girls went straight into work from school, with the majority leaving at the age of 14. They were hired as delivery boys, shop workers and lift-boys, and Lestrange called them 'blind-alley children' as there was little chance of their progressing on to something else.

Lestrange met a 19-year-old called Joe at a boys' club in London, who was thrilled at receiving a 10s a week raise, because he could now buy an outfit to impress the girl he was 'nuts' about. Yet, the 1931 Means Test meant that Joe's father lost public assistance money due to the extra family income, and Joe had to support his family with his wages. 'Fat chance I'll have of ever getting spliced with a ready-made family to look after,' he said. With no money for leisure time or for hobbies, Lestrange reported the 'hideous boredom' of youth unemployment and 'the lounging listless groups of youths at the street-corner encouraged by friends, "Let's knock off a car and get out and have a bit of fun"'.

Work opportunities for young women during the interwar years were limited. Domestic service accounted for 30 per cent of girls' work, while more than 40 per cent were employed in low-skilled factory work. By 1939, 7,600 girls were employed at J. Lyons and Co.'s tea rooms across Britain, as 'Nippies'. These waitresses wore a distinctive white headdress, black buttoned-down dress, and white collar and cuffs. They were provided with two meals a day and had special opportunities for a social life and recreation, with many getting married to fellow employees. *Picture Post* wrote of the typical Nippy, 'She is young, enthusiastic, hard-working, attractive … They are selected on deportment, condition of hands, and a variety of other qualifications.'

American culture seeped into Britain with Woolworths stores, dance halls, cafés, cocktail bars and, of course, Hollywood cinema. Bored young men terrorised the cinemas and dance halls dressed in the American gangster style of Oxford bags, winkle pickers and bowler hats – they were the pre-war Teddy Boys, who emulated James Cagney or other tough guys on the screen. Movie theatres offered a cheap form of entertainment in the midst of unemployment, and with the advent of mass-produced clothing it was easier than ever for working-class people to choose how to dress.

George Orwell, in *The Road to Wigan Pier*, illustrated how the magic of the movies in the thirties allowed for escapism. He wrote:

> The youth who leaves school at fourteen and gets a blind-alley job is out of work at twenty, probably for life; but for two pounds ten on the hire-purchase system he can buy himself a suit which, for a little while and at a little distance, looks as though it had been tailored in Savile Row. The girl can look like a fashion plate at an even lower price. You may have three half-pence in your pocket and not a prospect in the world, and only the corner of a leaky bedroom to go home to; but in your new clothes you can stand on the street corner, indulging in a private daydream of yourself as Clark Gable or Greta Garbo, which compensates you for a great deal.

It's often reported that the consumption of cheap luxuries often surges during times of depression, with lipstick and nail polish becoming a way to buy a small moment of happiness. As Orwell noted in 1936:

> A luxury is nowadays almost always cheaper than a necessity. One pair of plain solid shoes costs as much as two ultra-smart pairs. For the price of one square meal you can get two pounds of cheap sweets. You can't get much meat for threepence, but you can get a lot of fish and chips …

The glamour of the silver screen also shaped how young women dressed. The twenties had seen a revolution in female fashions. Corsets were loosened, hems raised and waists lowered, and hair was bobbed and shingled. This 'flapper' look answered the call for increased freedom of movement. The Depression led to a return to the feminine, with floor-skimming, luxurious gowns and waved hair that came straight from the pages of *Film Weekly*. It was a romantic look that offered a nod to the prosperous pre-war Edwardian era.

British youth often suffered from poor health, whether through smoking, diet or childhood illness. A 1937 Mass Observation study found that 56 per cent of male smokers started before they were 14, while 58 per cent of women began smoking between 15 and 21. With such behaviours inspired by film stars and royalty, men who didn't smoke were treated suspiciously.

Joining the army could be one option for the unemployed, but up to 45 per cent of young men failed the medical tests as they were unfit and undernourished. Unfortunately, it was these boys who would eventually be expected to be booted up and trained to battle Germany at the outbreak of war. George Orwell bluntly wrote in *The Road to Wigan Pier*, 'If the English physique has declined, this is no doubt partly due to the fact that the Great War carefully selected the million best men in England and slaughtered them, largely before they had had time to breed'.

Young people in the 1930s were political, speaking out against the older generation who appeared to be leading the country into another war, and choosing the extreme right or the extreme left as representatives of their idealism. At Oxford and Cambridge universities, pacifism and communism became increasingly popular. Strong anti-war beliefs led to what became known as the 'Oxford Pledge', when in 1933 the Oxford Union vowed that 'under no circumstances will we fight for King and Country'. It was a cry of youth, and many across Britain strongly agreed.

As a handsome Oxford University student at Trinity College from 1938, Battle of Britain pilot Richard Hillary considered being a conscientious objector, as he, like his friends, believed war only led young men to their deaths. In his 1942 memoir, *The Last Enemy*, he wrote, 'We were held together by a common taste in friends, sport, literature, and idle amusement, by a deep-rooted distrust of all organised emotion and standardised patriotism, and by a somewhat self-conscious satisfaction in our ability to succeed without apparent effort.'

He and his friends were members of both the university rowing team and the University Air Squadron, which had been formed between the wars to create a reserve of trained officer pilots. With youthful arrogance, they called themselves 'the long-haired boys', for their rebellious image and attitude. But as war grew closer, it was inevitable they would do what was expected. He wrote, 'We were cliquey, extremely limited in our horizon, quite conscious of the fact, and in no way dissatisfied about it. We knew that war was imminent.

There was nothing we could do about it. We were depressed by a sense of its inevitability, but we were not patriotic.' Richard and all his Oxford University friends who joined the RAF were killed in the war, demonstrating the sheer devastation of the young students of the thirties.

With mass unemployment came anger and resentment at the government, and the need to find a scapegoat. Fascism was an attractive prospect through its supposed promotion of family values and patriotism. Oswald Mosley, a former minister in Ramsay MacDonald's Labour Government, set up the British Union of Fascists (BUF) in 1932. Tall and dashing, with a severe moustache and his dark hair parted down the middle, as was the fashion of his public school, Winchester College, Mosley was often described as a 'Savile Row Fascist'. He was at Sandhurst when war broke out in August 1914, keen not to miss 'the adventure of a lifetime', and as he later recalled, 'never had men appeared more eager to be killed'.

Mosley spoke for the 'Trench Generation' and had at first championed socialism. A conservative MP at the age of 22, he switched to the Labour Party as he believed in housing, health and child welfare for all. After being deeply inspired by Mussolini's blackshirts, he founded the BUF to promote a 'Britain First' policy.

Mosley, like Mussolini and Adolph Hitler, believed it was the youth who held the key to revolution, embracing aviation as the future and promoting the importance of agriculture and a return to the soil. In his biography of Hitler, Wyndham Lewis defined Nazism as 'a hatred of parliamentary and bourgeois democracy, a horror of money and finance and a cult of youth'.

Under the Nazis, the future was the *Sonnenkind*, or the 'Sun Children', who were bronzed and strong and devoted to the Fatherland. They were nurtured at youth camps, where indoctrination took place under the guise of camping and hiking expeditions. There were 50,000 members of the Hitler Youth at the beginning of 1933, and by the end of the year there were over 2 million. This number grew as other groups such as the Boy Scouts were banned.

Mosley was influenced by the Nazis to establish the Biff Boys, the youth wing of the BUF. Many of those who signed up felt disenfranchised, angry at the older politicians, and had lost fathers in the First World War. According to Mosley, the BUF aimed to appeal to the 'little people, the shopkeepers, clerks who wore a white collar under their black coats' – the class 'most threatened by the economic crisis because they were not organised as were the blue-collar workers'.

The black BUF uniform, launched in October 1932, was a symbol of posturing masculinity, taking inspiration from the Italian blackshirts and Mosley's own black silk fencing tunic, with the button fastened on one shoulder. Their heavy jackboots menacingly clomped in unison. Mosley saw fencing as chivalric and potently masculine, envisioning himself as an 'Elizabeth swashbuckler' in his clinging outfit. And when Mosley described his concept of his 'Storm Troops', Prime Minister Harold Macmillan told him, 'You must be mad. Whenever the British feel strongly about anything, they wear grey flannel trousers and tweed jackets.'

Mosley adopted the Fascist symbols of the bundle of sticks and the axe, representing unity and the power of the State, but it was perhaps too much for the British population. He was told by Harold Nicolson, 'If we ever have fascism in this country, it will creep in disguised in the red, white and blue of patriotism and the young conservatives'.

Mosley encouraged his blackshirt stewards to be as aggressive as possible at meetings, as he believed that by provoking his opposition into retaliation, he would achieve victory for his party. At rallies across the country, in Manchester, Birmingham, Glasgow and Rochdale, his blackshirts forcefully ejected protesters, most notably at Olympia in June 1934. At this notorious rally, many on the anti-fascist side were charged, despite the strong evidence that the blackshirt stewards were the aggressors. *The Times* reported that Nellie Tuck, a 17-year-old factory girl from Shepherd's Bush, was fined for using insulting words and for assaulting a woman who was wearing the blackshirt uniform.

Women formed 20 per cent of the blackshirt membership and were trained by the St John Ambulance in jiu-jitsu in order to protect themselves from 'communist women'. Male and female blackshirts paraded through London, inspired by the youthful military demonstrations in Italy and Germany. The BUF Women's Drum Corps marched to the beat in their black berets, black sweaters, black leather gloves and grey skirts.

Many former suffragettes were attracted to the British Fascists in the 1930s, seeing it as the modern incarnation of their revolution. Mary Allen was considered, according to Stephen Dorril in his book *Blackshirt*, to be 'part of an upper-class lesbian subculture among militant women's groups on the extreme right'. She dressed in a dark blue tunic and breeches, black boots and peaked cap and visited Hitler and Goering in Germany to discover the truth 'of the position of German womanhood'. But masculinity was at the heart of fascism, and women were expected to know their place – with men dictating policies on birth control and abortion.

Rich society women were drawn to the 'charms' of Mosley's brand of fascism. At the wedding of Pamela Dorman and Ian Dundas, Mosley's chief of staff, the bride trimmed her gown with golden Fascist symbols to match the wedding cake, and the groom proudly wore his black tunic and shining belt buckle with the BUF insignia.

Diana Mitford was willing to sacrifice everything for Mosley, the man she called 'the Leader'. Like many young people in Britain, the six upper-crust Mitford sisters, the children of the 2nd Baron Redesdale, were divided by politics. Their parents regarded educated, intellectual women as 'rather dreadful', and so the girls were schooled at home. The girls rebelled in different ways against their staunchly conservative parents, each representing a different aspect of 1930s life.

Born in 1904, Nancy came of age in 1920 and quickly took up the burgeoning flapper fashion trend. Jessica wrote in her memoirs of:

> … the hushed pall that hung over the house, meals eaten day after day in tearful silence, when Nancy at the age of twenty had her hair shingled. Nancy using lipstick, Nancy playing the newly fashionable ukulele, Nancy wearing trousers, Nancy smoking a cigarette – she had broken ground for all of us, but only at terrific cost in violent scenes followed by silence and tears.

Beautiful, glacial Diana Mitford, born in 1910, gained a reputation as one of the Bright Young Things when she married Bryan Guinness in January 1929. Her group of spoiled socialites held decadent themed parties, such as 'baby' or 'bath and bottle' parties. After meeting Sir Oswald Mosley at a dinner party in 1932, Diana fell hard for the womanising Fascist. She believed he held the answers to Britain's problems and sacrificed her high-status marriage to wed Mosley in 1936 at Joseph Goebbels' Berlin home.

Nancy and husband Peter Rodd considered themselves left wing, yet they flirted with fascism by attending BUF rallies and buying their own blackshirts. In a letter to Evelyn Waugh, Nancy wrote that Peter 'looked very pretty in his black shirt'. But she added, 'We were younger and high-spirited then, and didn't know about Buchenwald.'

The three younger Mitford daughters, Unity, Jessica and Deborah, were teenagers of the 1930s, and at a time of greater political awareness, they represented that era's conflict between fascism, socialism and conservatism that defined the decade. Conceived in the Canadian town of Swastika and born just four days after the outbreak of the First World War, Unity Valkyrie Mitford's name was quite prophetic. At 6ft tall she had the appearance, according to Jessica, of a 'flaxen-haired war maiden' and a 'huge and rather alarming debutante'.

Sensitive and creative, Unity rebelled against the boredom of her first debutante season, taking her pet snake Enid with her to dances and stealing writing paper from Buckingham Palace and using it to write to friends. But, as Jessica wrote, 'Her efforts to brighten up the social scene gained few adherents … to try that sort of thing in, say, 1926, it might have caught on. But the debutantes of 1932 just weren't in the mood.'

After enrolling at art school in London in 1933, Unity would often visit Diana, and it was here, at her sister's home, that she met Oswald Mosley. Unity was immediately enthralled by his debonair charm and enthusiastically signed up to the BUF, soon dressing in black shirt, leather gauntlets and BUF badge. Unity tried to persuade Jessica to be a Fascist too, as Jessica recounted in her memoirs. '"It's such fun," she begged, waving her brand new black shirt at me. "Shouldn't think of it. I hate the beastly Fascists. If you're going to be one, I'm going to be a Communist, so there."'

Jessica, teasingly nicknamed a 'ballroom communist' by her family, was moved by the plight of workers in Britain during the Depression, and with youthful idealism, she decided to become a socialist. 'The little I knew about the Fascists repelled me,' Jessica wrote in her memoirs. 'Their racism, super-militarism, brutality. I took out a subscription to the *Daily Worker*, bought volumes of Communist literature … rigged up some home-made hammer-and-sickle flags.'

At their family home of Swinbrook, Unity used a diamond ring to carve swastikas into the windows, while Jessica embellished them with rival hammer and sickles. Their drawing room became a microcosm for Britain. One side was decorated by Unity with Fascist symbols, photographs of Mussolini and Mosley, and a record collection of Nazi and Italian youth songs, while Jessica's side was a communist library, decorated with a small bust of Lenin.

With an obsessive ambition to meet Hitler, Unity's fanaticism led her to Munich on the proviso of learning German. Both Diana and Unity had been warned by Ernst 'Putzi' Hanfstaengl on arrival in Munich that they wore too much make-up to please Hitler, as he liked women to be pure and traditional. Yet Unity successfully found her way into the Führer's inner circle by going daily to the Osteria Bavaria where he regularly ate lunch.

Back home, Unity would use the 'Heil Hitler' salute on 'family, friends, the astonished postmistress in Swinbrook village', and her collection of Nazi souvenirs and postcards of the Führer grew and grew. Nancy sent Unity a cheque for her twenty-first birthday in 1935, teasingly to 'buy yourself some pretty little Nazi emblem with'. Gathered round the family after dinners, Unity would sing loudly '*Deutschland über Alles*', while Jessica blasted out rival words of communist songs to the same tune.

Unity, Deborah and Jessica were taken on a Mediterranean cruise by their mother in the spring of 1936. Disembarking at Granada, Unity insisted she wear her swastika brooch. Locals gathered to take a look at the tourists, but when they saw the brooch, rage grew and soon Unity was surrounded by an angry crowd who tried to rip the symbol from her blouse.

'I no longer found their antics funny,' Jessica recounted of Diana and Unity, and held a fantasy that she could pretend to convert to fascism, accompany her sister to Germany to meet Hitler, then pull out a pistol and shoot him dead. 'Unfortunately, my will to live was too strong for me actually to carry out this scheme, which would have been fully practical and might have changed the course of history.'

Jessica, as a card-carrying socialist, was intrigued by her rebellious, blue-blooded cousin, Esmond Romilly, who ran away from school to publish a left-wing underground journal for schoolboys, called *Out of Bounds*. Nancy later described Esmond as 'the original Teddy Boy'. Esmond wrote, 'I had a violent antipathy to Conservatism, as I saw it in my relations. I hated militarism, as this meant the OTC [Officers' Training Corps], and I had read a good deal of pacifist literature. Like many people, I mixed up pacifism with Communism.'

Philip Toynbee, a football and cricket player at Rugby, took a stand against class systems by resigning from the OTC and wearing a hammer and sickle on his lapel. He also made the decision to run away from school, in search of the editor of *Out of Bounds*, who ran the publication from Parton Street Bookshop. Philip spent days at the bookshop, as 'beautiful visitors' drifted into the shop, including 'a man with a beard and leather trousers who drank whisky from a flask, smoked cigars and talked about "Jimmy Joyce" and "Ginny Woolf"'.

Philip and Esmond became firm friends and, to prepare for Mosley's meeting at Olympia, they bought 'knuckle-dusters at a Drury Lane ironmonger, and I well remember the exaltation of trying them on. We flexed our fingers. "A bit too loose here." "Not very comfortable on the thumb." We were expert knuckle-duster buyers.'

They crowded into the packed auditorium at Olympia, where they came face to face with the 'black-jerseyed stewards with hands on hips, complacent and menacing'. As protestors were ejected from the meeting, Philip remembered the 'coarse rub of a jersey against my cheek' and was left 'tearful, bruised and broken'.

Idealistic British youths like Esmond and Philip were fascinated by news of the Spanish Civil War and went to join Franco on the front line. Knowing little about the International Brigade, Esmond cycled to Marseille and boarded a cargo ship for Spain. His battalion was sent to the Madrid front, and a week before Christmas all but two of the English fighters had been killed. He was invalided home but remained a committed fighter of fascism.

Picture Post reported in November 1938:

> Over 2,000 English, Scotch, Welsh, Irish, went out to join the battalion, over 1,200 were wounded, many more than once, their reasons for fighting, the politics of anti-fascism. A cloth tied around their neck, a beret, they looked rough around the edges, with an army jacket or leather jacket to make do.

Jessica, on hearing of Esmond's exploits, was also occupied with thoughts of the Spanish Civil War. She cut pictures of female revolutionaries from the papers – 'determined, steady-looking women, wiry, bright-eyed, gaunt-faced, some middle-aged, some almost little girls'. These revolutionary women fought alongside men wearing culottes, workers' dungarees known as the '*mono*', and handkerchiefs around their necks, which became a symbol of the rebellion.

In 1937 Jessica met Esmond for the first time at a dinner party, and she persuaded him to take her to Spain, where he was returning as a *News Chronicle* correspondent. For Jessica, 'he seemed part hero, part adventurer, part bad boy' and, despite her parents' horror, they ran away to join the fight and made the decision to marry. She selected 'a good running-away outfit', based on the images of Spanish guerrilla women fighters in the weekly illustrated papers. 'I knew exactly what I wanted, and found it; a brown corduroy ski suit with a military-looking jacket and plenty of pockets.'

Leaving behind her life of privilege, Jessica sold off the items that she didn't require in order to fund her adventures with Esmond. She wrote to Deborah in April 1937, 'You know my Worth satin dress that's been dyed purple? Well I don't suppose I shall need a dress like that for ages by which time it'll be out of fashion so I wonder if you could very kindly try and sell it for me?'

The October 1936 Battle of Cable Street saw 3,000 blackshirts, three-quarters of whom were under 18, clash with a 100,000-strong counter-demonstration of communists, socialists and Jewish groups. Mosley had unveiled a new military-style outfit with peaked cap, jackboots, SS-style coat and an armband with the red, white and black lightning flash. However, as a response to political skirmishes, in January 1937 the government introduced the Public Order Act, which prohibited the wearing of political uniform in public places.

Pop culture continued to hold a grasp on young people in the late thirties, and it was this lure that was said to have prevented the country from falling into the Fascists' grasp. In 1938 the Spanish War was driven off the front pages by events in central Europe, as Hitler reoccupied the Rhineland, but George Orwell noted, 'Fascism and the threat of war aroused hardly a flicker of interest locally'. He explained:

The post-war development of cheap luxuries has been a very fortunate thing for our rulers. It is quite likely that fish and chips, art-silk stockings, tinned salmon, cut-price chocolate (five two-ounce bars for sixpence), the movies, the radio, strong tea and the Football Pools have between them averted revolution ... a sort of 'bread and circuses' business to hold the unemployed down.

London was the centre of youth culture, and at its heart was Piccadilly Circus, described in *Picture Post* in 1938 as:

... the most brilliantly lit corner in the world. It is tawdry, with flashing lights, roaring sounds of traffic, the Piccadilly escalator lit up, queues forming for a dozen theatres and cinemas, buskers playing the fiddle, while thousands arrange to meet friends outside the landmark shop Swan and Edgar's.

Hot chestnuts were sold for 2*d* on street corners, while milk bars were a new craze for young people, inherited from the United States.

London was particularly irresistible for undergraduates with money to spend, and Richard Hillary and his friend Noel Agazarian would go to the Bag O Nails club in Soho, or the Cavendish Hotel in Jermyn Street to mix with debutantes. Upper-class girls of 17 or 18, having been brought up in isolation from other classes, went through a 'coming out' in London, where they attended lunches, cocktail parties and balls to meet eligible men and new female friends. They wore red lipstick with their pale couture gowns and delicate ostrich-feather headdresses and would regularly catch-up at the soda fountain at Selfridges to gossip about what happened at the ball the night before.

As a debutante in 1936, under the short-lived reign of Edward VII, Diana Barnato, who would become a pilot with the Air Transport Auxiliary (ATA), enjoyed every moment of her season, wearing glamorous gowns by Madame Emilienne and meeting the eligible 'Debs' Delights' – the suitors who were acceptable to their parents. Many of these men would go on to sign up to the RAF, fight in the Battle of Britain, and become dinner companions for Diana at the 400 Club during the war, where they would spend all night talking about flying. Diana said:

> Those last years of peace I remember well. There were parties and dances, skiing holidays in Switzerland, with all sorts of friends. I met and danced with any number of young men who, in just a few short years, would make names for themselves in the coming war.

Propaganda poured out of Germany to demonstrate the might of their air force, and with the sense of a gathering storm in Europe, the Ministry of Labour opened 'Reconditioning Camps' for boys from derelict areas who were demoralised and undernourished. Following the Munich Agreement in September 1938, gas masks were issued to civilians, bringing back memories of the terrible injuries to young soldiers during the First World War. The mask came in a box, and these would soon become a fashion currency in themselves, which could be decorated in elaborate ways.

The government, in 1937, announced a recruitment drive for volunteers to sign up to the Air Raid Precautions (ARP) wardens' service, designed to protect civilians from air attacks. In May 1939, *Picture Post* described how 'the younger volunteers will drive ambulances, act as messengers, become Air Raid wardens. Older women will roll bandages, cook, look after children.' The magazine depicted the new female ARP wardens in their shiny jumpsuits, wellies and gas masks, looking like something from a science-fiction pictorial. This was a taster of the uniforms that women would soon be stepping into.

In 1938, as planning for a likely conflict took place, inevitably women would be needed in non-combatant roles. The women's services of the First World War were revived with the aim of recruiting tens of thousands of much-needed workers. The ATS (Auxiliary Territorial Service), based on the earlier WAAC (Women's Auxiliary Army Corps), was founded in September 1938. In spring 1939, the WRNS (Women's Royal Naval Service or, more commonly, Wrens) was reformed, although only women aged 18 to 50 who lived near naval ports were at first considered. The Women's Auxiliary Air Force (WAAF) was created in July 1939, based on the Women's Royal Air Force (WRAF) of the First World War. By December 1939, 43,000 women and girls had volunteered as Wrens, WAAFs and ATS, most of them having signed up in the first three months of war.

In May 1939, it was reported that '150,000 women were needed to train as nursing auxiliaries, between the ages of eighteen and fifty-five. They were given first aid training and then practical training in hospitals.' Nursing was the respectable choice for women who wished to help with the war effort, either by volunteering for the Red Cross or St John Ambulance, or by joining one of the services, such as the Queen Alexandra's Royal Army Nursing Corps (QAs).

In the Second World War, nurses worked on the front line, carrying out vital but dangerous work. At least 3,076 nurses lost their lives in the conflict, and they were expected to treat the enemy, as well as Allied soldiers. The QAs were posted around the world, including in North Africa, Hong Kong and Singapore. They treated troops on the front line, initially in the traditional grey dress and grey cape with red trimming and white headdress until they were upgraded to tin hats and battle dress. Their uniform didn't always protect them, and 236 died during the war when the ships they were travelling on were torpedoed, or during the invasion of Hong Kong and Singapore.

Cities across Britain were soon transformed into a sea of khaki and blue, with the flash of a red cross and white headdress on the many nurses now assigned to hospitals. With national rearmament, conscription was all but a foregone conclusion, and Esmond Romilly was certain that Britain would be transformed into a military camp, 'One vast OTC, with overtones of an eternal Boy Scout jamboree'. He had admired the International Brigade for its lack of discipline but shuddered at the thought of regimented army life.

Because of the threat of war, Jessica and Esmond made the choice to move to the United States in February 1939. They knew little of the country, except for the strange-sounding food, such as hot dogs and cookies, or from watching movies like *The Petrified Forest*, where Jessica 'gathered that Americans often made love under tables while gangster bullets whizzed through the air'.

Philip Toynbee's last escapade with Esmond and Jessica took him to Eton, where they decided to steal the top hats from the school's chapel. Once they had filled their arms with hats, they sped off in a motor car with top hats on their heads and crammed into the boot. They felt it was symbolic of 'our hatred of Eton, of our anarchy, or our defiance'. Esmond sold the hats the next day to an old clothes dealer to raise money for his and Jessica's trip to the United States.

Those who had been enjoying the summer season of 1939 found it difficult to imagine the changes that were coming when Britain and France declared war on Germany on 3 September. 'It seems quite hopeless doesn't it,' wrote Unity to Diana, on the news of Germany invading Poland. 'I think Chamberlain and co. are criminals and should be hanged … I fear I shan't see the Führer again.' Unity would shoot herself in the head in despair when she heard the news that Britain and Germany had gone to war.

Diana and Oswald Mosley, like other members of the Fascist Party, were arrested and interned for the duration of the conflict. She asked for her luxurious fur coat to be sent to her freezing cell, so she could at least be a little more comfortable.

Diana Barnato was given a Bentley from her father for her twenty-first birthday and in the winter of 1939 drove with a friend to go skiing at Megève. On the way home, she visited Paris where she stayed with Gogo, daughter of Elsa Schiaparelli. It may have been wartime, but she splurged on a new wardrobe from the outrageous designer, including a pink satin evening gown, two silk afternoon dresses and a heavy wool tweed coat lined with patriotic red, white and blue silk. 'People were beginning to die for their country whilst I was buying clothes,' she recalled.

Instead of going into his final year at Oxford University, the life path he had once envisioned, Richard Hillary joined the Royal Air Force Volunteer Reserves in August 1939 along with his Oxford friends, Peter Howes, Peter Pease, Colin Pinckney and Noel Agazarian. 'We were expected to be superior; we were known as week-end pilots; we were known as the Long Haired Boys; we were to have the nonsense knocked out of us,' he wrote, reflecting on his own path to war.

2

Battledress and 'Brown Jobs'

In the first weeks of war, the mood in Britain was optimistic. Joining the armed forces guaranteed a weekly salary and was a counterpoint to the unemployment that had marked the last decade. Frederick Carter, who signed up to the Royal Engineers, said:

> When I heard war had broken out, I didn't really worry. It was rough in England at the time; unemployment was very bad, and I thought, maybe, if we had a war, something might happen. I was out of work, and I thought I'd join the Royal Engineers and work as I was used to working – as a concreter. Nobody seemed upset about the war starting. The way old Hitler was taking over the world, we thought we should finish him off.

With the immediate introduction of the National Service (Armed Forces) Act, all men between the ages of 18 and 41 were asked to register for service and choose which branch of the forces they preferred; otherwise, it would later be decided for them. With its prestigious blue uniform, the RAF was by far the most popular, followed by the navy, but the army absorbed the majority of men.

Many British men suffered from a poor diet and lack of exercise, and in their rough, ill-fitting khaki uniform, some of which dated from the First World War, they were nicknamed the 'brown jobs', indicating their status as just another cog in the machine. With only a short time to prepare for war, their skinny, malnourished bodies couldn't compete with the bronzed Germans.

American journalist William L. Shirer, who had been reporting from Berlin in the lead-up to war, travelled into France and Belgium in summer 1940 to witness the German invasion. Returning from Brussels through Holland, he met a group of captured British soldiers and was struck by the poor physical condition of these boys, who had worked in offices before the war. Yet he admired their friendliness and humour, in comparison to the robotic Nazi youth, and noted it was this cheerfulness in the face of unimaginable horror which kept them going. 'They were a sad sight,' he wrote:

> Some obviously shell-shocked, some wounded, all dead tired. But what impressed me most about them was their physique. They were hollow-chested and skinny and round-shouldered. About a third of them had bad eyes and wore glasses. Typical, I concluded, of the youth that England neglected so criminally in the twenty-two post-war years when Germany, despite its defeat and the inflation and six million unemployed, was raising its youth in the open air and the sun ... I could not help comparing them with these British lads. The Germans, bronzed, clean-cut physically, healthy-looking as lions, chests developed and all. It was part of the unequal fight.

These six youngsters were the last survivors of their company, and one of them had lost an eye. But on the whole, he wrote:

> [They were a] cheery lot. One little fellow from Liverpool grinned through his thick glasses. 'You know, you're the first Americans I've ever seen in the flesh. Funny place to meet one for the first time, ain't it?' This started the others to make the same observation, and we had a good laugh. But inside I was feeling not so good ... I gave them what cigarettes we had and went away.

After war was declared, Arthur Ward and his friend Bill Turner signed up and reported to Gibraltar Barracks, Leeds, on 12 December 1939. Arthur observed the intake of 'pale looking young lads having just left home for the first time, looking a bit bewildered and lost ... we looked a motley crew dressed in all types of civvy clothing and carrying suitcases, bags etc. which did not help us to "march" very well.'

He and Bill were posted to Scarborough as gunners in the 70th Field Regiment Royal Artillery. Their first time away from home proved to be a sobering entry to life in the armed forces. They slept on the floor above a stable and were expected to wash and shave at a row of cold-water taps outside.

The recruits were issued with their army service uniform, which, for Arthur Ward, 'included long vests and long johns, which were supposed to keep our legs warm. We also had heavy boots, which I soon became used to, but some of the lads who had been used to working in offices had a terrible time breaking them in.' These boots caused blisters and sores as they spent hours marching around the surrounding countryside and villages.

One of the greatest issues for the government was being able to produce enough equipment for every soldier, and many of the new recruits were given the service dress of the Tommy in the Great War. Trials for a new field uniform were carried out in the 1930s to better suit modern warfare, including an innovative 'overall', similar in style to the fashionable ski suits of the time. Production of the new 'battledress' began in 1938, but they weren't issued until 1939.

Initially the short blouson jacket and baggy trousers were made in light denim, but the fabric wasn't tough enough to withstand long periods outdoors, and so a rough but warmer khaki wool serge fabric was used instead. This new battledress, considered the most efficient of army uniforms, would inspire the US Army's field jacket, and would also be copied by members of the RAF, who asked for their tailors to run up a blue version for them.

In preparation for being sent to France, the army's British Expeditionary Force (BEF) was issued with a full kit, consisting of battledress, Glengarry cap, socks, jerseys, long johns, heavy boots and puttees, which were long khaki bandages wrapped around the bottom of trousers. To wear under their steel helmet they were given cap comforters, which were an adaptable wool garment that could also be worn as a scarf or turned partially inside out to be worn as a hat. During the war, they became an unofficial symbol of the commandos.

Despite gripes that the puttees were uncomfortable and the jacket and trousers of the battledress came apart, they felt proud to wear their uniform. Sergeant John Williams, of the 6th Battalion Durham Light Infantry, recalled, 'We felt sorry for people who weren't in the army. We were having such a good time! We were being soldiers, and all the girls thought we were smart and handsome, and these poor sods were still working in the pit and the office.'

Ray Ellis was born in 1920 in Nottingham to a father who survived the First World War, and he was brought up 'to know where my duties lay. First to serve God by trying to be good. Then to be fiercely patriotic and to serve the King by being brave.' Coming of age in the 1930s, he was exposed to images of the Nazi rise to power, their swastika banners and Nazi salutes, and realised he would have to fight. 'It was in 1938 that we all began to waken to the idea that the country was in danger and every young man worth his salt wanted to play some part in its defence,' he wrote in his memoirs.

That year, at the age of 18, Ray signed up to the Territorial Army. When he saw the red, yellow and blue of the 107th South Nottinghamshire Hussars with its silver acorn and oak leaf insignia, it immediately appealed. He was issued with his uniform of service dress tunic, riding breeches and spurs, a leather belt, peaked cap and a white commemorative lanyard. 'It was all very exciting; I was brim-full of patriotism and regimental pride and found every possible excuse to wear my uniform,' he recalled.

Both of Ray's brothers, Rupert and George, also signed up to the Territorial Army, having been lured by the promise of adventure, an escape from the humdrum of civilian life and the chance to wear the virile uniform. Ray found that when he was given leave, the girls at home 'were not loath to be seen on the arm of a soldier'.

The Territorial Army were mobilised in preparation for war, and they marched daily in full kits and army boots, which chafed their feet until they were broken in. 'The short period that we remained in Nottingham was something like a holiday,' Ray said:

> Almost every evening I was able to return home and strut about in uniform with buttons and badges shining, winged riding breeches and puttees, and gleaming spurs which clinked and jangled as I walked proudly around the town. I was a real homespun hero who had never fired a shot in anger but I enjoyed every minute of it. Sadly it did not last very long.

In January 1940, they were given orders to move south, in preparation for going into France to push back the Germans. After squeezing aboard the train with their kit bags, rifles and webbing equipment, the 107th South Nottinghamshire Hussars were transferred to the SS *Devonshire*, bound for the Mediterranean and the North Africa campaign.

Arthur Ward recalled that his fellow recruits were from all walks of life, with many from inner-city slums like the Gorbals in Glasgow. Their life experience was in marked contrast to the army officers, who were often from the upper classes and raised on country sports. One weekend, when some of the officers took part in a fox hunt, many of the lads like Arthur were horrified at the barbarity of the creature being chased and torn apart by dogs:

> The huntsmen in their red coats thought it very amusing and the young ladies with them were just as bad, one of them proudly carried away the fox's tail which was covered in blood. Our officers who took part lost our respect for quite a long time.

The obvious class system was evident in the army, more so than in the RAF and navy. When undergoing their training at Sandhurst, army officers, almost all having attended prestigious schools, were officially known as 'Gentlemen Cadets' and, with few disciplinary rules, they were even treated deferentially by their instructors. Once in the army, they were assigned a 'batman', whose responsibility included ensuring their uniform was pristine.

The raw recruits may have been given baggy khaki, but officers could have their uniform fitted by Savile Row tailors. The officer greatcoat, which was double-breasted and in smooth Melton or doeskin fabric, remained unchanged from the First World War. The cuffs, originally designed for turning down over hands in cold weather, were now for decoration and rank insignia were emblazoned on the epaulettes. Officers could also wear their own double-breasted, belted trench coats, and tended to choose a manufacturer depending on what was fashionable in their unit. The most popular was from Burberry, the quintessential English brand that had first introduced the trench coat in the First World War. The 'British warm' greatcoat was tailored to order, and these became quite fashionable amongst officers in particular units, who added their own individual touches, such as coloured linings, and were available in a range of fabrics and shades.

Robert Edberg, an American radar expert in the Royal Corps of Signals unit, was stationed in Aberdeen with several British officers and loved every minute:

[of being] served by a batman who woke me in the morning with a large cup of hot tea and whilst I slowly woke he finished shining my shoes and uniform leather belt and he laid out my uniform for the day. I don't know how he did it, but they were kept spotless and creased to a knife edge.

Some soldiers chose to wear their uniform with particular flare. When couturier Neil Monroe 'Bunny' Roger joined the British Rifle Brigade, he brought with him his unique dandy style. As a clothes designer, he was particularly fastidious about his looks, buying fifteen suits a year from Watson, Fagerstrom & Hughes, favouring tartans, Edwardian-cut suits in pastels, or a statement scarf. So when he donned a khaki uniform, he added a silk scarf, some rouge to his cheek, and kept a copy of *Vogue* magazine close at hand.

Bunny was the second of three sons of an Aberdonian telecommunications magnet, Sir Alexander Roger, and a society beauty Helen Stuart Clark. They grew up in luxury at Ewhurst Park in Hampshire, as tenants of the Duke of

Wellington. After miserable schooling at Loretto, near Edinburgh, he was determined to become a clothes designer and enrolled at the Ruskin School of Art. With a reputation for eccentricity at Oxford, he dyed his hair, wore make-up and carried with him a Pekinese puppy, but he was summoned before a tribunal for suspicions of being 'a homosexual', and expelled from Oxford.

Bunny was a regular at Chelsea parties and, using his illustrious connections, he learnt tailoring skills at Fortnum's tailoring, and soaked up knowledge from his friend, Edward Molyneux. With backing from his father, he was able to open his own couture house, Neil Roger, in 1937, boasting clients including Vivien Leigh and Princess Marina.

He could also deliver a one-liner with aplomb. In bombed-out Monte Cassino in 1944, he ran into an old friend, who asked, 'What on earth are you doing here?'

'Shopping,' Bunny quickly replied.

After the war, Bunny became manager of the couture department at Fortnum's. Having served in Italy, he returned to the country frequently, and it was while on holiday in Capri he was said to have invented Capri trousers in 1949. He was also a promoter of the neo-Edwardian silhouette, worn on Mayfair gentlemen after the war, which would influence the Teddy Boy youth movement of the 1950s.

While all identifying regimental features on their uniform were to be disguised in case of capture when on the front line, troops wanted to stand out as individuals amongst a mass of khaki. The colour of a service cap or regiment sleeve flashes showed loyalty to their own tribe and became increasingly popular as war progressed. Scottish regiments had a long tradition of wearing their regimental tartans on their kilts and trews. In the First World War, the Highland Division was christened the 'Ladies from Hell' by the Germans for their kilts; but the traditional uniform was considered by the War Office not to be suitable for modern warfare, and soldiers were expected to hand in their kilts.

Lieutenant Colonel Douglas Wimberley, of the 1st Battalion Cameron Highlanders, wrote:

> The kilt as a battledress was being attacked from three angles. On grounds of security, on grounds of its inadequacy in case of gas attack and on grounds of difficulty of supply in war. There was also the tinge of jealousy – why should the kilted regiments be given preferential treatment to wear a becoming kilt. The thickness of the kilt and its seven yards of tartan was extra protection. It was traditional in all Highland regiments never to wear any garments in the way of pants under the kilt. But anti-gas pants were issued.

After training, the clue to where regiments were being sent was often in what kit they were issued. If they were given the tropical uniform, they were likely to be sent to Burma or India, or if they were issued the cold-weather kit, including the heavy canvas 'Tropal' coat, balaclavas, scarves and thick woollen socks, they thought they might be sent to Norway or the Arctic.

For those arriving in Cherbourg as part of the British Expeditionary Force, they were met by cheering crowds as they marched with their haversack slung on their shoulders, which contained a woollen pullover jersey, mess tins, cutlery, emergency rations, a water bottle and a green anti-gas cape, treated with linseed oil. 'Once we were in France, we were issued with battledress,' said Sergeant John Williams. 'Away went our regimentals. There was no longer any sign of the Durham Light Infantry, and no buttons to polish. We felt as though we'd slipped down the social scale.'

Despite the innovations of the battledress, they felt that their uniform wasn't a patch on the Germans. 'Our battledress didn't compare with the Germans' field dress for smartness,' said Alfred Baldwin, signaller with the Royal Artillery. But in these first days of war, a lot of the men had no idea of what a German soldier even looked like. 'We knew roughly that the Germans wore grey-green uniforms, that they had different-shaped helmets, but we didn't know very much else,' said John Williams.

Author Brian Jewell described those in battledress as looking like 'an animated sack of potatoes. Those of us with long backs found it impossible to keep the two parts of the uniform together whenever we had to bend over, this manoeuvre being attended by a pinging of buttons and a rapid cooling of the area above the kidneys.'

Sapper Frederick Carter recalled, 'My battledress was very dodgy. You went to the quartermaster's stores, and he issued you with a uniform, and you had to do the best you could. Mine was three or four sizes too big. I had to shorten the trousers myself.'

From 1941, the original 1937 battledress, as it was known, was updated with features to make it more practical, such as a collar lined with fabric, following complaints that the blouse collar was abrasive on the neck. There was also a new pocket on the trousers which was useful for holding maps. But, as the war dragged on and the army needed to economise, the battledress was simplified by dispensing with concealed buttons, tightening tabs and replacing brass with cheaper gunmetal.

When British troops first arrived in France, during what became known as the 'Phoney War', there was a holiday spirit amongst the men. Sergeant John Williams was billeted in a Normandy village with a plentiful supply of apples, eggs and bread; a welcome change from the rationing back home. 'When we got to France, it had been like a holiday at the beginning,' said Sapper Percy Beaton of the 218 Army Troops Company Royal Engineers. 'It wasn't until the German breakthrough came and we started getting shelled and bombed and shot at that we realised we might lose our lives.'

There were few entertainments available, and to occupy their time they got drunk on beer and sampled the wine, often for the first time in their lives. And without the regimental rules of army life at home, dress codes relaxed. John Williams said:

> Up until October, November, we'd been polishing our brass buttons and wearing our service dress. Then we got into this battledress which had no buttons to clean. Our gaiters had to be blancoed and our boots polished, but discipline's a strange thing. We weren't the smart, button-shining people we'd been a month before, but we still knew how to march and conduct ourselves in a proper fashion.

The French soldiers were not the formidable sight that the young Brits had hoped. Many still wore their red and blue uniforms of 1914, and they were underequipped and losing morale. They 'all seemed so sloppy. Baggy, unkempt clothes, hands in their pockets, necks open sometimes, cigarettes hanging from their mouths. They seemed like caricatures,' said John Williams. 'I certainly still had memories of the Great War when the French had put up such a good show at Verdun and places like that, and I was thinking to myself, "I hope they're better soldiers than they look!"'

The Phoney War came to an abrupt end in mid–May 1940, when the Germans advanced across the Maginot Line. Sergeant Leonard Howard of the Royal Engineers' 210 Field Company, billeted near Douai, was woken at 4 a.m. by bombing, dressed only in vest, pants and army greatcoat, due to a lack of pyjamas. Outside they could see the German plane swooping down, the pilot touching his forehead and then opening fire. 'That was our first initiation into real combat. One minute we were saying, "Why the hell's that plane got black crosses on it?" and the next moment we hit the deck.'

'I recall going that afternoon to the village barber and having a haircut. It seemed a sensible thing to do before the start of a battle,' said Peter Martin, lieutenant in the 2nd Battalion Cheshire Regiment.

As the thousands of refugees made their way along the roads with horses and carts, prams, wheelbarrows and piles of suitcases, a German Messerschmitt machine-gunned them down. It was a tactic to block the roads and to prevent the Allies from progressing, but it was an awakening to the brutality of the Germans. 'We realised the mentality they had. I couldn't understand it!' said Ernest Leggett, a private in the 2nd Battalion Royal Norfolk Regiment. 'These poor people were getting away from them. They weren't fighting them. They had no weapons. It was just murder. That sight is still with me. I still dream about it.'

More than a quarter of a million men were pushed north by Hitler's blitzkrieg, where they would be trapped by the English Channel. As they pulled back, with the threat of attacks from the Germans, they had to eat where they could, finding food in abandoned farmhouses, picking up blankets and sheets for their bedding as they moved on.

The Germans used disguise to cause disruption and to push forward. Some dressed themselves in nuns' habits or stripped British prisoners of their uniforms and then put on the clothes to impersonate them. Private Edgar Rabbets said:

There were German infiltrators – in British uniforms – who were well briefed and knew the regiments in the area. They'd come along and say they belonged to a regiment on the right or left flank of where you were … When they were challenged to produce their papers, they couldn't. I took one back to the unit he claimed he belonged to, and as the colonel didn't know him, that was the end of that one. I shot him.

As Sergeant Leonard Howard's company were preparing bridges for demolition over the Escaut Canal, they saw two nuns pushing a pram over the bridge, along with a group of refugees. When they got to the other side of the bridge, the nuns pulled out a sub-machine gun from the pram, spraying the refugees with bullets. They were German soldiers in disguise, and rumours soon spread to Britain that the Germans were parachuting into France dressed as nuns, and even as hula dancers.

After an exhausting, bloody battle, Ernest Leggett, two other privates and a lance corporal were the only survivors out of twenty-five in his group. In a lull in the fighting, they smoked and talked, picking off any Germans they saw moving in the distance. But as Leggett walked across the floor of a building he was caught in an explosion and seriously injured. His friends cut off his trousers, dragged him out to the railway line and, in his 'rough old pair of pants', he crawled and crawled along the line to the safety of his company headquarters.

After being given pain relief, he woke up on the beaches of Dunkirk on a stretcher in the dunes:

> I had nothing on me except a filthy old blanket and dirty bandages. I was given jabs every so often. I remember shells and bombs. I was very hazy, but when danger became very close, I can remember people falling on top of me – to shield me from further harm. That's comradeship.

By the time they reached Dunkirk, the men were hungry, exhausted and with much of their equipment lost. On 26 May 1940, Calais fell to the Germans, who were evidently better equipped and uncompromising.

Lance Corporal Edward Doe from the 2nd Battalion King's Royal Rifle Corps said:

> What amazed us was that when you looked at the German soldier, he had his jackboots on, a belt round his uniform, a canister at the side, but he wasn't lumbered down. He wasn't tied down with packs and equipment like we were. Furthermore, he was armed with an automatic. He could just point it and let go! We had to fire a shot and eject the cartridge and reload again. We were not only outnumbered in Calais, but out-armed in every way.

The rearguard was the last line of defence, protecting the BEF from the German onslaught as they retreated to Dunkirk; but they only had a slim chance of making it to a boat themselves. Many British troops were taken prisoner, but if they fell into the hands of the ferocious SS, or *Schutzstaffel*, a paramilitary squadron, their fate was worse. Even the imagery of the SS was designed to provoke terror, with their black uniform marked by lightning flashes and the symbol of skull and crossbones. The Waffen SS, known as 'Death's Head', were known to have carried out two massacres of surrendered British troops. One of the few survivors of the massacre at Wormhout was Private Bert Evans, who had recognised the SS by the lightning flash and skull and crossbones on their clothes.

After an air raid on his group, Private William Ridley of the 9th Battalion Durham Light industry helped search for casualties. He came across a boy who was down on one knee, still holding his rifle. When he touched him, he toppled over dead:

There was another one I couldn't move, so we went to get a shutter off one of the houses, and brought it over. We tried to lift him on, but when we lifted the top part of him, the bottom half stayed where it was. It was only the buttons on his battledress and his pants that were keeping his body together.

When his battalion abandoned their trucks, Private Victor Burton, from the East Lancashire Regiment, placed bandoliers of ammunition around himself and stuffed cigarette tins down his battledress shirt. Without underwear as protection, the cigarette tins dug into his chest, but with his frayed nerves, ditching the cigarettes wasn't an option.

After taking over a farmhouse, where they would be positioned as the rear-guard, Victor and his good friend Phil tried to cover themselves as they came under fire. 'I heard a tinkle on my helmet, and a bit of shrapnel dropped on my hand. I turned to Phil by my side, and said, "Hey, I've been hit, Phil!" And when I looked, the back of his head was blown in.'

With the BEF now trapped on the beach at Dunkirk, Churchill launched an ambitious plan to rescue them. Operation Dynamo began on the evening of 26 May, and the next morning every available craft was sent across the Channel to Dunkirk. By 4 June, 338,226 Allied soldiers had been rescued by 222 Royal Navy and Allied ships, and over 800 civilian vessels, including a two-man canoe.

'Dunkirk had the stink of death. It was the stink of blood and cordite,' remembered Private William Ridley. Groups of British soldiers sat on the sand playing cards, or shaving, despite the German planes spraying the sand with bullets. Some found champagne for sale and spent their last French francs on getting drunk. As the boats came in, the British soldiers formed orderly queues for a quarter of a mile running up the dunes, holding their place despite the relentless bombings.

Items of uniform and equipment had been lost on the long journey to Dunkirk, but some were given orders that they were expected to have full equipment before they would be rescued. Private Sidney Nuttall recalled:

We were told that no man of the Border Regiment would be evacuated to the UK until he was in possession of a full set of equipment. There was material all over the place – people had thrown stuff away. So we made up our kit with whatever we were short of from what people had thrown away. He then said we had to shave – but there was no fresh water. We had to shave in sea water, which we did – and which was very painful.

Sergeant Leonard Howard had picked up a dead corporal's overcoat to wear over his jacket with sergeant's stripes. But when he got into the water to reclaim an abandoned canoe, a beachmaster pulled out his gun to order him out of the water, thinking he was a corporal abandoning his men. Leonard said:

> They landed some beachmasters who were in service dress with red bands on their arms to try to organise the evacuation, and frankly the chaps who'd made it to Dunkirk didn't want chaps in service dress and Sam Brownes and red bands trying to organise them.
>
> A revolver bullet slipped into the water very, very close to me. I was livid. I'd got my own revolver in the top of my jacket and I swung round and shouted to this chap, 'I'm not a corporal! You can't judge people by what they're wearing on the beach today!' To my surprise he put his revolver back in his holster and saluted very smartly and said, 'I'm sorry.' I said 'That's all right, sergeant major.'

Douglas Williams reported for the *Scotsman* on the mass evacuation, describing 'an amazing flotilla of boats of all sizes and descriptions' ferrying home the BEF:

> From dawn this morning I stood for hours on the dock and watched a succession of vessels unloading endless columns of tired, hungry, dirty, but cheerful British and French soldiers, rescued as by a miracle at the eleventh hour from what had, a couple of days ago, appeared to them inevitable elimination.

Once on board the navy destroyers, Williams described how:

> … cabins were opened indiscriminately for the use of Army officers, their wet clothes were dried, and hot tea with rum was served out to all ranks … I was impressed by their wonderful condition and good spirits. Many sang 'Roll out the Barrel' as they waited in line to disembark, or gave three cheers for the ships' companies. All showed the strain of the past few days of hunger, sleeplessness and constant attack, and there were imprinted on their faces heavy lines of fatigue.

While many of the men were still in their uniform, those who were forced to swim from the beaches to the boats had shed most of their clothing and were now wrapped in blankets. Once on board, the men collapsed with exhaustion or showed signs of shellshock. The extended use of Benzedrine, supplied to them in their kitbags to help them stay awake for days, led to jitters and double vision. 'There was an officer in his pyjamas for some weird reason – standing up, waving his arms over his head and shouting, "Survivor! Survivor!" at the fighters and then he started making engine noises. I tried to ignore him,' said Reginald Heron, an able seaman serving on board HMS *Keith*.

Lance Corporal John Wells from the 6th Battalion South Staffordshire Regiment was on board the SS *Princessa* when it was hit and sunk. He found himself on a cobblestone quayside with half a dozen corpses in grey uniform:

> They were the first ruddy Germans I'd seen! And the souvenir hunters had all got their knives out and cut out the swastikas and badges from the Germans' uniforms. I felt for my Staffordshire brass knots – yes, I'd still got my buttons and emblems. I was very wet, but it was a nice, sunny day and I dried out fairly quickly.

Lavinia Holland-Hibbert, an ambulance driver in the First Aid Nursing Yeomanry (FANY), transported the Dunkirk survivors to hospital. She described how 'they were in torn, oily, wet uniforms – one officer had nothing on but a blanket and a monocle – and their faces were black and covered with oil.' She and her fellow FANYs spent hours talking with them, cleaning up their buttons and belts and posting letters to their loved ones.

The British Army in France had been completely depleted by the onslaught of the Germans. All that was left was a ragged convoy of tired, exhausted men who had lost much of the British Army's new equipment. They had replaced their kit with scavenged pieces of German or French clothing and weaponry that they had picked up on their journey. They had gone from uniformity, to a ragtag of survivors in clothing adapted from what they could find.

'I arrived back in England with a pair of French gumboots, my battledress trousers, an anti-gas cape, my jacket, and a French beret I'd got from a house somewhere,' recalled Lance Corporal Kenneth Carver, of the 5th Motor Ambulance Convoy Royal Army Service Corps:

> I remember getting on to a train, but I don't remember getting off it. I was told, three days later, that I was in Hampshire, where I woke up in a tent with my head in a nurse's lap. I was crying my eyes out and was absolutely bewildered as to why I was doing this.

Eileen Willis, a Red Cross nurse, was only 19 years old when she treated survivors from Dunkirk, and it was a major shock to her unaccustomed eyes. 'I'd never seen anything like it. Of course they were in an awful state, filthy dirty, exhausted,' she said:

> A lot of them had been lying on stretchers on the beaches for twenty-four hours and there had been an abnormally high tide so a lot of them had been washed out to sea. They had been bombed and starved and they were wounded. I remember we got them all into bed and they had the first dressings. But they just slept and slept, they woke up and had some food then went back to sleep again. There was a young chap, he'd got white hair and I looked on his notes and he was twenty-one. I said to one of the auxiliary sisters, 'Why has he got all this white hair?' She said, 'It's what he's been through.' But within about six weeks it had all grown through in his own colour which I found extraordinary at the time, but a lot of us found things like that.

The Dunkirk evacuees boarded trains at Dover, where they were packed into carriages with people going to their office jobs in London. While civilians had little understanding of the trauma these men had experienced, they welcomed them home as heroes. As Captain Anthony Rhodes recalled, 'These people in the train were very sympathetic to us. They wanted to know what had happened. They could see that we all had about three days' growth of beard. They could see that our clothing was falling to pieces and that we'd had an unpleasant time.'

Private Victor Burton, who had earlier witnessed his best mate's head blown off, found his way onto a boat, still in possession of his rifle, cigarettes and bandoliers. He woke to find himself in Ramsgate, being given tea and a corned beef sandwich. He was put on a train to Pontefract:

> When we arrived it was a lovely day and we sat in the grass and had these lovely boiling hot showers. We had all clean underwear. When I came back, we shaved, and I thought I'd go and have another bath – and I had about half a dozen good baths before I put the clean clothes on. Then we only had one problem – between a few of us we only had a few francs, and we wanted to buy a pint, so I thought I'd sell one of my two pistols. We went into this pub and I sold a pistol to get some beer money for the lads. I got £6 for it, which was a lot of money then – but we had a lot of beer out of it.

More than 140,000 British troops remained in France, having failed to reach Dunkirk in time for the evacuation. Not long after, a second expeditionary force was sent to France. On 9 June, Arthur Ward's regiment went with the 52nd Scottish Lowland Division with the objective of saving Paris. They docked at Brest and marched into town, where they were greeted by cheering crowds who handed out fresh strawberries and flowers, thinking they would be rescued by the Brits from the advancing Germans. 'The trucks came up with our spare clothing and equipment and we were not very pleased to find out that most of our kit had been stolen by the French people who were fleeing from the German advance.'

After less than a week, the news came that Paris had fallen to the Germans, and they were given instructions to get to Cherbourg as quickly as possible to be evacuated. There was chaos as they waited for orders, but Arthur was evacuated on 16 June, when ships arrived to take them out of France. 'We looked a motley crew – unwashed and unshaven for nearly a week as we only had the kit we stood up in, but we had all kept our rifles.'

Winston Churchill hoped they could rescue 45,000 soldiers from France, yet ultimately over 338,000 Allied troops were saved from the beaches of Dunkirk between 26 May and 4 June 1940. There were also huge losses to the RAF during the Battle of France, but the khaki-clad soldiers, having spent hellish days on the beach at Dunkirk, bitterly complained that the boys in blue, in their arrogant tunics embellished with wings, were nowhere to be seen.

3

The Boys in Blue

On what would have been her son Richard's fortieth birthday in April 1959, Edwyna Hillary reminisced about the last summer holiday he and his University Air Squadron friends had spent together before the outbreak of war. 'They all knew the war was coming,' she said. 'I'm glad he had that last summer.'

That summer, Richard Hillary and his fellow long-haired boys signed up to the Volunteer Reserves, and after completing RAF training at the base at Kinloss in May 1940, they relished the attention they would receive from their pilot's wings now sewn onto their tunics.

They all felt the thrill and promise of adventure, yet none would survive the end of the war. Richard, who found fame for his wartime memoir, *The Last Enemy*, was posted to Montrose, in north-east Scotland, as part of 603 Squadron with Peter Pease, Peter Howes and Colin Pinckney in 1940.

Noel Agazarian was posted to a different squadron. He was the son of an Armenian father and French mother and had a slight accent, which made him even more attractive, and during the war he grew a small Errol Flynn moustache. Noel, who had been refused admission by Trinity College in Oxford because of his ethnicity, was one of the top fighter pilots in the Battle of Britain while serving with 609 Squadron. His brother, Flight Lieutenant Jack Agazarian RAFVR (Royal Air Force Voluntary Reserve), became a member of the Special Operations Executive (SOE) and was executed in 1945 by the Nazis.

Richard Hillary and his 'long-haired boys' enjoyed appearing 'slightly scruffy' in upmarket restaurants, shocking the 'pink and white cheeked young men' of the infantry regiments. This carefree, irresponsible attitude would be put to the test during the Battle of Britain, where the stress and trauma on these young men was masked by hard drinking and black humour.

The summer of 1939 was sweltering, and Guy Gibson had also been enjoying the heatwave that year. Gibson had always dreamt of being a pilot as a child, keeping a picture of First World War flying ace Albert Ball VC on his wall, and after some time at St Edward's in Oxford, he signed up to Bristol Flying School in 1936. In 1937, he moved to RAF Uxbridge for basic training, and was awarded his wings in May of that year.

By 1939 he was preparing to leave the RAF in order to become a test pilot, but as the likelihood of war grew closer, he found himself called back from summer leave on a blacked-out train, packed with soldiers and civilians, heading to the RAF bomber base at Scampton, Lincolnshire, to rejoin 83 Squadron. 'Now Hitler had ruined my summer leave and was likely to do the same thing for many more summers to come.'

In the lead up to war, Gibson recalled that his days at camp were marked by heavy drinking and sleeping off hangovers in the English summer as they waited to be called up for war. 'Those gramophone records, the heat. Extra-large headlines in the newspapers every day, including a memorable "No war this year",' he remembered.

Like many in the RAF, both Battle of Britain legend Richard Hillary and Guy Gibson, hero of Bomber Command's May 1943 dams raid, conveyed suave sophistication and flamboyance in the way they walked, spoke and dressed. With their slate-blue uniform, embellished with silvery fabric wings sewn above the breast pocket, peaked caps over sculpted hair, and a gleaming identification bracelet on their wrists, they were the celebrities of the war. With a tendency towards being scruffy, they personalised their uniform to showcase their individual style. Their image offered a colourful escape from the drab khaki of the Home Front, and their battles played out over Britain, where the public could watch their dogfights with the Luftwaffe in the skies above.

In his memoirs Gibson revealed how he and his bomber boys lived, ate and faced death together, drinking heavily and partying hard to cope with the huge losses of their friends. Both Guy Gibson and Richard Hillary were the last ones standing of their group of friends at the start of the war. The death toll was enormous – around 93,000 RAF, Dominion and Allied aircrew were killed in the war on operations or in accidents, compared with 9,500 RAF crew killed on the ground.

Looking death in the face every day, these men sometimes questioned the reasons for the war, despite their unwavering sense of duty. Geoffrey Page, another member of 603 Squadron, said:

> I have since wondered about the underlying motive that led us to don uniform without hesitation to range the skies in defence of the homeland. Was it for King and Country? Or was it more fundamental than this well-worn recruiting cliché would have anyone believe?

Being a member of the RAF had traditionally been for the upper classes. The training centre at RAF College Cranwell cost £100 a term, plus extras for uniforms and books, and this was generally unattainable for working-class and middle-class boys. However, as Germany expanded its air force, the British Government needed to build up the RAF to ensure a firm footing in case of war. The RAF Volunteer Reserve (RAFVR), introduced in 1936, opened up flying to the lower-middle classes too. These auxiliary squadrons had a reputation as 'weekend flyers', and the public in the 1930s was shocked by their rebelliousness. They drank heavily, drove fast sports cars and recklessly performed aerial stunts.

In the summer of 1939, Tony Bartley trained at No. 13 Flying School in East Lothian, Fife. He and his friends bought a sailboat they named *Pimms No. 4*. He went into Edinburgh every Saturday for 'drink safaris', flew right under the Forth Road Bridge and 'fell madly in love with the Lord Provost's daughter'.

Bartley was born in Dacca, Bengal, to an Irish district judge in the Indian Civil Service. At 14 he was sent to school in England, but he was uninterested in studying and planned to work for the East India Company. However, after a soul-destroying apprenticeship at a chartered accountants firm, he began taking flying lessons. As well as the sense that he must protect Britain from the Luftwaffe, his decision to join the air force was triggered by a visit to Germany, where he witnessed the maltreatment of Jewish citizens.

When the draft was introduced, the RAF was by far the most popular service to sign up to. Between September 1939 and January 1942, 789,773 men and women were enlisted. By 1945, over 1 million men and women were in one of the strands of the RAF.

Fighter Command protected the skies above Britain by holding back the German Luftwaffe. Bomber Command led dangerous bombing raids to target strategic sites in occupied Europe, while Coastal Command kept the sea lanes open, preventing Britain from being starved into surrender. Friendships were formed within these strands, with shared experiences and rituals and their own distinctive styles. According to Cecil Beaton, who carried out a photographic study of the RAF, bomber pilots seemed 'to possess a reserve born of their great responsibility to their crew', while fighter pilots were 'the gay, more reckless ones, more temperamental, perhaps a bit selfish'.

Members of Fighter Command left the top button of their uniform tunic undone, which became known as 'Fighter Boy style', while bomber pilots were slightly resentful of the public hero-worshipping of the 'scarf-flapping glamour boys'. Gibson, having served as both a fighter and a bomber, opted to keep his top tunic button undone to mimic the style.

However, there could also be great rivalry. Guy Gibson, in *Enemy Coast Ahead*, described inter-RAF rivalry between the 'the Bomber Barons' and the 'Fighter Glamour Boys':

> Even in the cities, the fighters seemed to have all the fun, walking off with the women and drinking the beer, mainly because their stations were always close to a town, while a bomber base is miles from anywhere. Naturally all this irked the boys of Bomber Command quite a lot.

Gibson's 83 Squadron flight commander, Oscar Bridgman, was also quite unconventional, and new recruits, as Gibson noted, did not expect 'to see their Flight-Commander with his tunic undone and his hat on the back of his head, his feet on the table and behaving so casually'.

As well as being nicknamed the 'Glamour Boys' for the way they wore their uniform with desirable panache, they were also called the 'Brylcreem Boys', because of their movie-star hairstyles. County Chemicals of Birmingham, who produced Brylcreem, jumped on the association and used an RAF man in tunic and cap to advertise their products.

Richard Hillary was particularly vain about his hair, becoming paranoid when some of his crewmates made a joke about dandruff. Gerald Stapleton, who served in 603 Squadron with Richard and was nicknamed 'Stapme', after a phrase from his favourite comic strip *Just Jake*, said:

> Hillary was a very nice chap; he was a year older than I was. He was very well dressed, very good-looking with a typical university hairdo – long hair! Not long as we know it today, with a pony-tail, but much longer than our hair, although ours wasn't too short. But Hillary's was over his ears and over his collar, and we weren't allowed to have that!

The prestige of their uniform also meant they could be arrogant – they referred to the boys in the army as 'the brown jobs' for their poorly fitting khaki uniforms and for their lack of freedom in comparison. But their blue uniforms, with the silver wings sewn onto the tunic, were incredibly alluring.

Colin 'Hoppy' Hodgkinson, an acquaintance of Richard Hillary's, lost both legs in an air accident in 1938, and after being posted into 131 Squadron in 1942 he felt rehabilitated by his new uniform. He wrote in his autobiography, 'Air Force Blue, at that time the most famous colour in the world … I smoothed the wings above my left breast pocket, prinked like a mannequin up and down before a glass. My God! Nothing could stop me now. I was irresistible!'

Joan Wyndham and her friends, who had signed up as WAAFs, referred to the men who worked on the ground as 'wingless wonders' – they were invalidated because they weren't operational flyers. 'I can't describe the effect wings have on a WAAF,' she wrote. 'Our theme song should really be "If I Only Had Wings".'

For those serving in the RAF, there was a special camaraderie, where secret language indicated they were part of a club. Eric Partridge, a New Zealand-born linguist and member of the RAF, collected a 'Dictionary of Slang' during the war, which was published in 1945. Eric noted that during wartime, combatants developed a richer slang than civilians – because they were living a more exciting life and dealing with new situations, their language became 'youthful, energetic, adventurous'.

Those in the RAF called the ground crew 'erks', which, Partridge noted, was a corrupted abbreviation of 'air mechanic'. A 'scramble' or a 'party' was an aerial fight, reflective of the humour in downplaying incidents. To crash a plane was to 'prang' it, and an easy early morning bombing was a 'milkround' and an 'egg' was the nickname for a bomb or mine. To 'get some flying hours in' ironically meant to sleep, and 'Happy Valley' was a similarly ironic expression for an area much bombed.

The RAF slang may have been only understandable to those on the inside, but many of the words trickled down to become used in everyday English.

'Sprogs' (from frog spawn) meant new recruits and 'goons' were those who weren't very bright. When landing, someone would ask 'any joy?', meaning any luck, and 'it's a piece of cake' was an RAF catchphrase for an aerial combat which was an easy victory.

The individual heroes of the RAF became household names. In March 1940, after claiming his fifth victory, the first ace proclaimed by the press was New Zealand fighter pilot Edgar 'Cobber' Kain. In one photograph, he's suavely cool with his wavy hair brylcreemed, a little curl down his forehead, and his cream roll neck worn under his tunic, with the top button undone.

The 'colour bar' was dropped in October 1939 and in November 1940 recruiting began in the West Indies and Africa. Nine squadrons from the Indian Air Force fought in the Second World War.

Flying Officer Akin Shenbanjo was a wireless operator with 76 Squadron, and his crew named their plane 'Achtung! The Black Prince' after him.

Actor Cy Grant, from Guyana, served as a navigator with 103 Squadron before being shot down on his third trip during the Battle of the Ruhr. He spent the rest of the war in Stalag Luft III.

'Sas' de Mier was one of the few Mexicans in the RAF, and his brother 'Mo' de Mier was, according to Diana Barnato, the 'only Mexican in a kilt', as an officer in the Gordon Highlanders.

After earning his wings, Tony Bartley was posted to the infamous 92 Fighter Squadron, where he met Squadron Leader Roger Bushell, 'a South African and a bull of a man with a damaged eye from an accident with a ski pole which somehow didn't detract from his rugged attraction'. He was ten years older than Tony and nicknamed the 'Führer'. As Tony got to know his new squadron over beers in the local pub, he noted in his memoirs, 'A new life was starting for all of us. Few were to survive it.'

92 Squadron, based at Biggin Hill during the Battle of Britain, had a reputation for daredevil bravery and hedonism. Flyers like Bartley, Robert 'Bob' Tuck and Brian Kingcombe became household names as they fought off the Luftwaffe in air battles multiple times a day. They headed to London's nightspots in fast cars powered by aviation fuel to drink away their stress.

Bob Tuck was known as a wild aerobatic pilot and a fighter. As painter Cuthbert Orde said, 'Everyone knows Bob Tuck: flat-out for fighting and flat-out for parties.' Tony Bartley recalled first meeting Tuck 'lounged out of his cockpit, a silk scarf draped around his neck, a monogrammed handkerchief drooping from one sleeve. He lit a cigarette in a long white holder, and strolled towards our CO.'

In May 1940, the squadron protected the retreating British Army from swarms of German fighters at Dunkirk. They lost men and Bushell was downed and taken prisoner of war. Later, he would lead the infamous escape from Stalag Luft III and was captured and killed by the SS. During the defence over Dunkirk, Bartley had a close call, counting eighteen bullet holes in his Spitfire, his body aching from the centrifugal forces, and his eye bleeding from a burst blood vessel:

> That evening developed into a party, God knows why. We hadn't much to celebrate except rumours we were being temporarily rested. We had lost our CO, five pilots … wounded but we wanted to forget the battle and make merry. That was the spirit, initiated at the Battle of Dunkirk, which prevailed amongst fighter pilots throughout the war.

Winston Churchill coined the nickname 'The Few' for the men of the RAF who pushed back the Luftwaffe during the Battle of Britain. They were, as Tony Bartley wrote:

> … a generation born to war, as a generation earlier our fathers were. Some of us were men, but most still boys … we were fit and fearless, in the beginning. By the end, we were old and tired, and knew what fear was … We expected to die, but, in the meantime were determined to live every minute of each day. Aeroplanes were our first love, followed by girls and alcohol. All three were indispensable to our existence.

The Glamour Boys often mixed in celebrity circles and dated London stage actresses. As 'The Few', the exclusivity of the RAF attracted celebrities like Richard Attenborough, Richard Burton, Denholm Elliott, Rex Harrison and Christopher Lee. Guy Gibson married actress Eve Moore, after meeting her backstage at a show; Richard Hillary and Hollywood star Merle Oberon had a love affair during his visit to America; and Tony Bartley married Deborah Kerr in 1945, after being introduced in Brussels when she was putting on an ENSA (Entertainments National Service Association) show of *Gaslight* with

Stewart Granger. He remembered her 'strawberry complexion, a shy warm smile and a little plumpness accentuated by the Khaki uniform she wore'.

Legend recounts that it was stage actress, Lily Elsie, who chose the blue colour of the uniform for the newly launched service in 1918. The precursor to the RAF, the Royal Flying Corps, was established in May 1912, with a khaki service uniform of folding cloth cap, double-breasted tunic, cord breeches, brown ankle boots and a Sam Browne belt.

Admiral Mark Kerr, consulting on the design of the new RAF uniform, was dating Elsie, who was starring on stage in *The Merry Window*. When he asked her views on a new colour to replace the existing khaki, she picked out the shade that 'matches the colour of my eyes'.

However, another story was that Bradford's textile mills in 1917 received an order for 1 million yards of light blue cloth for the Tsar of Russia's cavalry, but when the October Revolution broke out the order was cancelled, and instead the cloth was used to dress the RAF when it was formed on 1 April 1918.

A whole range of kit was provided by the RAF, and this could be adapted to follow the style of their particular squadron. A typical pilot's equipment was a flying helmet, goggles, oxygen mask, leather Irvin jacket and 'Mae West' life jacket. A blue-grey greatcoat was worn over their service dress. NCOs (non-commissioned officers) were issued with a heavy serge coat, while officers could have theirs tailored, belted and made from a lighter fleece cloth.

They were also issued with a Sidcot suit, a one-piece flying suit in light-weight waterproof green cotton, lined with fleece and based on a design from the First World War. Group Captain Douglas Bader, who lost both legs before the war, liked to wear a 1930 pattern flying suit, as he could keep his artificial legs in one, ready to scramble. Some chose to buy their own white or black 'Prestige' one-piece flying suits, or to custom-make a version of the army battledress uniform in blue.

However, the majority of pilots chose to fly in their service uniform of shirt, tunic and trousers, partly down to the hot weather during the summer of 1940 when the Battle of Britain raged. Flying officer Harold Bird-Wilson of 17 Squadron said:

We flew in ordinary uniforms. We had no overalls in those days. We had jolly good sheepskin lined flying boots, leather gloves and helmets. We had sheepskin leather jackets and Mae Wests … we sometimes used to sleep at our dispersal points. Some pilots actually scrambled and flew in their pyjamas.

While the Irvin jacket and matching Irvin suit trousers with braces were often seen in press photos, they were bulky and restricting, and not popular for flying. Originally manufactured by the Irvin parachute company, the jackets were made from thick-pile sheepskin, dyed brown, and with 'Made in England' on the zips to the front and cuffs. Some pilots also felt the black leather fleece-lined boots were too cumbersome, and instead preferred to wear their service shoes which were quicker to remove in an emergency.

A hazard of wearing a shirt and tie under their Mae Wests during combat was that if the pilot landed in the sea, the shirt collar shrank in water and they could be throttled by their tie. The RAF issued new shirts with detachable collars, but some preferred to wear their cream woollen crewneck, which was much softer on the neck. Many pilots chose a debonair silk scarf around the open neck. They bought their own scarves, usually with a silk side for appearance and a wool side for warmth, and in school stripes, paisley pattern or polka dots. It was a prized possession for a girl to be given one of these.

'Air combat was a personal, individual challenge, because we fought alone, man against man. A contest of gladiators in the vast arena of sky,' wrote Tony Bartley. The isolation of a pilot meant they were more individual in their style. Guy Gibson, for example, recounted he wore two watches, 'because one looks good and the other one tells the time accurately'. He described the night of the dam raids, being in a 'Lancaster cockpit in the light of the moon, flying just above the earth'. It was warm in the plane, and so he opted to be in shirt sleeves with his life jacket worn over it. 'Incidentally, my Mae West was a German one, pinched off some fellow shot down back in 1940, and the envy of the whole squadron.'

RAF pilots often tried to salvage Luftwaffe life jackets from crashed German pilots when they could. Group Captain Brian Kingcombe noted, 'The German life-jacket was in many ways superior to our British issue, being, among other things, inflated by a small compressed air bottle rather than by lung power. It was also less bulky and far more comfortable.'

The rear turret gunners were in the coldest position of a bomber plane and they piled on the layers – vest, pants, shirt, pullovers, roll-neck sweater, four pairs of socks, tunic, flying clothing, a scarf, and a heated suit when it was later introduced. During the Dambusters raid, Richard Trevor-Roper chose to wear his old teddy-bear flying suit because of its comforting, familiar smell. Gibson wrote:

> All clothes which have been on a lot of raids have a smell, a peculiar but not unpleasant smell which shouts aloud to all bomber crews who are in the know that the wearer, or owner, whichever the case may be, is pretty experienced … A wife or loving mother would send the thing to the laundry if she had her way, but you try to do that with the boys. As far as I can see the stronger the smell the better it is liked!

The RAF had a reputation for not keeping their uniform pristine. Miles Tripp, a Lancaster bomber, remembered, 'My hair hadn't been cut for months and I never wore the standard forage cap; my dress was a mixture of flying gear and ordinary uniform topped by the red scarf'. In his memoirs, Richard Hillary described how 'Stapme' Stapleton was 'always losing buttons off his uniform and had a pair of patched trousers which the rest of the Squadron swore he slept in'.

Another fashion was for a moustache, which was an attempt to pay homage to the established RAF pilots of a generation before. Stapleton said:

> It was a trend that I believe came from the fact that a number of older, although not necessarily more experienced, pilots came to us from Army Co-operation squadrons after the battle for France. We simply decided to grow moustaches in order to make us look older. We were conscious of how much younger we looked than them.

Despite the individualism, there was also a certain degree of conformity and tribalism in the RAF. In the briefing rooms, bombers all tended to wear roll-neck pullovers. 601 Squadron lined their tunics with bright red silk, as did Richard Hillary. In a pastel portrait, Eric Kennington depicted him with his battledress deliberately left open revealing a slash of luxurious red lining.

Sometimes the choice to go without the full gear could prove hazardous. Hillary recalled in his memoirs that one of his squadron, Sheep Gilroy, was in the middle of a bath when he was scrambled and, in his rush, didn't put on his tunic and identifiable wings. When his plane was hit and caught fire, he bailed out by parachute and landed in a London slum. Badly burnt, and only in his shirt and Mae West, he was surrounded by a mob who initially assumed he was a German. When Brian Kingcombe's plane was hit, and he floated down on his parachute, wearing a German Mae West, he was worried that 'peasants with pitchforks' would mistake him for the Luftwaffe.

Goggles were an essential part of the kit, but some versions had flaws. The MKIII and MKIIIa goggles, made from celluloid, were not fireproof, and so the next version, the MKIV, introduced in June 1940, was made from protective glass with flip-down tinted lenses to protect from the blinding sunshine.

Pilot Officer Keith Gillman appeared on the cover of *Picture Post* in August 1940, wearing his own Luxor goggles, more comfortable and light-weight than the military's, and these were often privately bought by Battle of Britain pilots. Tragically, the magazine article was published a week after he was killed.

Like other fighter pilots, Richard Hillary felt claustrophobic wearing his goggles, so he slipped them up onto his forehead. Richard also chose not to wear his leather gloves and RAF silk liners underneath, and for this, like many other pilots, he would pay a stiff price.

As the Battle of Britain raged in August 1940, Richard Hillary's 603 Squadron was sent to Hornchurch. They arrived on 27 August, and were immediately in the centre of the action. Group Captain C.A. 'Daddy' Bouchier remembered the arrival of this unlikely auxiliary squadron, hands in pockets, hats perched on the back of their head, and who he described as 'the motleyest collection of unmilitary young men I had seen for a very long time'.

In *The Last Enemy*, Richard described those in his squadron, such as Noel 'Broody' Benson, who was smart and clean-cut, 'nineteen years old, a fine pilot and possessed of only one idea, to shoot down Huns, more Huns, and then still more Huns'.

Yorkshire-born Ronald Berry, born in 1917, was nicknamed 'Ras-Berry' after somebody wrote 'Ras' before his surname on his flying logbook. He had joined the Volunteer Reserves after seeing an advert in 1937 looking for flyers and was thrilled that someone from his background could be given the chance to experience the exhilaration of flying. He sported a distinctive heavy moustache and became one of the most renowned of the flying aces of the war, excelling as a squadron leader in North Africa.

While they had spent the first months of the war in Montrose, where Richard, 'Stapme' Stapleton and others in the squadron regularly entertained local chil-dren in the hamlet of Tarfside in Angus, Hornchurch was a baptism of fire. The day after they arrived, 603 Squadron were thrown right into the intense battles, and on this first day they lost three of their men, including Benson.

As the most popular and brightest character in the unit, the death of Flying Officer Robin 'Bubble' Waterston on 31 August was devastating. But as Stapleton later said:

> With no time to grieve we just got on with our job. We had to, we were fighting for our lives, our freedom and that of the country. Despite the casualties, today, when I look back, I recall we also had great fun. It was an exciting time and we made the most of our opportunities to live it up.

After one air battle, Richard witnessed Colin Pinckney floating down in a parachute. 'He was a little burned about his face and hands but quite cheerful. We were at once surrounded by a bevy of officers and discovered that we had landed practically in the back garden of a Brigade cocktail party.' Their planes were salvaged, and they were handed double whiskies by the party guests to soothe their nerves.

Richard Hillary recalled that 'the first Hun attack usually came over about breakfast-time and from then until eight o'clock at night we were almost continuously in the air. We ate when we could, baked beans and bacon and eggs being sent over from the Mess.' Similarly, Guy Gibson also noted that coming back from a night bombing raid, there would always be a breakfast of bacon and eggs as a treat for every airman who survived a mission. A common joke, to reflect their black humour, was to ask, 'Can I have your egg if you don't come back?'

Drinking was their outlet when off duty. According to Tony Bartley, to cope with the unrelenting wave of Luftwaffe and the loss of their friends, they needed 'the alcoholic tranquilizer and stimulant in order to keep going, all the time'. He described the cycle of fighting during the Battle of Britain:

> My batman called me at 4.30 a.m. with a cup of tea. I struggled into my clothes and bumped into Wimpy Wade in the corridor. He had thrown on his uniform over his pyjamas. It was cold and dark outside. The boys converged from various rooms of our barrack block, dressed in polo-necked sweaters, corduroy trousers and flamboyant scarves.

In the dispersal hut, heated by the pot-bellied stove, they waited for the warning that the enemy were coming. 'I watched the boys lying on their iron cots in Mae Wests and flying jackets, some tossing in uneasy sleep. Others played nervously with flying helmets and oxygen tubes or studied enemy aircraft identification charts.'

Another survival technique was to treat death as a joke. Irish nurse Mary Morris, whose diaries recorded her time in the Queen Alexandra's Royal Army Nursing Corps (QAs) in London and overseas, knew Irish flying hero Brendan 'Spitfire Paddy' Finucane, as both their families had fought the British in the 1916 uprisings. She noted that he played 'the game of nonchalance as usual, as he drank beer from his own special pot', and the RAF were 'a special kind of people, outwardly talking in clichés and using their own "in" language. They are a law unto themselves, top tunic button undone, droopy moustaches.' She added:

> The RAF are the heroes of today, but too much is expected of them. The pilots have their mugs hanging above the bar, and if somebody fails to return from a mission, the mug remains there, but his name is never mentioned, not even by his closest friends. They are a strangely superstitious bunch of boys, many just down from Oxford. The 'few' are now becoming fewer so we must hope that Jerry eases up for a while. They are all so brave and so desperately tired.

92 Squadron was nicknamed the '92nd Night Club' because they held dances in their mess, entertained celebrities including Laurence Olivier, Vivien Leigh and Noel Coward, and even had their own jazz band. Their partying caused alarm to senior RAF officers and a psychologist was sent to assess them. He declared that, despite their antics, they were still able to do their job. However, in order to implement greater discipline, a curfew in the mess and uniform rules were enforced. They could no longer wear check shirts, suede shoes, red trousers or pyjamas under their flying kit.

Benzedrine was issued to airmen to keep them alert during missions, yet, because it was a stimulant, it was also used as a party drug. Tony Bartley recalled parties in the mess at RAF Hornchurch in May 1940, when Spitfire pilot Bob Holland knocked back his Benzedrine with whisky and hammered out frantic music on the piano.

When Bartley was awarded the Distinguished Flying Cross (DFC), he went to his tailor to have it sewn on, but it was a mark on his uniform that he felt uneasy about:

> I felt supremely conscious of the blue and purple striped decoration under my wings. As I made my way to my parked car, pedestrians looked, stopped and then smiled. A young girl stranger ran up and kissed me. The public wanted to shake our hands, touch us, idolise us.

The RAF even managed to overshadow the Americans who arrived in Britain in 1942. Norman Poole recounted how in early 1942, he and his friend Archie Mackinnon were visiting a pub in Swindon on their way to delivering planes. Sitting at one of the tables were four girls and half a dozen US servicemen. Although Poole and Mackinnon 'didn't have nylons, we had an advantage that others didn't possess. We had "Wings"! We were still the glamour boys of the services and you couldn't blame us for trading on it.' They sent a message to the women that they should make their excuses with the Americans, and they swiftly ditched their dates and met Norman and Archie outside the bar, where they spent the evening drinking together and then a night in a hotel.

Guy Gibson, like many of the RAF men, saw women as a distraction, and before he met his wife Eve, he dismissed them as 'things that just came and went in parties. Sometimes they were dumb, sometimes they were too intelligent, rarely had I been impressed by any one.'

Tony Bartley had similar attitudes to women. He wrote, 'With peace offerings of their femininity, part sexual, part maternal, part masochistic in making love to a young man who could be killed on the morrow. We accept their gratuity, but feel more secure in male chauvinistic companionship. Drinking with our tribe.'

Richard Hillary's plane was hit on 3 September 1940, and after managing to escape the burning plane despite terrible injuries to his face and hands, he was rescued from the English Channel. His severe burns allowed him entry into the so-called 'Guinea Pig Club', a group of RAF men who had suffered disfiguring burns and were treated by pioneering plastic surgeon Archie McIndoe at the Queen Victoria Hospital in East Grinstead.

In the summer of 1940, McIndoe found he was dealing with a new kind of injury known as 'airmen's burn', where the severity of an aviation fuel fire caused severe burns to the areas not covered by protective clothing. A total of 4,500 airmen were burnt during the war, and those who suffered the worst burns had chosen not to wear their protective clothing, particularly during the hot summer of the Battle of Britain.

Pilot Officer Geoffrey Page, shot down on 12 August, recalled that he and Richard both suffered the same injuries to their hands as they had not been wearing gloves. 'In 1940 an unofficial order had gone out that you must wear gloves and you must wear your uniform jacket under your flying jacket,' he said:

The burns cases were so much worse, some were burnt to death, because all that they wore was a cotton shirt. When the aircraft caught fire you only had a few seconds in which to get out. If you didn't get out in that time you never would. There was an appalling number of hand burns. When I finally returned to flying I was always careful and put gloves on, in fact I had a pair specially made with zippers running down one side to enable me to put them on easily.

Richard, who had grown up with the reassurance of his own good looks, was now faced with painful and life-changing injuries as his eyelids, cheeks and lips had been destroyed. In his memoir, he recalled that his mother, sitting by his bedside, told him that he should be glad this happened to him, as 'too many people told you how attractive you were and you believed them. You were well on the way to becoming something of a cad. Now you'll find out who your real friends are.'

During his time recovering in hospital, Richard received the news, one by one, that his friends were killed – first Peter Pease and Peter Howes, then Noel Agazarian, and Colin Pinckney in January 1942. 'That left only me – the last of the long-haired boys. I was horrified to find that I felt no emotion at all.'

Richard was a memorable figure in the East Grinstead ward, wearing bright red pyjamas for good luck, a long dressing gown and a varsity scarf, and with a gold cigarette holder in his mouth, described by Page as 'the fried Noel Coward look'. The ward sister disapproved of his flamboyant pyjamas. 'It's the wrong address you're at with those passion pants,' she told him. 'This is the hospital, not an English country house weekend.'

After multiple operations and almost two years recovering in hospital, Richard chose to visit the United States with a plan to give morale-boosting talks in factories across America. However, Sir Gerald Campbell, minister at the British Embassy in Washington, feared that women, particularly in the Midwest, would be horrified at the results of war on young men. But Richard's burns proved to be an aphrodisiac, as they were a mark of his bravery.

William Simpson, suffering burns when crashing in France in May 1940, wrote, 'Those silver embroidered wings on the smoke-blue RAF uniform, and the little flashes of coloured ribbon beneath them … the uniform was redolent of glamour and courage. Even the breaking of our bodies was accepted as part of success rather than failure.'

After meeting in New York, Richard embarked on a passionate affair with Hollywood actress Merle Oberon, who felt a degree of affinity, as she had been injured in a car crash. Despite the pride he felt in his blue uniform, embellished with wings, and the burns injuries which branded him a hero, Richard was haunted by the deaths of his friends and, feeling like a failure, he knew he wanted to go up in the air again to experience the comradery of the mess once more.

Richard should not have been permitted to return to flying, since his hands were so severely burned, but on 15 November 1942 he was posted to RAF Charterhall for operational training. His book, *The Last Enemy*, had been published to great plaudits and success, and Richard was a celebrity amongst the new group of young men who looked on him with awe. But his hands were not strong enough to control the twin-engine planes he was flying. In a letter to his girlfriend Mary, he described being helped into flying suit and boots by his radio operator and waddling to the plane looking 'like an advertisement for Michelin Tyres'.

A few weeks before he died, Richard ran into an old friend, Colin Hodgkinson, who recorded their last conversation.

'Goodbye Colin, I don't think I'll see you again.'

'Why?' I asked. 'We might run into each other.'

'No,' he said, smiling with his twisted lips. 'I don't think I'm to last it out.'

Richard was killed a couple of weeks later, on the night of 7 January 1943, along with his radio operator, when their plane crashed onto Crunklaw Farm in the Scottish Borders. Reporting his death, *The Scotsman* newspaper wrote, 'Hillary called himself, in mock disparagement, the "last of the long-haired boys". He used the term to describe a band of Oxford undergraduates who all joined the RAF together and of who he was the sole survivor.'

Guy Gibson became the last survivor of the original members of 83 Squadron when Oscar Bridgman died in a big raid over Bremen, and James Anderson Pitcairn-Hill was killed at the age of 24 during a raid on Le Havre in 1940. 'We would go on and on until the whole squadron was wiped out, then there would be new boys … new people – different – with different views on life – different jokes and different ways of living.'

By March 1943, with the introduction of target-indicated bombs, the decision was made for the RAF to strategically bomb the Ruhr dams. Pulling together all the aces from Bomber Command, Squadron X was formed, later to be called 617 Squadron and nicknamed the 'Dambusters'. There were twenty-one crews, consisting of 147 men from Great Britain, Australia, America, Canada, New Zealand, and led by Wing Commander Guy Gibson.

Also in the squadron was Gibson's good friend, John Hopgood, or 'Hoppy' as he was known, and Richard Trevor-Roper, who was 'one of the real

Squadron characters. At night he might go out with the boys, get completely plastered, but would be always up dead on time in the morning to do his job.'

The night before the dams raid, they gathered in the mess at Scampton, drinking whisky and placing down a bowl of beer for Gibson's labrador, as was their custom. However, his dog was hit by a car and died instantly. It felt like an omen, and while the raid was a success, many of the men were killed, including Hoppy, who was only 21.

'They die bravely and they die young,' said Gibson, as he thought of all those who were lost during the raid. 'Why must men fight? How can we stop it? Can we make countries live normal lives in a peaceful way? But no one knows the answer to that one.' Guy Gibson argued that these young men who were dying must have a say in the future of the country. But he was killed before the war ended, in a flying accident over France.

4

Where Were the Boys in Blue?

In May 1940, as the Dunkirk evacuation was playing out over the water, Guy Gibson visited Brighton to see his actress wife Eve Moore starring in a revue, *Come Out to Play*. It was hard to believe what was happening over the water, as Brighton's promenade was almost as it had been in peacetime. In the cafés by the sea, girls in pinafores and black stockings served tea, the hotels were open and the beach was packed with bathers. The only clue that the country was at war was the barbed wire and the presence of soldiers.

One evening, when Guy and Eve had met up after her performance, the shrill sound of sirens cut through the air. They rushed into the Grand Hotel for a drink, while a bombing raid played out in the distance. The bar was crowded with civilians and khaki uniforms and Gibson, dressed in his RAF blue, stood out.

As he and Eve were standing in the bar, they were approached by an army officer, whose eyes were blazing with anger. Guy prepared himself for another inevitable argument with a 'brown job'. But Gibson recounted that 'this chap wasn't drunk. He had had it. He had just come off Dunkirk that morning, after spending four days on the beaches.'

'Where was the RAF at Dunkirk?' the officer said, having clocked the uniform. 'I only saw one Spitfire in four days. It was absolute hell. Bomb after bomb rained around us and we couldn't do a thing about it.'

During the mass rescue operation at Dunkirk, many in the army felt they had been neglected. Airmen commonly dismissed those in the army as 'brown jobs' or the 'unemployed', and there was an obvious resentment about this snobbery which came to a head during Dunkirk.

Richard Hillary, Noel Agazarian and Peter Howes drove to Brighton on their day off. Richard wrote that the beaches, streets and pubs 'were a crawling mass of soldiers, British, French, and Belgian. They had no money but were being royally welcomed by the locals. They were ragged and weary.' They encountered two French soldiers and a Belgian dispatch rider, and took them for a drink at a bar, which was:

> … [a] seething mass of sweating, turbulent khaki. Before we could even get a drink we were involved in half a dozen arguments over the whereabouts of our aircraft over Dunkirk. Knowing personally several pilots who had been killed, and with some knowledge of the true facts, we found it hard to keep our tempers.

When he arrived back at his Bomber Command station, Guy Gibson discussed in the mess the rumours that the RAF had been negligent when it came to Dunkirk. 'Well, the Army are pretty browned off about it,' said one of the members of the squadron. 'I came up from Salisbury yesterday and the chaps down there say it isn't safe to go into a pub unless in convoys of two or three. The brown jobs are beating up anything in blue they can see.'

The Dunkirk evacuation brought serious losses for Fighter Command, but because the fighting took place out of sight, keeping the Germans away from the ships at Dunkirk, soldiers thought they had been abandoned and let down by the RAF. 85 Squadron faced the greatest losses, with twenty-five Hurricanes downed in a couple of days. It was also said that pilots who parachuted onto the beaches found they were confronted by soldiers who demanded to know where the RAF had been.

Mary Morris recorded in her diary the resentment they felt at the RAF, with one soldier telling her, 'The only time we saw the bloody RAF they were dropping supplies behind the German lines.' Lavinia Holland-Hibbert, a FANY, also recalled that the men she looked after in hospital after Dunkirk said, 'Where were our bloody planes? Never saw one. Don't you girls go out with an airman.'

'Frankly, if it hadn't have been for the RAF, the troops would never have got off. Because the German Air Force quit the beaches,' said Tony Bartley:

> We turned them back. I'm damned sure that Fighter Command had a hell of a lot to do with it. A fighter pilot I knew was shot down at Dunkirk and went in the sea. He swam out to a boat and he got on board and the navy chap said, 'Get back! We're not picking you up, you bastards! We're only picking up the soldiers!'

Tony Bartley wrote a letter home to his father in India, 'The BEF have started stories that they never saw a single fighter the whole time that they were being bombed. The feeling ran very high at one time, and some fighter pilots got roughed up by the army in pub brawls.' Tony explained the reason they couldn't see the RAF at Dunkirk was they had been forbidden to go below 15,000ft, while the German dive bombers were operating below them. 'Little do they realise that we saved them from the "real bombs", 500-pounders carried by Heinkels.'

New Zealand fighter pilot, Alan Deere, spent time among the BEF during the Dunkirk evacuation. In a tiny wardroom, surrounded by army officers, he was met with hostility because of the belief that the RAF had done nothing. In fact, seventeen pilots in Deere's squadron had been lost during Dunkirk, and he was angered that they received no acknowledgement or thanks.

Hostilities between the RAF and the army grew during Dunkirk and beyond, accentuated by the differences in uniform and the RAF's sense of superiority, enhanced by their wings. However, by August and September 1940, during the Battle of Britain, attitudes to the RAF changed and they were soon hero-worshiped for their actions in protecting Britain's skies.

In summer 1941, Philip Toynbee was working as a junior intelligence officer in Southern Command Headquarters when he met up with his old friend, Esmond Romilly, who had joined the Canadian Air Force as a pilot officer. Esmond disliked wearing an officer's uniform because it was like 'parading the mark of the beast', and he was still preoccupied by social structures, with his displeasure at how the airmen at his station talked down to the ground crew. Toynbee recalled:

It was a time when the infantry often regarded the air force with a gnaw-ing and unconfessed hostility. Home-based infantry officers had done no fighting at all, at least since Dunkirk, and they were secretly jealous of the glamour and publicity which has been won by air-crews and fighter pilots.

Esmond guessed this at once, and 'in a mess of disconsolate and half-hostile young officers, he at once won affection and gratitude by brazenly deprecat-ing the role of bomber crews and insisting that the infantry would have the most dangerous and the most important work to do.'

Esmond was reported missing after a raid over Hamburg in November 1941, at the age of 23. Philip wondered at the tragedy of him being killed, when he had been so desperate to stay alive.

5

Women in Uniform

Stephanie Batstone always dreamed of going to sea. During her time assisting in a London hospital, she would rush to London Bridge whenever she could to soak up the smell of the Thames, gaze at the ships and imagine that one day she would be on a boat. She had looked admiringly at the poster for the Wrens, with a clear goal that she would one day wear the smart navy uniform. 'I had nothing against the ATS or the WAAF except that they didn't have telescopes and generally lacked the special glamour of the Navy,' she wrote.

When Stephanie came across a leaflet appealing for recruits to train as visual signallers, she jumped at the chance. 'As soon as I saw the photographs of girls signalling with lamps and doing semaphore and hoisting flags up masts, I knew that was what I was going to do.'

On 25 May 1943 Stephanie arrived at HMS *Cabbala* with her school friend, Dorothy, along with forty new Wrens who came from as far away as Brazil. These included:

… Marianne from Barclays Bank in Aberdeen, Joy from Sainsbury's cold meat counter in Birmingham, Clodagh from milking her father's cows near Kinsale in County Cork, Maureen from being a hotel chambermaid in Dublin … I guessed that a lot of us had left school at fourteen. Our clothes were different from one another's and our accents were different and our backgrounds were different. We only shared one thing in common – our dreams. We had almost all spent every Saturday afternoon of our youth at the pictures, with Clark Gable and Cary Grant and Leslie Howard and Fred Astaire and Gary Cooper and Tyrone Power.

Whether they were Chelsea socialites, fresh out of school, a secretary or chambermaid, women from all walks of life signed up to non-combatant roles in the armed forces, where they played a vital part in serving the country as members of the ATS, the Wrens or the WAAF. When they put on their uniform for the first time, it immediately stirred within them a different feeling; a sense of authority and certainty that they should now be taken seriously. Wearing a uniform also protected them against harassment, as it automatically commanded respect from men because these women were doing their part in the war.

As well as the armed forces, voluntary services would also be vital for the war effort. Most popular with married and older women was the Women's Voluntary Service for Civil Defence (WVS). Launched in June 1938 and accepting women between 16 and 80, the WVS already had 165,000 volunteers when war broke out. They set up mobile canteens and respite centres for bombing victims, they organised the Government Knitting Scheme for office workers and munitions girls to knit children's clothing on their lunchbreaks, and they helped evacuate 1.5 million mothers and children from the cities to the countryside.

The founder of the WVS, Stella Isaacs, Marchioness of Reading, persuaded couturier Digby Morton to design a stylish uniform to make the service as attractive as possible, which could be purchased at shops like Harrods and Fenwick's at the volunteer's own expense. This meant that the service was mostly inaccessible to poorer women, who couldn't afford to buy an expensive new uniform.

Digby Morton initially created a tweed grey-green overcoat and a dark green felt-brimmed hat with red band. By December 1939, this was expanded to a herringbone tweed jacket lined with green artificial silk and matching skirt, red Viyella wool blouse and red artificial silk blouse, scarf and light green cotton overalls, which were not to be mixed with a civilian wardrobe.

At first, volunteers could collect their uniform on production of a WVS badge. However, with the suspicion that unauthorised people were trying to collect the desirable pieces, a printed card was to be shown. In spring 1940, a lightweight summer uniform was manufactured and distributed by Lillywhites. It was an attractive grey-green flannel shirt-waist dress with two large pockets on the skirt, and a breast pocket with a red embroidered WVS cloth badge. It also came with a red crêpe de Chine collar, to compliment the red of the WVS logo. Further uniform innovations included epaulettes for sewing onto overcoats and suits to attach gas-mask straps, a

WVS dark green beret and, as a response to the 'Make Do or Mend' campaign, spare buttons and leather elbow patches for mending them when
they wore out.

Serving food and supplies to the armed forces was the Navy, Army and Air
Force Institutes (NAAFI). As part of the ATS, NAAFI girls, in their snappy
brown belted jacket, caps and skirts, served in mobile canteens, operating the
tea urn and dishing out buns to the troops.

Gladys Saunt, called up in 1944 when she turned 18, was assigned to the
NAAFI at Garrett's Hay, near Woodhouse Eaves:

> I didn't like the uniform. The jacket had dull buttons so I asked my brother,
> Louis, who was in the Army, to get me a battle-top with brass buttons. I had
> it altered by a tailoress so that it would fit me properly. I didn't like the shoes
> either – horrible brown, flat heeled things and we had to buy them our-
> selves. We weren't paid very much.

Off duty, a soldier wishing to escort a NAAFI girl was given a receipt for
her, having to deliver her back to her base by a stipulated time – but at least
they could wear their civilian clothing to dances, unlike the other services.
'We were lucky, we were allowed to wear Civvies,' remembered Rhoda
Woodward, who worked at an RAF base in Oxfordshire, from 1942:

> Our hair had to be kept above our collars on duty. We used to make a head
> band out of the top of an old stocking and roll our hair round the band. This
> style was known as the 'Victory Roll'. Afterwards, when brushed out, our
> hair turned under into a pageboy style quite easily.

The Air Raid Precautions (ARP) wardens' service was created in April 1937,
and along with older men, members from the WVS were assigned to take
on the role of ARP wardens. They enforced the blackout and dealt with
bombing incidents, putting themselves on the front line. Another vital job
for women was in the National Fire Service, which was formed in 1941,
for which recruits were issued a navy uniform with tapered trousers and
rubber boots.

For younger women looking for excitement, overseas travel and a pay packet, the armed services were the most appealing route, if they could get the permission of their parents to do so. Otherwise, they might be stuck with munitions work. There was a definite hierarchy when it came to the different uniforms. The swish grey-blue of the WAAF was the most respectable, the Wrens' navy suit was the most desirable, combined with the inspiring recruitment poster that promised the chance to see the world, while the ATS, with its rough khaki, was the least discerning. From December 1941, all single women between the ages of 20 and 30 were conscripted into service.

Hazel Williams, 14 years old at the outbreak of war, moved to Danbury in Essex from Bilbao to escape the Spanish Civil War. She and her grandfather, a Boer War and First World War veteran, both tried to sign up to the armed forces by fibbing about their age. Instead, they settled with being the oldest and youngest fire watchers in the village. They had a close call when Danbury was hit by bombs but, Hazel said, 'it was great being a teenager and putting fires out and blowing a whistle madly!'

Moving to Chelsea with her family, she joined the Girls Training Corps, an organisation run by FANY officers who taught teenagers Morse code and first aid. 'We wore navy skirts, white stiff linen tunics, berets and leather belts and were nicknamed "Hitler's Maidens" for we looked quite tough!'

Once Hazel turned 17 she was finally accepted as a WAAF. She had previously tried to join the Wrens but a requirement was to have a connection to the Navy. 'I didn't make any attempt to join the ATS which weren't a very attractive service to join. A saying went, that the Wrens were the tops, WAAF a reasonable second, but the ATS – Yuk! We were a snobbish lot, I regret to say.'

While uniforms served to strip away their individuality, Stephanie Batstone, working as a visual signaller with the Wrens, wrote:

> Inside the buttoned jackets and under the round caps, which looked so identical, were separate seething, bubbling cauldrons of emotion – patriotism, desire to win the war, pride in the Navy, confidence in the training we had received, belief that ours was the best job in the world, hunger for food and hunger for male company, and the sentimental mishmash of daydreams which had also shaped our youthful minds.

Access to military-issued uniform also served another purpose. With clothes rationing introduced in mid-1941, joining up meant young women could get hold of brand-new, quality clothing. Their full kit typically included sets of underwear, two pairs of shoes, blouses, skirts, stockings and a warm greatcoat.

For some girls from deprived areas, to receive new, properly made garments and extra pairs of knickers was a revelation.

But the complete control over what they wore and how much make-up they were allowed to use took some getting used to. In the 1930s, almost every woman wore petticoats and girdles under neat dresses, a pair of high heels, silk stockings, and their hair long and waved. Femininity ruled supreme, and trousers were reserved for only the wealthy and most daring of women. As Hilda Newman, a lady's maid in the 1930s, who joined the ATS, noted, 'Trousers were, in the inter-war years, only worn by "fast women" and not really respectable until the war, when women went into the forces.'

For all services, the regulation length of hair was 2in above the collar, and if they were pulled up on parade for contravening this, they would be ordered to cut it straight away. As it was spun in the propaganda booklet, *Eve in Overalls*, 'Whether under a cap or a steel helmet, their hair – and this is generally beautiful in England – is arranged to show the permanent waves at the very best advantage.' Sylvia Drake-Brockman said:

> Rita Hayworth and Dorothy Lamour wore their hair cascading onto their shoulders, so civilians did the same. But on joining up, you either had to have your hair cut, or else dress it in such a way that it not only fitted under your cap but was also well above your collar.

Dame Helen Gwynne-Vaughan, Chief Controller of the ATS from 1939 to 1941, was adamant that make-up should be natural and inconspicuous. Red nail varnish was not acceptable, but women could get away with pale colours. Miss Ainsworth, Chief Commandant for Northumberland, felt differently: 'It won't do the country any good if we turn out a lot of drab-looking girls. I prefer make-up.'

For upper-class girls, life in the services was a shock to their often unregulated lives. As Anne de Courcy wrote in *Debs at War*:

> Girls who a few months earlier had dropped evening dresses on to the floor when they returned from balls at 3.00 a.m., knowing that a servant would later pick them up, mend anything torn, deal with stains and return them fresh to a cupboard, and that breakfast would be served at a civilised hour in the morning in the comfort of luxurious surroundings, now caught crowded, smelly Underground trains in the uniforms they had worn all day to dance for a few hours in a basement nightclub.

Advertising that was aimed at women switched focus from promoting maximum femininity to adapting the way one dressed in order to support wartime work. The corsetry industry ditched frills, lace and embroidery, and instead incorporated useful pockets into corsets for keeping money safe. In one example, an advert for 'Eve' shampoo explained, 'Already you've probably sacrificed your elaborate up-swept hair style to accommodate your uniform cap – but there's no need to sacrifice the health and the beauty of your hair as well'.

Picture Post reported in October 1939:

> New lipsticks to go with every kind of uniform have now been worked out by the experts – and even if forbidden, the Sergeant-Major cannot notice them! War changes everything – even lipstick. And the demand for it. Since the beginning of September, there has been a 'run' on lipstick. Manufacturers and beauty specialists say they have never sold so many in their lives.
>
> So plentiful are they that already new colours are being put on the market to attract war-time buyers. 'Burnt sugar' and 'sporting pink' are brand new shades especially designed to wear with khaki … For Air Force blue, there's a special dark crimson – Redwood – and for the navy or the Fire Service, a clear scarlet known as 'Stop Red'. Deep, glowing shades are now ready for wear at 'black-out parties' and 'shelter socials'.

Despite the restrictions, it was still expected that women should be glamorous, and there were countless stories promoted like that of Valerie Hudson, a showgirl at the Windmill Theatre in London. As *Picture Post* recounted, when war broke out, she didn't want to give up her job as a showgirl, so she joined the ARP as a part-time voluntary worker. She fitted in ARP training, lectures and classes around her rehearsals at the Windmill. 'For a showgirl with rehearsals, five performances a day and the all-important job of keeping fit and beautiful cannot be a whole-time Air Raid Warden,' said the article. It described how she would go straight from ARP to the Windmill, hanging her steel helmet on the peg and changing into her costume. 'A siren suit zipped up, and Valerie Hudson is once more the perfect Air Raid Warden,' it continued.

During what was known as the Phoney War, before the German invasion of France in May 1940, the anti-gas clothing women were made to carry seemed unnecessarily cumbersome, with 'a five-times-too-large coat and a colossal hat. In all this, plus goggles and gas mask, I certainly shan't die of a gas attack. I'll be suffocated long before that,' said Joan Bawden, the mother of composer, Tim Rice.

Gas mask cases also became a fashion accessory. Hazel Williams travelled from London to Shropshire to be kitted out. As she was waiting to collect her uniform, she discovered a healthy trade in gas mask cases:

> As we walked in, still in our civvies, and with our civilian gas masks I noticed a WAAF NCO and an air woman standing at the entrance, with dozens of gas mask cases slung over their shoulders … most women tried to make the cardboard boxes, containing their gas masks, look attractive … some of the cases were in real leather, others mock croc or attractive water proof covers. As we passed these two women, they said to each of us, 'You won't want those civvy gas masks any more, we will take them'. What a racket! I wonder how much they made selling the cases out of each new intake of WAAF?

The largest number of women – over 200,000 during the war – joined the ATS. Their work included driving, typing, administration, cooking and working on anti-aircraft and searchlight batteries. But the khaki uniform was universally considered dowdy and unflattering, despite the flash of pink underwear. Even their stockings were khaki; a marked contrast to the glamorous black stockings of the Wrens.

Later in the war, Princess Elizabeth signed up to the ATS as a driver and mechanic in spring 1945. Lesley Whately, who had known Princess Elizabeth since childhood, said her enrolling with ATS gave it cachet, 'I was absolutely staggered because we had all taken it for granted that she would go into the Navy as a Wren.'

With fewer restrictions than the WAAF and WRNS about who could join, the ATS offered girls from deprived backgrounds a better life. On arriving at training centres, they were deloused, issued soap and toothbrushes, given three meals a day and their own bed, and in their kit, along with four pairs of lisle stockings, they could find three pairs of khaki lock-knit knickers, two pairs of men's blue and white striped pyjamas, eight starched collars and two studs, three pink bras and two pink boned corsets.

'I was well aware that we in the ATS were the rough, tough ones – we got all the dregs,' said Judy Impey, an upper-class girl from an army family, who signed up to the ATS at the age of 18 in 1942. At her training camp in Yorkshire, she said, they arrived:

… ragtag and bobtail in civilian clothes, no table manners – you didn't have to teach them that but you hoped it brushed off a bit – and some of them hungry. One of the awful jobs was delousing them. Also inspecting their feet. They had to have baths in disinfectant and they were given coarse underclothes.

But she also gained new experiences from the girls from very different backgrounds to hers. 'I learned so much about the ways of life the others had. I learned that you ate fish and chips in bed, you smoked in bed, and if you went out you picked up a boy.'

Lady Meg Colville, later a lady-in-waiting to Princess Elizabeth after the war, was sent to the Royal Scots barracks near Penicuik as an ATS officer in 1941:

I hated that job because I wasn't qualified enough for it. We got the conscripts then, the slum dwellers from Newcastle and Glasgow, who were fairly dicey. The ATS were issued with sanitary towels, paid for by money provided by Lord Nuffield. But we had to teach them to be clean. At Glen Cross we had a 'head hut' where their heads were deloused. With a new intake we used to have a sweepstake on how many dirty heads out of a hundred there would be.

The ATS uniform, styled after the Motor Transport Corps outfit of the First World War, consisted of a lightweight serge belted khaki tunic with brass buttons and a mid-calf skirt, lined with khaki cotton. With it they wore a khaki shirt and tie and for active work they were given trousers, brown leggings, brown boots, a greatcoat and a tin helmet. The uniform was ill-fitting and baggy, and girls pulled in their belts in an attempt to create more of an hourglass silhouette.

With a shortage of available uniforms, girls were issued overalls to wear until they could be supplied with the full kit. There were also major shortages in greatcoats and Mackintoshes with fleecy linings, and so they shivered at their anti-aircraft batteries over the winter of 1939. To make up for inadequacies, by 1941 tailored battledress, boots and gaiters were issued, and a faux fur coat, known as the 'teddy bear coat', was introduced.

Elizabeth Oldham, in the all-women's 93rd Searchlight Regiment, was pleased to have the fur coat to wear with the tin hat. 'Official-issue fur coat – just something you pulled over your head and it came down round your bottom and kept you warm. Teddy-bear fur, actually!'

Initially, there was opposition to female Anti-Aircraft Commands, as it was thought too dangerous to allow women to fire guns, but with a shortage of officers and other ranks at the start of 1940, there was a recruitment drive to attract women to these 'Ack-Ack' stations. Olive Helyer, from Norton-on-Tees, was sent to Plymouth after being assigned to the searchlight division of the ATS:

> My mother wouldn't sign for me to go abroad – your parents had a lot of say then – so I joined the ATS. You were frightened, naturally, but after the alarm you just got out of bed with your Dinky curlers in and you got your steel hat on – you didn't have time to take your curlers out. Then you got your battledress on, pyjamas underneath, and said to yourself: 'They're coming over here – and we're going to hit them!'

Doris Batley joined the ATS in October 1942 and volunteered for Ack-Ack duties. She was sent to join the elite 93rd Searchlight Regiment, training in Rhyl, on the North Wales coast. Doris said, 'It was November and the nights were cold, but we were issued with boots, trousers, battledress tops and leather jerkins, and later, when we were sent out to operational sites, fur coat with hoods.'

Many of the girls worked on the searchlight batteries alongside older men who were unfit for service, and who sometimes gave barbed comments about the character of these young women in uniform. The ATS developed a reputation as 'officers' groundsheets' and were given lectures on pregnancy and STDs. With shared dormitories in barracks offering more freedoms than ever before, they were judged for drinking too much and flirting with men; it was enough to put off many parents from letting their children join the armed services. 'Up with the lark and to bed with a Wren', was one common saying. Mona McLeod, who would become a land girl, recounts how her father, an expert in venereal disease, forbade her from being stationed at an RAF base because of all the cases he had come across.

Ursie Barclay, an officer in the ATS, was reluctantly given permission by her mother to sail to Italy in 1942 with the army. Before departing, Lady Maud Baillie, in her kilt and uniform jacket, gave the girls a sermon, 'If you get asked out to dinner by twelve young men on the same night when you get wherever you are going, it's not because you are popular. It's because you're scarce.'

The First Aid Nursing Yeomanry (FANY) was considered the chic wartime service. It may have been a division of the ATS, but the girls felt independent – a cut above. When war broke out, this was the service, along with the Motor Transport Corps, that the debutantes wished to join, and it gained a reputation as a service solely for posh girls to drive cars. All members could drive or fly, as they were wealthy enough to have been able to afford lessons or were taught by their chauffeurs.

Ordered from their fathers' tailors, they ensured their khaki uniforms were distinctive, with a dyed blue and pink lanyard worn on the left, a flash on the shoulder and straps over their caps. Their officer-style Sam Browne belts also set them apart. 'When we did anything official,' said Lavinia Holland-Hibbert, 'we were made to remove all these things – and how we resented it.' She added, 'During my first Season, in 1938, I joined the FANYs run by all these lesbian ladies with trilby hats standing in front of the fire with their skirts hiked over their bums, and the rank and file very aristocratic young women.'

The FANY had their origins as mounted nurses in the Boer War, riding horses close to the battlefield to treat injured soldiers. They played an important role in the First World War, where instead of horses, they drove ambulances in the battlefields of France. They continued to operate in peacetime, when driving became the focus of their work. In 1938 the Women's Legion, the Women's Emergency Service and the FANY were merged into the new ATS, but the FANY kept their London headquarters and retained their exclusivity by only attracting the well-bred.

Lavinia Holland-Hibbert, who drove officers from the Oxfordshire Yeomanry, had the upper-class belief that rules didn't apply to her:

> I was pretty insubordinate, always losing my car and going to London and dancing all night and being late on parade. My attitude was that if I wasn't found out there was nothing wrong. I always tried to make whatever I was doing, or wherever I was, fit in with my ways.

After Lavinia arranged to be posted to Italy, she met Denis Healey, a second lieutenant in the Royal Artillery, and later the deputy leader of the Labour Party. He described their love affair in his autobiography, *The Time of My Life*, when they went on sightseeing trips together. He wrote, 'We spent weekends at the medieval town of San Gimignano and later at the enchanting fishing village of Positano, south of Naples. The FANYs were an exceptional lot, with much broader views and wider interests than I would have then expected.'

Later in the war, because of their language knowledge and driving skills, the FANYs became a cover for those recruited as spies in the Special Operations Executive (SOE). Thirteen of these women were killed by the Gestapo, including Noor Inayat Khan, Britain's first Muslim war heroine.

6

Dreaming of the Sea and the Sky

Lady Elizabeth Scott, the eldest daughter of the 8th Duke of Buccleuch, decided the Civil Nursing Reserve didn't suit her, and switched to the Wrens with a friend on a whim. 'I think we both fancied the navy-blue uniforms,' she said. 'We Wrens did look marvellous whereas the other services, through no fault of their own, didn't.'

The Wrens was the most desired service for its chic, flattering navy-blue skirt and jacket, cut in the same way as a naval officer. The uniform was topped with a black felt tricorn hat with the laurel, crown and anchor emblem on the front. The kit also included white shirts, black ties, black stockings and knee-length elastic navy-blue silk knickers, which were nicknamed 'blackouts' and were a source of ridicule for those in the Wrens. 'The enterprising ones among us promptly cut off the legs and, hey presto: trench knickers! We kept one pair intact for inspection though,' said Maxine Woodcock.

The Wrens had the motto 'Never at Sea', as they weren't permitted to operate from ships at sea until 1943, much to Stephanie Batstone's disappointment. However, they worked in many different roles, as visual signallers, messengers and administrators.

Sheila Mills joined the Wrens just two weeks after her eighteenth birthday, after training at St James Secretarial College in London. She arrived for her first posting in Dunfermline in October 1940, excited and apprehensive about the enormity of uprooting her life, and with the dream of going overseas. Sheila described her uniform in a letter home to her mother: 'We have to wear knickers "closed in at the knees" for the morals of the Navy must be kept up!'

Due to the delays in receiving her kit, she continued to wear her civvies:

When I am in uniform life will be hell, tho! No lipstick or nail polish, hair cut short; even tho' it's very tidy now, and skirt to my ankles, and you're not even allowed to wear your hat at an angle. Oh, I'm thoroughly fed up with them all. Surely, if you're willing to serve your country they should let you look as attractive as possible?

As a new recruit at HMS *Cabbala*, Stephanie Batstone was expected to wear the training uniform of bluettes and lisle stockings. 'Bluettes would have looked at home in a penal settlement,' she wrote. 'They were boiled out blue overall dresses of a kind of sponge cloth, buttoned up to the neck. Worn without slips, they rucked up in front, sticking to our stockings as we walked.' When parading the semaphore flag signal, the strain of lifting their arms at different angles would split the fabric under the arms.

Stephanie loved being a Wren, from learning the unique naval language, such as 'tiddley' for fine, and 'Jimmy the One' for first lieutenant, to being taught how to use the Aldis lamp, which flashed Morse code from shore so that passing ships at sea could be guided to safety.

She wrote of her excitement at finally receiving her full uniform, for 'now we should look like the girl on the poster'. They queued up to be presented with a pile of clothing, which included two skirts and two jackets, 'a tiddley one and an everyday one'. She was also given:

> … two pairs of black lisle stockings; two pairs of shoes, a raincoat, a greatcoat, a tie, six collars and six shirts, and the hat with taffeta ribbon …
> And, because we would work outdoors, two pairs of thick navy woollen blackouts, two pairs of bellbottoms, a seaman's jersey, and woollen gloves and socks.

Deciding they wouldn't be seen dead in their woollen knickers, she and her friends packed them up and sent them home, but by winter in the Hebrides they wished they could have them back.

The bellbottoms had been the item of clothing Stephanie had most wanted to get her hands on, as they 'were our badge of office, our passport to a man's job, and in them we intended to swank around the camps and bases of the future with our bottoms cheekily outlined and our waists nipped in'. However, reality proved a bit different. Stephanie's bellbottoms were just sailor's trousers, 'enormous thick things, all padded with lumps of wadding, hundreds of buttons, blue and white stripe linings and enormous let-down flap on the stomach'. In a letter back home, she included a sketch of the bell-bottoms and the 'ridiculous hat' which was to be worn over one eye. 'It isn't as bad as I had expected,' she reassured her family. 'I have been getting quite used to putting it on over one eye.'

The only item they didn't need to alter was the seaman's jersey. 'It was perfect. It came down to our knees. It was warm and comfortable and inde-structible. It could be boiled, scorched, scrubbed, slept in, lived in, and would last a lifetime.'

Stephanie's memoirs reveal a girl who was naive and much less knowing than other girls her age. Sharing a three-bed dorm room with Stephanie and Dorothy was a glamorous Wren called Roberta, with a blonde Veronica Lake curtain of hair, who accessorised her skirt and shirt with an RAF silk scarf knotted around her neck, given to her by her 'sweetie-pie'. Stephanie and Dorothy may have had new striped pyjamas, but Roberta wore a pink satin nightie with blue ribbons. Roberta may have gone on dates with different men, but Stephanie and Dorothy held a midnight's feast for a friend's twenty-first birthday. With cakes sent in from their mothers, they dug holes into the sponge with nail files, to pour condensed milk into.

Roberta was bored being stuck at camp and was desperate to go overseas. She had something in common with Sheila Mills. As well as a keen interest in having the right clothes at all times, Sheila also looked down on some of the other girls. She wrote to her mother:

Everyone seems terribly young. When they hear I type and do shorthand they think I'm most accomplished, which makes me laugh, and I feel quite a grandmother – at 20! They are very young, or about 25 or 40 and missed their chances! I'm afraid I must be rather blasé or a terrible snob because I don't feel inclined to run around with any Tom, Dick and Harry like these girls do. Any soldier or sailor does for them.

While they had hoped to be posted to Portsmouth, the centre of action for the Wrens, Stephanie and Dorothy were drafted to Oban in October 1943. They travelled all night from London to the Highlands, making a stop at Bletchley, where 'eight Scottish Royal Engineers got in, in a welter of great-coats and kitbags and respirators'.

On arrival in Oban, they found their accommodation was in cold, damp cabins in the grounds of Raasay Lodge, struggling, in blackout, to travel between the camp and the lodge where they showered and ate. Stephanie and

Dorothy were unhappy about 'being so far away from the war, and the food, and the lack of men, and the cold of the damp'.

Ganavan War Signal Station was a mile out of town and up a steep hill, and they trudged through wind and rain to reach it, with their wellington boots and raincoats not enough to keep themselves dry. The signal room had an iron cylindrical stove, which they used to dry their constantly damp clothing, and 'after a few weeks our bellbottoms had a circular burn mark round each thigh where we had leaned over the stove and scorched them on the top rim'. Later, as they got used to their workstation, they worked out they could use the stove to make marmalade and dye old knitting wool.

Over the winter it was so wet that they were issued with stiff oilskins, which made it difficult to sit and bend their knees. 'We had four pairs of trousers and four jackets between us – when we put them in the cupboard they stood up all on their own. We couldn't really wear them, they slowed us up so.'

When they got a call that they were to be inspected by the signal officer, they realised they had fallen some way below the image of the ideal Wren:

> I had on a pre-war school sweater with frayed cuffs which had unsuccessfully been dyed navy from yellow, over a shrunk white pullover in which my father had once gone on a boat in 1912. My bellbottoms were shapeless and stained with coffee, and my toes were sticking through a pair of ancient plimsolls. Joan was wearing bellbottoms and a fluffy pink angora jumper and very old silver sandals.

The RAF would occasionally send a van to Oban to collect the Wrens for a dance at their base, where a three-piece band was set up in a blacked-out hut playing the foxtrot and waltz. Stephanie and her friends wore their uniforms to the dance but had spent hours starching their collars and pressing their shirts. 'We sat in serried rows, our clumping black shoes and thick black stockings hopelessly out in front of us, our sensible hair rolled off our collars, our faces scrubbed and weather-beaten, and lightly powdered with Tokalon, looking wholesome and dull …' Stephanie had once made an attempt to find 'battle red' lipstick in Oban, to no avail.

Then the 'Civvy Transport' arrived, and the RAF men cheered and perked up as girls streamed into the hut:

> [with] Betty Grable and Hedy Lamarr and Ava Gardner and Lana Turner hairstyles, piled up curls in front and long at the back, shiny, brightly coloured, faintly grubby dresses which shot up their thighs as the airmen lifted

them over the tailboard, scarlet Cupid's bows, navy blue eye shadow, padded shoulders, sheer stockings with black clocks, high heels. They were a renta-cutie mob, and the airmen just loved them.

She recalled the smell of sweat and Californian Poppy in the room, air force blue against jewel-coloured satin. They did the 'Hokey Cokey' at 10 p.m., before being taken away on their transport. She described the fixed smiles and faraway eyes, feeling disappointed that not all wartime dances were satisfying when it came to finding love. Instead, she longed for 'the cool, quiet, dark sea at Ganavan, the feel of the Aldis in my hand, the pencil of light answering. I wished I'd been on duty.'

At the signal station in Oban, Stephanie and her friends would occasionally meet men from overseas. The South African Air Force seemed otherworldly, bronzed and broad-shouldered and clean, like film stars in their dazzling ochre uniform with a leaping springbok insignia on the shoulder.

They were also taken on a boat trip with a couple of men from the US Navy, changing out of their bellbottoms and seamen's jerseys for skirts and clean white shirts. 'Joan's Yank was the fastest worker, but was having difficulties – he obviously wasn't used to dealing with a tiepin and tie, or a collar stud, and it slowed him up.'

In May 1944, a convoy of US merchant ships began filling up the anchorage in preparation for D-Day. Stephanie developed a friendship with a signalman called Jack Campbell, despite communicating solely with their Aldis lamps. They talked of missing home, of school, which they had only recently left, and where they had been in the war. Even though he was anchored offshore, they were forbidden to meet each other – he was not allowed on shore and she was not allowed on a ship. On 31 May, she arrived at the signal station to find that all the ships had gone to the D-Day manoeuvres. She didn't know if she would ever hear from Jack again, and it would be fifty years later that they would meet up for the first time.

Life in the Wrens was a culture shock for Sheila Mills, who felt a step above the other girls in maturity. Because of her glamorous image, always fastidious about her clothes and make-up, rumours went around that she was a former chorus girl:

I do wish we could meet people of our own kind whom we could visit or go out with. Life is so mundane and dull mixing with the servant class the whole time. Not that they aren't nice people – they are. But you get so tired of living with them and they scream about the place so.

Still waiting for her uniform, she asked her mother to send clothing from home: 'I exist on only two jumpers, a navy one and a pink one, which is miraculous for me. Stockings are indeed a problem, because all mine have gone at once, and I've only got two pairs left and can't get any more.' She was pleased that her sister Rosemary sent her fur coat to her, because she could slip it on 'when dashing out in the evenings, and really it's got quite cold lately.'

When Sheila was finally issued with her uniform, she found the shoes 'damned uncomfortable (I've had to put plasters on my heels) and they squeak'. The greatcoat, however, was 'terribly nice and I feel most smart. I've only got to adjust the belt at the back and it will be a perfect fit. I changed the shirt at M&S for a 14½ which is very nice; they tend to shrink and I loathe them tight.'

In June 1941, Sheila was given a place at the Royal Naval College in Greenwich to train as an officer, before being sent back for a posting at Methil, Fife. With the promotion, she could now have her uniform tailored by Moss Bros. 'They are supposed to be very good,' she wrote. 'And also are most reasonable. I've ordered 2 suits, one bridge coat and a hat, and if I don't pass out all right they take responsibility. The suits I have ordered in superfine as I hate serge and the difference in price is negligible.'

Back in Fife, she enjoyed the sherry parties, hockey matches and walks on the beach. But Sheila was yearning for adventure overseas and finally, in 1942, she got her wish and was posted to Egypt for the North Africa campaign.

'A great crowd are the WAAFs,' wrote Guy Gibson in his wartime memoirs. In the bomber ops room, he said, 'the only thing that holds your interest in it is, perhaps, the pretty girl behind the telephone and the large blackboard on the wall.'

Chelsea bohemian Joan Wyndham was one of these plotters at RAF Barton Hall. The underground Filter Room was 'huge and hectic, like a newspaper office in an American movie', where the WAAFs wore headphones connecting them to radar stations to plot the position and height of planes on the map. They scrambled over the map as they charted their course, with the Fighter and Bomber Command officers observing from the level above. Gibson said,

'Some of these girls are extremely pretty and have in Fighter Command been known since time immemorial as "the beauty chorus".'

And while their earphones were placed on their carefully styled hair, they struggled to stay cool. It was very hot in the underground Filter Room, especially in their heavy tailored uniform. 'I'm not wearing anything under my uniform except thin pants and a suspender belt, but still my shirt comes off wringing wet. It's awful but thank goodness we are allowed to work in our shirt-sleeves,' wrote Joan in her memoirs.

By 1943 there were 181,835 women in the WAAF, doing a wide range of roles. As well as plotters, they worked as cooks, waitresses, radiographers, mechanics, and manned the enormous barrage balloons suspended in the sky by ropes, which were designed to stop enemy aircraft. There was hierarchy amongst the different factions. After training, Hazel Williams became a plotter for Fighter Command, and discovered they 'were very snooty' to the other WAAF trades. 'In fact, the signals girls and plotters didn't like each other very much.'

Joan Odette Bawden, born in 1919, had a comfortable middle-class childhood growing up in the Surrey village of Claygate. Before the war she attended secretarial college, one of the few educational options for women, but harboured a desire for more:

> I wanted to write; I wanted to travel; I wanted to be famous. But all I got were rejection slips from editors, and how could I save up for a world trip on £2 10s a week? Then, in September 1939, war was declared. This was my opportunity, I seized it immediately. I joined the Women's Auxiliary Air Force.

She wrote in her diary of her reasons for joining: firstly, 'doing one's bit', secondly it would get her away from home and 'make me adult and independent', thirdly, ' it's a change and adventure', and fourthly, 'I want to swank around in a uniform'.

Joan Bawden was initially posted to RAF Hendon to work as a secretary, and when she received her first promotion she not only earned a small raise but she could also order a second uniform from Moss Bros, surreptitiously in officer's cloth. In March 1940, catching a bus to a friend's wedding, she felt she 'was looking very smart and clean with my hair newly set, my buttons shining and I was wearing my Moss Bros best blue.'

Joan met up with an old friend who had joined the ATS, at a Lyons Corner House café. They compared their uniforms, agreeing that the WAAF's was much superior, 'so much so, in fact, that she's going to see if she can't get a transfer to the WAAF'.

The WAAF uniform brought a sense of prestige to those who wore it. The jacket was cut like the male RAF jacket, but tailored to suit the female figure, and featured four brass buttons, a fabric belt and flapped pockets. They wore a light blue shirt and black tie, in mourning for the men of the Royal Flying Corps who died in the Great War, black lace-up shoes and a peaked cap, with a cap badge almost identical to the men's, unlike the other two women's services. Those in the WAAF held the equivalent ranking of the RAF, with officers wearing the same rank braid as their male counterparts.

Their greatcoats featured a white wool lining, with the idea that it could be spread on the ground to attract attention, in the event of having to bail out of a plane. However this was wishful thinking, as there was slim chance they would ever be in the air.

Like the Wrens, their thick knickers were a particular source of amusement, known as passion-killers as they had been purposely designed to be as unromantic as possible. The navy blue winter-weight knickers were referred to as 'blackouts', and the lighter blue summer knickers were known as 'twilights' to those in the WAAF and RAF.

As for the grey-blue lisle stockings, they 'must have lost more recruits than any other item', wrote Sylvia Drake-Brockman. 'All the girls loathed them. They were thick, a ghastly blue and made the slimmest legs look twice their size.'

Despite attempts by the top brass to stop flirtations, glamour was considered part of a WAAF's duty. Not only did they defy Hitler with lipstick, but it also helped them look their best for the airmen. 'Evening in Paris', advertised as for a woman who loves 'a soldier … a sailor … a marine', was the favoured perfume of the WAAFs, but it was in short supply. Given a new job as the messing officer, Joan Wyndham was in charge of the stock cupboard, allowing her to illicitly order make-up and scent for her friends. On her list was 'Cutex Cameo nail varnish, one Max Factor Pancake Natural No. 2, three refill Cyclax Velvet Grape lipsticks, two Coty Paris perfumes, and one Helena Rubenstein Apple Blossom perfume. I am now one of the most popular girls in the Mess.'

A Mass Observation survey of WAAF in 1941 found that the women kept 'a lively interest in clothes, fashion and general dress matters'. Most chose to ignore the rules that hair should sit above the collar, and they shouldn't wear nail varnish. While they were expected to wear their uniform when off base, one tactic when going to a dance was to feign illness and wear their greatcoats buttoned to the neck. Once safely outside, they removed the coats to reveal a glamorous civilian dress.

Kathleen Godfrey, the daughter of Rear Admiral John Godfrey, who was said to be the inspiration for Ian Fleming's 'M', was 16 when war broke out. Too young to join a service, Kathleen enrolled in domestic science school where she was taught basic cooking and dressmaking skills:

> I chose to make a pair of white satin pants, called 'French knickers' with fashionably wide legs. No elastic at the waist. They were kept up with one pearl button, the cause of much embarrassment some years later when the button flew off on the platform at Tottenham Court Road Station, allowing the knickers to slip to the ground round my ankles.

Over the summer of 1940, Kathleen worked as a land girl on her godmother's farm in the village of Spaxton, in Somerset. The village was without electricity and she lived in an old farmhouse next to the church, lit by brass oil lamps and candlelight. Jobs included feeding the hens and pigs, milking the cows and making clotted cream and butter by hand in the dairy:

> I worked on the land doing most of the things which the men did. The young farm workers had all been called up leaving a motley crew to work on the farm … I learnt how to drive a tractor and even learned how to sharpen and use a scythe to slice through the nettles.

When she turned 18 she joined the WAAF as she wanted to contribute more to the war, particularly after a close friend was killed. Kathleen's life was one of privilege, and after her medical exam she called up her father who took her for lunch at the Savoy. But as Aircraftwoman 2nd Class Godfrey, she had to queue up for her uniform like every other new recruit in Yorkshire.

The uniforms 'made no concession to our shapes as they were modelled exactly on the men's, even buttoning from left to right,' said Kathleen:

> The belted jacket in Air Force blue had four square pockets, eliminating any curves which might have been visible; then came a knee-length straight skirt and a blue cotton shirt with separate collar which, as it had to be stiffly starched, left an unattractive red mark on the neck … The rest of the outfit consisted of thick dark-grey cotton stockings, suspender belts, bras and even black knickers, with elastic at the knee known as 'anti-passions'. The black

lace-up shoes rubbed horribly, and all the clothes tended to be scratchy and uncomfortable. As snow lay on the ground, we were issued with thick double-breasted great-coats which had a full complement of brass buttons with embossed eagles on them. All of them had to be polished every day. Lastly came a peaked hat with RAF badge, yet another piece of brass to be cleaned. In addition, we carried cumbersome gas masks everywhere with threats of horrible punishments if we put anything else like a book or make-up in with the gas mask.

Her father, in his admiral's uniform, came to see her and took her for tea:

He hadn't ever seen me in uniform before and I suppose that must have been quite a surprise. Over a cup of tea he asked me how I was getting on. 'What are you doing with yourself all the time, Kathleen?' he asked me. 'I can't possibly tell you, Father. It's a secret,' I answered. He was of course delighted.

After a year at a radar station on the Isle of Wight, Kathleen was sent to Bletchley Park, where army, navy and air force worked in secret to break the Enigma code. Once she passed officer training, she could now have her uniform tailored in London:

It had a red silk lining and an almost invisibly thin stripe on the cuff which denoted my new status. Actually, most of us, while in the ranks, had already had our uniforms tailored in officers' cloth for wearing on days off. This, combined with the occasional pair of silk stockings and civilian shoes, meant that we felt quite presentable.

Kathleen turned 21 in October 1943, and for her birthday party at the Savoy Hotel, she recalled:

[I] wore my first long evening dress; sparkling black net with yards of material in the skirt. All the current boyfriends were in uniform, and we danced away the evening in the adjoining ballroom. The band made us forget about the dangers and uncertainties of the real world outside.

After being accepted into the WAAF in April 1941, Joan Wyndham and her three best friends, Gussy, Pandora and Oscarine, packed their duffel bags and travelled early in the morning to Preston. With the smell of fish and chips in the air, and the sight of malnourished children in the town, their accommodation felt grim compared to what they were accustomed to. The other WAAFs who were staying in their building seemed so different to these upper-class bohemian friends. A drunk peroxide blonde, naked except for a pair of satin drawers, began throwing up in the bathroom sink.

On their first night, Joan recalled in her diary, it was freezing cold and they all slept in their underwear, except for Pandora:

> … [who] changed into her oyster-grey silk pyjamas. She kept her pearls on too, because she says real pearls die if you take them off for too long. I lay shivering in bed, thinking of my lost studio in Chelsea, so warm and cheery with the oil stove, and Rupert playing his guitar.

As well as contending with fleas in the hay-stuffed pillows and lice in their hair, they always felt hungry. 'Our best bet is to take a penny platform ticket and go to the Free Forces Canteen, where if you fight your way through the hordes of sailors and tommies you can eat your fill for nothing, and stuff your kit-bag into the bargain.'

Their social life involved pub parties in the mess, which turned into 'Babylonian orgies', with the party ending with 'WAAF's collapsing and being sick on the road, airmen peeing against the wall, couples rolling in the grass'.

In preparation for a sergeant's dance, they spent the afternoon 'tarting' themselves up. They had one lipstick to share between them for lips and cheeks and Rubenstein's Apple Blossom to spray in their hair and, having to wear their uniform at dances, they used their best efforts to make it as attractive as possible, picking violets to place in their buttonholes. 'There is not much you can do to make a WAAF's uniform sexy (apart from pulling your belt in till you can hardly breathe), but jumping up and down on your cap to loosen up the brim does help to give it a rakish air.'

In March 1942, Joan was posted to Stanmore, the top fighter headquarters near London, where she was separated from her friends. She was struck by the WAAF officers in the mess, sophisticated and glamorous and into the latest swing music. They found Joan strange for reading Baudelaire in bed, and putting on an air of bohemianism:

> All my fellow officers are fairly glamorous, and a gay, wild lot, always talking about the Savoy and the Berkeley, and the nightclubs they've been to. They are mad about swing and play hot jazz all day. The Wrens, who share our Mess, are sniffy and stuffy, reading good books in one corner of the

ante-room while the WAAF's go trucking madly around the gramophone singing 'Bounce Me Brother with a Solid Four'.

Joan was later posted to Inverness where she was reunited with Oscarine and Pandora. It was quiet compared to London, with the only decent men in the area being the Canadians and the Norwegian sailors, who were 'gorgeous, sexy and very, very funny, and they drink like fishes and take over the whole town – it's like a Viking invasion'. Some nights the sailors climbed up the drainpipes of the hotel to visit the WAAFs in their rooms. The officer in charge of the WAAF mess was nicknamed 'Gloves' Gallagher, for her habit of 'leaving her leather gloves behind in glamorous places so that she can go back for them the next day and get chatted up by the top brass. So far she's scored with Bomber Command HQ, the Cameron Highlanders, and two battleships.'

Joan Bawden also enjoyed the independence and the camaraderie of sharing living space with a mixed group of WAAFs. Evenings were spent sitting by the fireplace in their slacks and jumpers, listening to the wireless, reading books and chatting about the airmen they met at dances. She enjoyed taking care of her uniform, pressing the skirt and jacket, polishing her shoes, and washing her stockings. With delays in issuing the full uniform to WAAFs, they didn't receive their greatcoats until January 1940, and had to wrap themselves up in layers and layers to try to keep warm:

> I am very dirty because it's too cold to wash but I don't care. I haven't made my bed for days because I have discovered that if I crawl out carefully it will still do. In short, the layers of ladylike-hood are peeling off pretty speedily and doubtless soon I shall smell. Oh well, what the hell.

In August 1940, during the Battle of Britain, when the country was raided by the Luftwaffe, Joan experienced directly the dangers of war when Hendon came under fire in a bombing raid. She wrote:

> None of us could find our clothes. We rushed distractedly around, pulling on whatever we could find, quantities of strange and miscellaneous attire, and finally I followed my household to the shelter, wearing pyjamas, slacks, jumper, jacket, an old dirty but warm dressing gown, tennis shoes and carrying somehow two blankets, pillow, a gas mask, a tin hat and my anti-gas equipment. I secured a corner of the shelter, wrapped myself like a cocoon in the blankets and prepared for sleep.

Love affairs flourished on RAF bases. But in November 1943 the Air Council issued a directive that male officers should observe a professional relationship with air women. Aircraftwoman Morfydd Rose was a waitress in the sergeants' mess:

> We young WAAFs would have to endure a barrage of good-natured banter: 'How is your sex life?' 'I dreamed about you all night' ... 'Please serve us in the nude'. We took it all in good part, because we knew the great strains they were under.

The WAAFs had no end of demeaning nicknames put on them by the men in the RAF, such as 'aircrew comforts'. They were referred to as 'bluebirds', from 'the blue bird of happiness', a 'blonde job' for a fair-haired WAAF, and a 'Huffy' was an unfriendly WAAF. A 'Chop Girl' was a WAAF who was considered bad luck as previous boyfriends had been killed in action and was therefore spurned at dances.

Many WAAFs who were in relationships with airmen knew the dangers and experienced the anxiety as they waited for them to return from a mission. Morfydd Rose's boyfriend, Flying Officer Phil Burgess, was a navigator with 617 Squadron and took part in the dams raid in 1943. She remembered serving food in the sergeants' mess to the crews who had returned from the raid, and the sadness when told that eight planes had been lost. 'We all burst into tears,' she wrote. 'The tables we had so hopefully laid out for the safe return of our young boys looked empty and pathetic.'

Sometimes WAAFs would have to chalk up on the board 'M' for 'Missing' beside their boyfriend's aircraft, trying to fight the shock and remain strong. Guy Gibson wrote in his memoirs:

> ... [a] girl called Mary Stoffer would climb the ladder to fill in the board. She was waiting for her husband Harry to return ... She just sat there, staring at that space, a funny look, an incredible look. Someone came in with a cup of tea, but it had long since gone cold before she noticed it was there. Then there was a quick ray of hope, the phone rang. It was the observer corps to say that a Manchester had just crossed the coast coming in our direction. Could it be Harry? Her face lit up in a smile, hardly daring to say anything; then we heard it go over and pass on its way. Her face fell, her eyes began to glisten as she fought back her tears ... In the end I got up and took her by the arm and led her to my car. She wasn't crying, she was very brave. She insisted on stopping at the Waaf Officers' Mess to collect

her things, little household things. She clutched them tightly as I dropped her at her house.

Going into a pub in Elstree in May 1940 with a group of pilots of 504 Squadron, Joan Bawden noticed 'people eyed me enviously in the bar, with the four of them so young, so good looking. They make you want to describe them as they do in silly magazine stories: knights of the air, gay gallants, splendid youth.'

At the Hendon Way, Joan and her friend Molly met two pilots, Mac, who 'was young and fair and trying to grow a moustache', and Red, a stocky, auburn-haired 19-year-old who had already downed eight Germans. They spent the evening talking and laughing, singing sentimental songs while bombs fell outside. 'When you're pretty drunk you just don't care.' Molly and Joan wrapped their warm flying jackets around their shoulders for the walk home.

But the tragedy of war hit home during the Battle of Britain, as the death toll for 504 Squadron rose. Joan later heard that seven of 504's officers had been killed since they left Hendon:

Seven of them: that's nearly all of the officers. It made me sick with shock. It's the wicked, pointless dreadfulness of their deaths; they haven't had any life at all … How can any of them be blamed for their ruthless living, their desperate cramming of every sensation into hours when, instead of the gentle years, they have only the rushing days?

Joan was a liberal thinker, and watching the terrible newsreels in the cinema and hearing of the men they knew who were all too suddenly killed, she reflected that her generation had been let down by the ones before; the leaders who took them on the path to war. 'We had twenty years to make away with war and through our own fault we failed. Those who did it deserved to die, but not us young.'

WAAFs were rarely given a chance to fly, but Joan was one of the lucky few, particularly with her new commissioned role as a photographic interpreter at Medmenham in May 1941. A pilot at Hendon promised to take her flying and she chatted with the squadron in the pilots' room, scattered with maps and books and pieces of flying kit. She said, 'They perched on the backs of their chairs, smoking, talking to me; their tunics were ancient, their wings frayed, they were young, untidy and contented.'

She was lent a flying jacket and helmet to wear over her uniform but her skirt made it difficult to climb into the cockpit, and almost impossible to wear a parachute and harness. They found a stepladder for her to get into the Lysander, and then she was airborne. 'It's a rare event (at Hendon anyway): a WAAF flying.'

Jackie Sorour's passion in life was flying. Born in Pretoria, South Africa in 1920, she took her first flight as a present for her fifteenth birthday after begging her mother to buy her one. Her entire family had been against her taking to the air. At 17, in 1938, she was the first woman to perform a solo parachute jump in South Africa, and in June of that year left to travel to England to train for her pilot's licence.

She stayed with friends of her family, the Hirons, at their farmhouse in Oxfordshire while she learned to fly. As war drew closer, she wept with envy as the men at the training school were summoned to do their part in the war:

I despised my body, my breasts, all the things that pronounced me woman and left me behind as solitary and desolate as a discarded mistress … That evening in bed I thought of the Amazonian women who were alleged to have cut off their breasts to enable them to sight their bows and arrows accurately. I looked malignantly at my breasts, symbols of weakness, rooted firmly on my chest and remembered Mr Hirons' cut-throat razor in the bathroom.

In the hope that she might be put to war work as a pilot, she agreed to sign up in the meantime as a WAAF. Her first role was as a personal batswoman to two WAAF officers; she 'envied their tailored elegance and the thin pale blue stripe on their sleeves'.

She was then asked to report to the WAAF training centre, where she observed how the individual personalities were homogenised when wrapped in air-force blue. She noted the groups of 'highly individual females were to be seen entering the gates. A few weeks later, the processing completed, columns marched uniformly out again … We were numbered, ranked, and drilled until even our expressions became uniform.'

She felt out of depth with the more sophisticated girls who bought exotic lingerie, drank and knew about sex. 'She thinks she's too good for us,' they told her. 'She's a Brylcreem girl. Officers only.' One of the girls, Vera, was a film extra who ignored the uniform regulations. Jackie described her 'hippy walk, long flaxen hair (despite orders to cut it), scarlet nails and lips, caricatured the severity of the uniform and brought agonized frustration to the faces of the airmen as she prowled around the camp.'

Finally, after months working as WAAF, including a stint at a radar station in Rye, where they sipped tea and shivered in balaclavas, greatcoats and scarves, she was asked to report to the Air Transport Auxiliary (ATA), at Hatfield Aerodrome in July 1940. To fly for a living had been her dream. She loved it for its 'glamour, its adventure, but above all for its elusive mysticism and solitude' – and no longer did she worry that her sex was getting in her way.

7

Bomb Girls, Land Girls and Lumberjills

In the first two years of war, it was reported with concern that incidents of female juvenile delinquency doubled and there was a 70 per cent rise in venereal disease. Constantly exposed to images of men in uniform, and with the message that a woman's duty was to boost the morale of men by being available, it was inevitable that girls were expected to grow up more quickly.

Yet, teenagers still loved the movies and their favourite stars were Judy Garland and Mickey Rooney, whose cheerful renditions on screen offered pure escapism. *Picturegoer* magazine noted that 'Veronica Lake and Lana Turner do more for the girl of fourteen than merely set her hairstyle'. They offered a sense of hope, and despite the rationing in place, girls would covet make-up and new clothes to look like the stars on screen.

Dancing was incredibly important to young Brits, and at halls across the country they created their own style and dance codes. Teenage boys took to the dancefloor in roll-neck sweaters and suits with brylcreemed hair, but it was the men in uniform that girls wanted to dance with.

Patricia McGowan was 17 when the war started and despite the threat of air raids, she would live for going to her local YMCA in Birmingham for ball-room dancing every Wednesday with her friend, Mollie. The chance to dress up was a real joy and, like other teens, she carried her dance shoes in a bag to ensure they were kept pristine. She said:

An air raid could start at anytime, anywhere, so each day was lived precariously. The melodic sounds of the dance band came across in a most inviting way; saxophones droning slow foxtrot tunes that seemed to give us itchy feet. The sounds from the band invaded the mind and one forgot about danger from outside that warm throbbing dance hall ... Oh, it was so good to be in the swim of things again! For weeks I had been moping about at home feeling somewhat stagnated, and to get myself dressed up for this occasion was sheer bliss.

One evening, as they made their way home, they heard the air-raid sirens wailing. They tried to catch the last tram home, but they found that all transport had been stopped because of the raid, and so they had no choice but to make the dangerous walk home. A woman offered for them to come into their family air-raid shelter, but the two girls decided to keep going, so they could get home sooner. As they ran down the road, they were crying like frightened rabbits, almost hysterical, and in the panic, Patricia realised she had lost her dance shoes.

The next morning, she surveyed the damage. There were piles of rubble from where houses had been obliterated. She also found out that the air-raid shelter which she and Mollie had been invited into had taken a direct hit and everyone inside had been killed. Teenagers lived with these near misses almost every day during the war.

When clothing rationing was introduced in June 1941, there were serious restrictions on the amount of new clothes that could be bought. The allowance was enough for only one new outfit per year, including shoes, hats and gloves, and girls quickly learnt ingenious methods to look good with limited resources. They used old sugar bags and parachute silk to make clothes, boot polish for mascara, beetroot juice or rose petals soaked in wine for blush, and to create the effect of tan stockings, they painted their legs with gravy browning or drew a line down the back to imitate the seam. A shortage of shampoos, kirby grips and hair styling products led to an increase in hairnets and complicated twists such as the 'V for Victory' rolls.

Turbans also became very popular in the war. They were worn by girls who worked in munitions or on farms and came to represent a sense of patriotism – it was a sign that they were working hard for the war effort.

The war offered girls the chance to escape a life in domestic service by filling the jobs normally taken by men. But many teenage girls who were too young or had been not been given permission by their parents to join a service, found that they were directed into the Women's Land Army (WLA) and the Timber Corps, or into munitions work. In the First World War, these roles earned women the nickname of 'Munitionettes', and in the Second World War they became known as 'Bomb Girls'.

Betty Nettle, from Bridgend in Wales, was still a teenager when she went to work at the Welsh Arsenal during the war. She recalled in 1941:

> There were uniforms everywhere. For a 16-year-old, that meant good fun at the dance. To an extent, all the changes around us – the building of the arsenal, the uniformed men everywhere, all the new people coming into the area to work at the arsenal – it all made life more exciting.

Like many young women, clothes were very important to her, 'even though I didn't have any money … when I heard about the jobs at the arsenal, I didn't think twice … When I started work there, I already wore trousers. You couldn't buy them, I just wore my brothers' cast-offs.'

She worked in the under-18s section, making the uniforms for those in the different sections, 'coats, belts, caps, turbans, jackets, waistcoats; trousers for the men. White coats for the women. The belts were in different colours for different shifts for the workers in the ammo section. Blue for one shift, green or red for another.'

Betty was also tasked with repairing the parachutes, where the fine silk panels would be removed and replaced. It was the perfect opportunity for girls to source much-needed fabric for making new clothes:

> One girl was so good at making things, she could literally just look at you and go: 'Oh, you're 36-24-38' and then she'd cut it out, without a pattern, and make something to fit you out of parachute silk or cotton. She'd make you a petticoat or cami-knickers. Of course, you'd have to put them on and wear them before you went home. You were always searched, every time you went in or left the arsenal.

The searchers would ensure nothing left the factory, often carrying out random checks and discovering that people were stealing items like powder bags, where the fabric could be recycled. Others collected the little circles of paper from the punching-out clock, smuggling them out in their bras so they could be saved and used as wedding confetti.

Making bombs and ammunition at Royal Ordnance Factories (ROF) was vital but dangerous work, with the constant risk of explosions or of the factories being targeted by enemy aircraft. Like the land girls and lumberjills, they were often sent miles away from home, living in purpose-built hostels. But they didn't receive the health benefits of being able to work outdoors and suffered exhaustion as they covered shifts for factories that were open every hour and every day of the week.

In 1943, the *Saturday Evening Post* ran the ad, 'She's 5 feet 1 from her 4A slippers to her spun-gold hair. She loves flower-hats, veils, smooth orchestras – and being kissed by a boy who's in North Africa. But man, oh man, how she can handle her huge and heavy drill press.'

On the factory floor they were dressed in white overalls or white jacket and trousers, and a white turban to avoid being scalped if their hair was caught in machinery. Strictly no metal was allowed as even the tiniest spark could trigger an explosion. Wedding rings had to be covered by tape and all clothing was made from cotton to prevent the possibility of static electricity.

On arrival for their shift, the girls lined up on the 'Dirty Side' to take off their clothing, jewellery and hairgrips and store them in their kitbags. They moved over to the 'Clean Side', where they were issued with rubber-soled shoes and fire-proofed overalls with rubber or wooden fastenings.

Margaret Curtis, born in 1922 in Lanarkshire, worked as a parlour maid from the age of 14, but when the war started, she wanted to help the war effort and found a job as a process worker at ROF Bishopton, an explosives factory on the outskirts of Glasgow. She described wearing a white jacket and trousers, a white turban and rubber boots, or wellingtons, all year round. 'But you could not leave the plant in your wellies – that was forbidden,' she said:

> There were lots of other things you were forbidden to take into the building. No metal anywhere, no safety pins, no hairpins, no matches, no ciggies – the tiniest spark could put everyone at risk from explosion. There were men, the 'danger building men', whose job it was to carry out spot checks for any dangerous items, going round all the time, double checking on us.

Yet, despite this hard work, they earned little recognition because they didn't have a uniform to wear outside of the factory. As a token, workers at Royal Ordnance Factories were given a small badge with 'ROF, Front Line Duty', to wear on their coats so that they could be given preferential treatment by shopkeepers and in cafés.

Laura Hardwick, who worked at Swynnerton Royal Ordnance Factory, travelled to work on a train that was always packed with soldiers in khaki:

We weren't in any kind of uniform. Munitions girls could not wear any uniform outside the shop floor, because they said there was a risk of contamination. So when we got to the station, the WVS wouldn't serve us tea. Cups of tea were only for those in uniform. In the end, we'd pal up with the soldiers, sitting on their kitbags. That way, they'd get us a cuppa from the WVS. The soldiers knew what we did in munitions and that we were part of it all.

Munitions girls could also be identified by the yellow hue to their hair and skin from chemicals like TNT, which led to their nickname 'canaries'. Some factories supplied creams to act as a barrier to protect their skin, but women found that wearing thick 'pancake' make-up was equally effective.

As well as keeping their hair safely contained, turbans also protected their locks from the harsh chemicals. 'You were foolish if you didn't get that turban on first,' said Betty Nettle:

If the powdery stuff got into your hair, it would change colour. Even if you had a little bit of hair showing, that was it, it became discoloured. If you were blonde or ginger, it went green. Black hair went red. You tried your best not to let it happen but there were still times when you'd get a little bit on your face.

There were rumours that cold tea could remove the tint, but no matter how hard they scrubbed, the yellow wouldn't come off. And under the electric lights of the dance hall, their yellow-tinted skin would look even more pronounced:

Being yellow didn't stop the men from coming on to you. There were mainly women working in my section at the arsenal but there were a few men, mostly men who had come out of working in the collieries because they had chest problems. They weren't physically fit or desirable but they'd still come on to us girls.

As well as the danger, munitions work was hard, and factory workers who were hunched over conveyor belts every day needed some support. In 1943, the Corset Guild of Great Britain petitioned Downing Street on behalf of the women of Britain to help fund supporting corsets.

To allow them some respite from the hard work, there were social and sports clubs, drama groups, cinema screenings and a canteen at the munitions plants offering subsidised hot meals. During their shifts they listened to the BBC's 'Music While You Work', the most popular wartime radio show which played continuous live popular music. Songs reminded the girls of the absent loves in their lives, such as 'We'll Meet Again' and 'There's a Boy Coming Home on Leave'. 'The Thingummy Bob' was a song dedicated to munitions workers.

Girls also shook out the aches in their muscles on the dance floor. Every town or village hall would put on a dance, with bands playing the waltz and the foxtrot, but in larger cities, dance halls would play the latest crazes, including the jitterbug. It also gave the factory workers the chance to swap their overalls and turbans for a glamorous dress and to free their hair from their turbans and headscarves.

Dances could be held in factory canteens or at hostels and the women were encouraged to invite 'a friend in khaki'. Like most other factory girls, Betty Nettle preferred the men in uniform, whether it was the army, air force or navy:

There were some Americans in the area, of course. I met some nice ones. But that was all there was to it. Sometimes the first thing a guy in uniform would say was: 'I'm married, this is a photo of my little girl', so you could be friends, sit down and have a chat with them. And they'd want to talk about their family back home. I liked the friendship of it, rather than the courtship.

'At times they'd organise a big dance with the soldiers from the base nearby at Trentham. I loved the quickstep; Glenn Miller's "Chattanooga Choo Choo",' said Alice Butler, who had been called up to work at Swynnerton as a teenager. 'I'd wear a favourite brown and cream dress with inverted pleats with very high heels. Now and again I'd resort to using gravy browning to draw a seam down the middle of the back of my stockings – that meant they were "fully fashioned".'

Socialising was also touched with sadness because dating members of the armed forces stationed nearby would inevitably mean saying 'goodbye', without knowing whether they would meet again. Sometimes, as they were packing up boxes of bullets to send to soldiers overseas, they would leave little notes for them to receive, such as 'Keep 'em on the run', or 'We all love you and we're here for you', as Iris Aplin recalled. In return, letters from troops fighting in North Africa were read out, which thanked the bomb girls for 'never sending out a single dud mortar bomb'.

Like many young women, May Lamont believed it was unpatriotic not to wear make-up and perfume, even when working outdoors as a lumberjill. The eldest of eight children and with a lorry driver father, she was born in 1925 in Glasgow. May, who left school at 14, saw how her mother struggled with so many children and knew as a teenager she didn't want to be in that position herself.

Once she had turned 18, May had hopes of being a Wren, having seen the inspiring recruitment posters:

I really loved the uniform, so I took out all the papers, got everything going, got brochures, but you needed a birth certificate to join and your parents' permission. There was no way on God's earth I was going to get that so I thought I'd try the WRAFs but the same things were needed, so the last one I wanted was the army, because of the terrible uniform.

In 1943 she saw an advert in the *Glasgow Herald* looking for girls to work with the Forestry Commission, based in Edinburgh – a job which didn't need parental permission or a birth certificate. In front of the interview panel, she announced that she wanted to join because 'I come from a big family and I want to go out into the world'. When asked what she knew about horses, considering she was from Glasgow, she informed them that her grandmother had bought a horse for her fruit barrow, and she'd therefore had experience cleaning him down.

When May was informed that she had been accepted into the Timber Corps, she was 'high as a kite' with the news. She received a travel warrant in the post to take the train from Queen Street Station to Mucherach, Dulnain Bridge, an estate owned by Lord and Lady Fleming.

The girls shared four to a room at Mucherach Lodge, and each girl chose their bed. May couldn't help but notice that the two girls from Edinburgh who were sharing the room opened their suitcases and unpacked their nightwear, underwear, towels and a toilet bag, which was something May had never come across before. May only carried with her a small suitcase with just a few belongings. Before running away from home, May had woken early to pinch three pairs of her sisters' knickers and two vests from the pulley, but hadn't managed to bring a towel. Embarrassed at their lack of possessions, May and another girl from Glasgow held back from unpacking their cases until the Edinburgh girls had left the room.

On arriving at the lodgings, May was issued with her uniform for the Timber Corps. 'We had khaki corduroy trousers, 2 green sweaters, 2 cream shirts, a beret, 4 pairs of socks and brown brogues and a greatcoat,' she recalled. Her two sets of overalls were enormous on her, and so she had to pull them up by their straps. While her uniform was too big for her, she and her friends adapted it to suit and May, with her own individual style, tied scarves around her head with a fashionable flare:

> We were woken at 6.30 a.m. and we were up and dressed, just a quick splash with water, there were no showers. The cook from the big house made breakfast, usually porridge, boiled egg, scrambled egg, toast and jam. I loved everything about it, great food … each morning the lorry would pick us up and take us right up to the woods.

As the Battle of Britain and the Blitz raged, and the country was under heavy bombardment, women working on farms or in forestry were a common sight across the country. Dressed in their green and beige uniforms, or old shirts and trousers, with a scarf tied around their heads, their mission was to ensure farm production continued in order to prevent Britain from starving. But it was more often than not a thankless job, and the girls were often treated with suspicion, in part because wearing trousers, living far from home and doing a 'man's job' seemed to be an indication of loose morals.

Wartime propaganda booklet, *Eve in Overalls*, claimed that farmers were a little afraid at first of the Women's Land Army and the Timber Corps, 'many on account of their crops and no doubt a few on account of their morals – of these women so pertly dressed up as men'.

Posters depicted a glamorous and healthy way of life, but it was often tough, back-breaking work with jobs including stone picking, beet pulling, stacking corn, building hay and leading the horses for the ploughing. The reality of what they wore for work was quite different from the smart green and beige uniform for parades and publicity.

In November 1940, *The Scotsman* reported from St Andrew's House, where a group of land girls took part in a War Weapons Week Parade, 'All of them seemed fit and full of zest … they looked remarkably smart in their Women's Land Army uniform – green jerseys, with broad-brimmed buff felt hats, knee breeches, and buff woollen stockings and shoes'.

Most girls worked in their baggy brown dungarees and jumpers, sometimes using warm sacking as extra insulation. Colourful knotted scarves were tied around their heads to keep their hair safely contained. This was sensible, particularly with reports of one land girl who was scalped when her loose hair was caught in a potato sorting machine.

Mona McLeod, a land girl in Scotland, was isolated on a farm in the Scottish Borders for long stretches at a time, suffering constantly from chilblains, and working so hard that all she could do was collapse in bed every night. It was far removed from the common notion of land girls working in gangs and socialising with one another. She found the uniform ineffective and, instead, she made up her own wardrobe by borrowing her brother's tweed jacket and sourcing a pair of waterproof trousers:

It really was a disgrace: short-sleeved Aertex blouses, one green woollen sweater, a hat, a very nice dress overcoat, which looked super over breeches, but you couldn't work in it, two pairs of cotton dungarees, which you wore over cotton breeches, which were so badly cut that if they fitted, you couldn't sit down and if they were comfortable, they looked like balloons. You got long woollen socks, a cotton coat and a dress raincoat. No gloves. It was totally inadequate for working out of doors all winter. I even had chilblains on my ears! Eventually, I got my brother's old sports coats and wore layers.

Doris Una Ball enrolled as a land girl in March 1944, electing to work in dairy and arable farming. She and two other land girls were sent to a farm in Nottinghamshire, managed by a jovial Scotsman who had farmed in Britain and Australia, and who assigned tasks to the land girls. Doris stayed with his family in a cold farmhouse only heated by the black iron cooking range in the kitchen. She remembered that there was often a newborn piglet in a box in the kitchen, which needed to be hand-reared. She would be out of bed at 5.30 a.m. every morning, and because it was so cold, 'I'd hurriedly struggle into khaki knee breeches, jumper and wellington boots and splash my face from the cold water tap in the kitchen … The farm manager brewed tea and after quickly gulping it down it was then outside, whatever the weather to begin the day's work.'

Amelia (Mitzi) Edeson joined the Land Army in March 1942 and was posted to Leominster in Herefordshire:

I received my uniform at home, trying on the corduroy breeches was a laugh, they were laced at the knees and trying to bend my legs was diffi-cult. There were knee length woollen stockings, brown leather shoes, cream shirts, green jumpers, a lovely three-quarter-length dark beige with white wool lining coat, beige hat, and a wide leather belt. We got the rest, wellies, overalls, big oilskin Mac's etc when we got to the hostel.

Mitzi had never travelled further than Scarborough, so getting on a train was quite an adventure. She was guided by one of her brothers to a compartment with other land girls, who, it turned out, were all going to the same place. When they met the farmers they would be working with, she found they 'weren't too keen to have us, but we were cheap labour, and it was war times. I expect their thoughts were mixed when they saw us town girls, most of us were around five feet two inches and weighed about eight stones.'

Emily Braidwood volunteered for the Women's Land Army aged 19, after reading in the paper that there was an urgent need for women to work on the land. Following an interview with an intimidating woman in a beautiful silk dress and with a 'five pound note voice', she was accepted into the Land Army and in October 1941 was sent to Clacton-on-Sea. It was, for Emily, 'a big change, having spent most of my life living in one room with my mum, dad and brothers'. It was also the beginning of 'the happiest days of my life because there was a purpose served, growing food for Great Britain'.

She and twelve other young women, from all across the country, were met by a member of the Women's Institute and taken to their new homes. Emily said:

> There was a kind of hostility in the village, servicemen were accepted, not the land girls. The general opinion held that land girls wore too much in the winter and too little in the summer! My uniform consisted of corduroy breeches, strong brown leather shoes, long woollen socks, fawn cotton aertex T shirts, fine cotton long sleeved fawn shirts and a tap tie band at the waist, fawn felt hat with a Women's Land Army Badge, dark green tie with WLA [Women's Land Army] letters and a dark green woollen jumper.

She was also given one pair of gumboots, two light khaki coats and a dark green oilskin, which crackled and smelled of disinfectant.

She and her colleagues were up at 6.30 a.m. on their first day to pick sugar beet. Freezing cold, and breaking the ice on the water jug, it was clear what she was in for. 'I wore umpteen layers of everything I could lay my hands on. I could hardly walk.'

Land girls found they were often judged for their relaxed uniforms and their freer lifestyles, living away from home in dormitory accommodation and fraternising with men, which sometimes ended in tragedy. On Kay Riddell's first day on the small farm where she was stationed, she noticed a strong smell of gas in the air. Despite feeling 'greener than my W.L.A. jumpers', she discovered that one of the land girls who had been staying in their hostel had gassed herself because she had fallen pregnant to a married man. 'She had been one of the hostel elite; a rat catcher. They always seemed to look glamorous. Maybe it was the Gabardine breeches they wore?' recalled Kay.

Barbara Beddow, from West Riding, worked in the Timber Corps. She had married her childhood sweetheart in April 1939 and, less than six months later, after joining the Irish Guards, he was killed in the war. On reading an article about women working in the Forestry Commission, she signed up and was sent to the Forest of Dean for training.

She was billeted in a hostel and was taught how to measure trees, fell them and replant. After six weeks, they were sent to Fearby in North Yorkshire. The presence of this group of girls caused consternation amongst the locals, with interest from village boys and suspicions from the women. 'I think older local people saw us as a threat, bringing a challenge to their own young people, who were still under discipline; the young ones were jealous of our freedom. We were probably seen as being a bit wild and too free,' said Barbara. Even her friend Nancy was disapproving: 'She was critical of me because I flirted with the boys, so soon after being widowed.'

Rosalind Elder became a lumberjill in the Women's Timber Corps in the winter of 1942. After training, she was sent to Morayshire, working to a quota of felling sixty trees day, but 'in the summertime it was quite pleasant and we did have beautiful tans'. She recalled that 'our uniform was most attractive, riding breeches, green pullover, beige shirt, green tie, riding coat and to top it all off a jaunty green beret with a badge depicting a tree.'

Despite their low wages, which only left enough for pocket money after the food costs were deducted, the land girls and lumberjills were proud of their work and that their contributions were helping to win the war. May Lamont loved working alongside Canadian and Norwegian civilian forestry workers who hauled the felled trees, while the girls would take the axe to clear off the branches. In every area was a portable sawmill to cut the trees to size. After her first day of working, she thought, 'This is for me!'

May recalled that the girls were not paid as much as the men, but the Canadians and Norwegians paid the 'Jills' bonuses from their own wages to recognise how hard they were working. Once the area was depleted, they would move to a new area. When they moved to the area of Black Mount, Bridge of Orchy, it was here that she would stay until the end of the war, and where her social life took off.

The Special Air Service (SAS) and the Highland Light Infantry were stationed nearby, and they would hold raucous dances. 'The Canadians were rubbish dancers, good at throwing you about but for individual dances, waltzes and foxtrots you needed a Scotsman,' she said. The Canadians would send trucks to collect the girls and take them to dances in Scout halls. 'Always records, Glenn Miller, Mantovani, the Foxtrot was my favourite dance. In the biggest hall of all, the one at Crianlarich, I won a Miss Lovely Legs competition!'

Catherine Speirs also remembered the fun of socialising at dances with the armed services:

There was an Army Camp a mile or two up the road from the hostel where the armed forces were gathering at Dundonald awaiting orders for the second front. These young men used to come down to the hostel on Tuesday evening and chat, play darts and sing etc. The girls looked forward to this and we had freedom to have fun and enjoy the male company.

8

The Desert Rats

For two and a half years in the Western Desert, the Allies fought to protect North Africa from falling into the hands of the Axis Powers in searing battles across Egypt, Libya and Tunisia. Egypt and the Suez Canal was a vital access route to India, the Far East and Australia, and it also provided the oil needed for fighting the war.

Fighting in the desert was the 7th Armoured Division of the Eighth Army, whose formation sign was a desert rat, or jerboa. This symbol came to personify them as one of the outstanding divisions of the war as they defeated the Italian Tenth Army in North Africa and came up against Rommel's fearsome Afrika Corps.

After having been given movement orders in January 1940, Ray Ellis and the South Notts Hussars were posted to British Palestine under the command of the 1st Cavalry Division and were issued with their tropical kit. He recalled:

> The uniform was made of khaki drill, a light cotton material much more suitable to the climate of the Middle East than the khaki serge we had previously worn. We wore pith helmets, shirts and puttees most of the time, but for more formal occasions the dress was tunics and slacks.

The temperature in the desert went from extremes: blistering hot in the summer, and very cold at night, particularly over the winter months. Sandstorms blasted through the camps, coating everything with dust and sticking to skin and hair. Alastair Borthwick of the Highland Division said the dust 'was diabolical stuff, orange in colour. It settled on the skin, smooth as face-powder and before long, skin, hair and clothes were in colour and texture a uniform matt orange. Eye shields of some kind were essential.'

The military uniform for those in the desert needed to be suitable for these conditions, with khaki drill shorts and shirts designed for the sweltering heat. They were often issued with warmer clothes, and sometimes even fought in their greatcoats and jerseys. The nights were cold, and to try and stay warm Captain William Boulton of the 104th Essex Yeomanry Field Regiment Royal Horse Artillery, would 'dig a hole and sleep with all my clothes on. But vehicles driving about couldn't see these holes, and we had at least one fellow killed by being run over at night.'

As Britain fought in empirical campaigns throughout the nineteenth century, it was realised that uniforms for hot climates needed to be practical rather than showy. The scarlet wool serge uniform may have been an impressive sight on a Victorian soldier, but by the end of the century, a lightweight camouflage uniform was introduced to be more comfortable and less conspicuous. From 1885, all regiments in India would wear a khaki drill uniform of tunic and trousers. By the mid-1930s these were replaced by khaki drill shorts in close-weave cotton, and shirts made from Aertex, which were lighter in the heat. The word 'khaki' originated from the Urdu word 'Khak', meaning dust, and was just one example of the Indian influence on British Army slang. 'Chai' was the beloved sweet tea made from condensed milk, which offered a moment of respite to soldiers, while 'Blighty' came from the Hindi word 'bilayati', meaning 'foreign'. A common expression used in the North Africa campaign was to refer to a 'Blighty one', slang for a wound that could result in being evacuated back to the UK.

Overseas, away from the parade ground, there was a more relaxed way of dressing, and soldiers added their own pieces to modify their uniform to adapt to the heat, dust and plummeting night-time temperatures. After being evacuated when he fell sick from malaria, Bombardier Stephen Dawson, of 104th (Essex Yeomanry) Field Regiment Royal Horse Artillery, was pleased to be sent back to Tobruk: 'It was like coming home. I hated the army in base areas, it gave me the creeps. It was quite different out in the field, you could wear what you like; there is an element of excitement.'

When on leave, they shopped in Cairo's bazaars, buying *kufiyah* scarves to protect their faces from dust, sandals with crepe soles known as *chuppli*, and sand goggles. Local tailors made a living by providing useful clothing, such as flannel bush jackets with bone buttons or non-regulation Aertex shirts, similar to the American style of blouse, fully buttoned and with unpleated pockets.

'Clothing was important,' said Major Ralph Bagnold commanding the Long Range Desert Group (LRDG):

There is a tremendous contrast in temperature between night and day in the desert. The sand radiates the heat, and it can get up to fifty degrees Celsius by day, and below freezing at night. So you need enough clothing and blankets for the night, yet in daytime just enough clothing to stop the sun burning your skin. All we wore was a shirt and shorts. The Arab head-dress was good as it flapped in the wind and kept one cool, and in a sandstorm you could wrap a piece of cloth round your face. We got the head-dress from the Palestine police, because we didn't want to risk breaking secrecy by putting out a contract in Cairo for Arab head-dress. I had sandals made, the Indian North-West Frontier chapli [also, *chuppli*], a very tough sandal with an open toe, so that if sand got into it you could shoot it out with a kick.

The *chuppli* sandal was originally worn by Pathan tribesmen in north-west India, before being picked up by the British Indian Army and spreading to the Eighth Army in North Africa. Reversed leather chukka boots with lightweight crepe rubber soles, also known as desert boots, were also popular. These boots would be worn by the troops back in Britain, earning the nickname 'brothel creepers'.

The Wolseley pattern pith helmet, made from khaki drill and covered in cork, was worn by all ranks in the First World War, and its deep brim was designed to protect the neck and shoulders. The crown was often lined with silver foil to deflect the sun's heat. However, it was considered impractical and was cast aside during the Second World War for something more lightweight like a Gurkha bush hat, khaki turbans or small-brimmed sun helmets.

Infantryman V.C. Fairfield of the 64th Field Regiment Royal Artillery bought a beret in Cairo as, 'the issue beret was, in my opinion, a disgrace. It had a thick band around it which was either too tight or too loose. It was shapeless and could not be made to look smart when worn and here in the desert it was unbearably hot.'

'We had long since given up the habit of wearing steel helmets,' said Ray Ellis, after months spent in the desert, following his arrival in the Middle East in early 1940:

For most of us it became a matter of pride to wear some other form of headgear, usually something informal. Some liked to wear the knitted cap comforter, others the normal khaki side hat; I had my favourite peaked cap with the wire removed, and there were some who preferred to wear the RHA [Royal Horse Artillery] dress side hat of red, blue and gold. Whatever hat we wore, it usually carried the regimental cap badge, of which we were all very proud. It was one of the very few cap badges in the British Army that carried neither name nor motto, and where other badges were made of brass, ours was silver in colour.

For the Highland regiments, the kilt was declared incompatible with modern warfare and its issue was suspended in 1939 in favour of battledress and the tropical khaki uniform. However, such was the pride in the kilt, Highlanders continued to wear them, sometimes with khaki aprons on the front. Eventually, the Army Council agreed that officers could purchase the kilts already held in storage and wear them as they wished.

During an initial period of intense training, before being sent to the Western Desert, Ray Ellis had been stationed at a camp at Hadera in British Palestine where they were merged into the 1st Cavalry Division. He considered it his happiest period during the war. Surrounded by a eucalyptus plantation, they drifted off to sleep each night under their mosquito nets with a chorus of a thousand frogs and spent their free time swimming in the sea or visiting cafés and the cinema. When Italy joined up with Germany to declare war on Britain on 10 June 1940, the 1st Cavalry Division was mobilised to take up position in the Western Desert at the Egyptian port, Mersa Matruh.

In North Africa, the Desert Air Force was essential support for the Allied war effort and the RAF's Middle Eastern Command covered an area of 4.5 million square miles. Instead of the air force blue, they were issued stone-coloured service dress and khaki drill bush shirts to keep cool, while ground crew in the desert wore khaki drill coveralls.

Also taking part in the North Africa campaign were 30,000 Australian and New Zealand Army Corps (ANZACs); an army of Sikh troops in shorts, sweaters and turbans; and the Gurkhas, known for sneaking up on the German lines and slitting their throats. As *Life* magazine noted in March 1940, many of the ANZACs were sons of First World War veterans and 'they were a raw, eager, fun-loving crew. They sang Roll out the Barrel and shouted "Cooee".'

At the camp bar, Ray Ellis met Australian soldiers for the first time:

We got on quite well together, although their manner of behaviour and their type of discipline were very different from our own. One thing we did have in common was a dislike of this particular place and the experience of drinking warm beer in a hot, dusty tent.

The 2/28th Battalion of the 9th Australian Division was from Western Australia. Most of the men were used to desert life from having worked the gold fields and were from tight-knit families and communities. 'We found the Australians very rough and ready. A filthy-dirty bearded chap addressed our CO as "Hey, mate",' noted Captain Peter Lewis, officer commanding for the 8th Battalion Durham Light Infantry.

When the 1st Cavalry Division arrived in Mersa Matruh, they were struck by the sand whipped up by hot wind and getting into their eyes, throats and hair. The only way to be able to find some relief from it was to wrap up in a blanket or cover their faces with scarves. With their hair always thick with sand, Ray's brother George suggested they shave their heads, 'I was the first to volunteer, sitting on an upturned petrol tin whilst George got busy with the scissors and cut off all my hair. When the others saw the final result they decided that it was not such a good idea after all!'

At the fortress of Mersa Matruh Ray Ellis described how they lived in a 'rough and ready manner', sleeping outside 'wherever the gun was placed', and where they ate, washed, shaved and slept:

> There was no shortage of food, but it was a monotonous repetition of bully stew, tinned pilchards and tinned bacon … our salvation was tea: hot, strong, sweet tea. How we loved our tea! We called it 'char', a Hindustani word borrowed, like so many 'army words' of the time, by the British Army in India.

The Western Desert Force and the British Armoured 7th Division launched a surprise attack on the Italian Tenth Army at Sidi Barrani in December 1940, but instead of engaging in combat, the Italians gave themselves up in droves, despite being five times the size. The British took over 38,000 prisoners, with a loss of 624 casualties to the Western Desert Force. Sergeant Emilio Ponti of the Italian Tenth Army was one of the first to enter Sidi Barrani by tank, 'We had no enthusiasm. We didn't believe we were doing the right thing. To get killed for some madman seemed stupid.'

The Italians wore green-blue uniforms with pith helmets, or elaborate plumes sprouting from their headwear, and carried suitcases filled with dress and parade uniforms. While they made up the majority of those who were killed in the immediate attack, there were also high numbers of Libyan casualties, distinguished by the colourful striped scarves wrapped around their heads. The victorious Allies placed rough markers to indicate which nationalities were buried where, but for the British they created individual graves, marked with a rifle in the ground, a steel helmet stuck to the top and their dog tags fastened to identify them.

As they sifted through the Sidi Barrani battlefield, the Allied troops salvaged what they could from the Italians, including plentiful Chianti and Italian groundsheets. Ray said:

> They were vastly superior to the British groundsheet, which was an abomination. The Italian version was of a closely woven fabric which was wind and waterproof and skilfully designed to be used not merely as a groundsheet but also as a sleeping bag and as a cloak. In addition to this there were buttons and buttonholes that enabled them to be easily fastened together to make anything from a two-man tent to a small marquee.

Signaller Ted Whittaker, from the 107th (South Notts Hussars) Field Regiment Royal Horse Artillery, said:

> We were marched to a place where there were piles of Italian kit, which we could take. I got a dagger. There was a large store of tinned food and condensed milk. My mother had always stopped me from eating condensed milk with a spoon, and there was no one to stop me there. We found a gramophone and a pile of opera records. So for some time we sat and ate tinned food with Nestlé's condensed milk and listening to opera. I found a nice silk black shirt. There were pullovers, black woolly hats with pompoms, small Beretta pistols and huge revolvers. After this we went back to Mersa in triumph wearing black woolly hats, and black shirts. We were soon told to 'take that bloody stuff off and look like soldiers; and have a wash and shave'.

After the victory at Sidi Barrani, Ray Ellis was granted leave to Cairo, arriving on New Year's Day 1941. The continual bombardment day after day wore them down, fraying their nerves, and the leave in Cairo offered a break from being perpetually under attack and living in the most basic conditions in the desert.

As soon as Ray arrived at the hotel, he was struck by the comfort it offered. 'It is hard to imagine the sheer delight we found in living again as civilised human beings,' said Ray:

> To be able to shower, and to wear clothes that were freshly laundered and smartly creased, gave us a wonderful feeling of well-being, whilst to sit

down to a properly laid table with a crisp, white tablecloth was joy beyond belief. The food: real butter, newly baked rolls, steak, chips, strawberries and cream – it was like something out of Alice in Wonderland. We ate well and slept quietly in clean, soft beds, far from the crash of battle and the fear of imminent death.

A visit to Cairo was a feast to the senses with its colour and noise. The countries of North Africa were exotic places, only read about in adventure books or atlases, and for the troops who were sent there, it was a far cry from life in rainy Britain. As well as peeping inside the brothels of Wagh El Burket, they visited the pyramids and the Temple of the Sphinx, travelling through open countryside from Giza to Cairo. Experiencing one of the seven wonders was on the checklist of every young person serving in North Africa. Getting there involved a drive through the countryside and, once there, they could scramble to the top of the pyramids or go inside at a time when there were no restrictions on where they could explore.

Sam Pritchard, a minister's son from North Wales, arrived at Fuka in the autumn of 1941 to join 216 Squadron and then 45 Squadron. They slept in tents on the ground and, to pass the time, they would sunbathe, play cards in the sergeants' mess, and knock back Cairo beer, Stella or Canada Black Label, which was extra strength and guaranteed to get them drunk.

North Africa was his first time abroad, and at first Sam treated it like an adventure, but the action was relentless and exhausting for airmen. Granted leave from their base at Gambut in Libya, Sam and his friends of 216 Squadron would collect a month's pay, which would be spent in three days in Cairo, enjoying good food and drink and staying in the best hotel rooms possible.

Arriving at the Cairo hotel he would 'luxuriate in the bath for about two hours from 9.30 a.m. onwards, during which a hotel servant brought me a succession of cold Stella beers'. Then, 'dressed in my smartest bush jacket, immaculate slacks and "brothel creepers" I rendezvoused with friends at Groppi's or the Exmorandi Bar'. In Cairo the best hotels, like the Continental and Shepheard's, were for officers only, but Groppi's, founded by a Swiss chocolatier, Sharia Soliman Pasha, in 1909, was open to everyone, and served coffees, ice creams and beers.

Sam and his friends would begin their day with an iced coffee, before switching to beer and spending evenings on the dance floor. They lunched on 'wonderful fresh sea-foods, covered in sliced tomatoes, cucumber and other salads', washed down with more drinks. He returned to the hotel for a siesta, before being awoken with a raw egg and brandy drink, which made him 'suitably refreshed and full of beans for another rendezvous with friends and another night on the town'.

After this luxury, for a minister's son, returning to the desert 'felt like a period of spiritual atonement and asceticism. Never again in our lives would we relish the ambrosia nor taste the nectar in quite the same way once the "desert" component had been taken out of the equation.'

The terrace at Shepheard's, with its potted palms and wicker chairs, looked out onto Camel Street, and south of the terrace entrance was a row of tourist shops. The hotel itself was an oasis of Moorish design, with Persian rugs, mosaics, and granite pillars. An article in *Life* magazine in December 1942 wrote:

The well-to-do British officers in Egypt, the ambassadors … the American with fat purses, the glamor girls of the Middle East, the Russian Commissars, the famous war correspondents and the civilian tank experts, all stay at just one hotel in Cairo: Shepheard's. When the war in the desert went badly, a favourite criticism back home was that it was being fought from the terrace of Shepheard's. The high officers did not stay there, because it was conspicuous, but nearly everyone else did.

The hotel had a habit of accumulating mementos from all these soldiers. In the storeroom, officers going to war in 1882, 1915 and 1942 checked their excess luggage. There would be many unclaimed bags left behind from those who didn't make it back alive.

The American Bar was nicknamed the 'Long Bar' because it was so overcrowded it took an extended amount of time to get a scotch and soda. A popular joke amongst Brits and Aussies, when it looked like Rommel may take Cairo, was 'wait until he gets to Shepheard's; that'll hold him up'.

By the end of January 1941, British forces took the port of Tobruk from the Italians and, reassured by an easy victory, Churchill transferred British troops to Greece. Over Easter 1941, the Germans sent reinforcements to take back Tobruk and, despite their ferocity, the Australian infantry defeated the German troops with bayonet fighting one-on-one.

The Siege of Tobruk was to last from Easter until Christmas. Ray and the South Notts Hussars had been sent to defend Tobruk, along with the 9th Australian Divisions. Both countries got on well, with the Aussies nicknaming the South Notts Hussars the 'Acorn Gunners', after their insignia. Cut off from the outside world, they found ways to differentiate themselves. 'I had named my gun "The Saint", after a character in the books by Leslie Charteris,' said Ray Ellis:

This idea became popular in 425 Battery and soon all the guns bore names chosen by their sergeants. Sammy Hall, one of the signallers, had been a signwriter in civilian life and he enjoyed painting the names on the gun shields for us. For me he painted the characteristic matchstick man with a halo and below it the words 'The Saint', in the regimental colours of red, blue and gold.

During this period in defensive position, settling into former Italian camps, there was little entertainment. No books, radio or film screenings were available and food was limited to corned beef or bully stew, army biscuits, tinned bacon, and vitamin C tablets. They were constantly under attack as planes screamed down on them, dropping bombs. The water shortages were an issue, with half a gallon of water issued to each person, for both drinking and washing. To conserve water after brushing their teeth and washing their faces, they took Italian gas-mask filters and put them on top of the tin, which would clean the water for reuse.

Captain Vernon Northwood of the 9th Australian Division recalled:

The dugouts left by the Italians were very dirty, and full of fleas. We threw out the rubbish left by them. The water situation was pretty grim. Tea was made centrally and brought up at night with the main meal. You had a water bottle a day for drinking. I used to shave in a tobacco tin, after cleaning my teeth I would spit the water back into the tin and shaved in it. I had a little piece of sponge. We shaved every day, to avoid sores … At midday a heat haze settled over Tobruk, and in places you could move around in the haze; you could walk about and talk to the men. The men took their boots off and walked about in the sand to clean their feet. You took your shirt off and the sun baked off any sweat.

Ray finally received a package from home that had been sent by his mother six months before. It contained a stale cake and some chocolate for his birthday, a magical healing ointment made from a recipe passed down by his grandfather and, for reasons he was never quite sure about, two packets of balloons. But their inclusion led to a tender moment of relief, as the warring sides shared a brief moment of playfulness. The Brits and Australians blew up the balloons and sent them up over the parapet to see what the reaction of the Germans would be to colourful balloons floating over no man's land:

> The front immediately fell silent. All firing in the vicinity stopped. The enemy must have wondered what on earth it was and their field glasses must have been working overtime before they realised that it was a joke. They were quick to respond and to join in the fun, and as we popped up the balloons, one at a time, they fired at them with their rifles. They entered into the spirit of the thing by not using machine guns. It went on until all the balloons were burst and then we sent up a red flare and they fired a flare in return. At least it made a change from trying to kill each other and the balloons had served a purpose after all: they had shown that we were all stupid human beings.

It was not always easy to tell the difference between allies and foe. Captain Hans-Otto Behrendt was an assistant to Lieutenant General Rommel, and as they travelled from Derna, they encountered a British soldier with a broken-down motorbike by the side of the road:

> When we drove up, he asked us if we were going to the Third Armoured Brigade, and I said 'Yes'. He got into my car, and after a while he said 'strange car'. 'Yes, you are right, this is a German car, and we are Germans,' I replied. All he said was 'Oh'. I admired him for his coolness.

By October 1941, the Australians were relieved in Tobruk by the British 70th Division, reinforced by the 4th Royal Tank Regiment. Rommel had formed the German Panzer Afrika Korps, sending them into Libya over summer 1941 to push forward at Tobruk. The Eighth Army was formed in September 1941, with new equipment arriving in Egypt to prepare to battle the German Afrika Korps.

When the 9th Australian Division were sent back to Palestine for a rest, they were now tired, thin and well bronzed from constant exposure to the sun. Captain Vernon Northwood remembered:

> We were badly dressed, a few wore German caps; there is always a clown in any military organisation. Everyone was ragged. Every man was given a bottle of beer during the night at a stop on the journey by train from Alexandria to Palestine. The effect was disastrous; it went straight to their heads. They wandered off the train into the desert. I wondered how we

would find them. In the end we had to put out a cordon and usher them back to the train. We were proud of what we had done: the 9th Division was the first force to stop Rommel.

Ray Ellis was promoted to sergeant while in Egypt, proudly wearing three stripes on his uniform. Because he and his brother George were both in B Troop, Ray had been moved to A Troop to avoid a situation where they could both be killed. For Ray, it was 'an unexpected and shattering blow', as he had bonded completely with that group of men. 'We had shared everything since the moment of our call-up nearly two years previously.'

As well as being separated from his buddies, Ray, at 22 years old, was becoming disenchanted with war. 'I was sick and tired of everything concerned with warfare. I was weary of military discipline, of striving to become more efficient in the art of killing and I was tired of the corporate life that is the thief of solitude.' He pitied the newest recruits who were experiencing warfare for the first time:

> I felt sorry for them because they were obviously all frightened … by that time I'd got past that stage. I was only twenty-two, but as far as warfare went, I was an old man. They were also homesick. It was only a matter of months since they'd been at home with their wives and sweethearts.

After retreating from Tobruk, Rommel launched a ferocious counterattack at the beginning of 1942, recapturing Benghazi and pushing towards Tobruk. The Battle of Knightsbridge was named after a spot in the Western Desert where two tracks crossed. It was an immediate, bloody battle, taking place on 6 June 1942, and it was here that Ray heard that the whole of B Troop had been wiped out during a ferocious onslaught of German tanks. These men had been like brothers to him. He had trained with them, travelled and lived in close quarters with them, and to find they had all been killed was an unimaginable trauma. He learnt that his brother George had been saved from death as he had fallen ill before the battle, but all his old friends were now dead:

> I remembered how we had joined the South Notts Hussars on the same day and how we had gone for a drink together at the Borlace Warren pub at the top of Derby road. Pat Bland, another friend from the earliest days, had also been killed. In fact they had all gone. Jack Tomlinson, 'Tommo' as we used to call him, had died most stubbornly. With both his legs shattered, this brave lad had remained in the layer's seat and fired a last shell point-blank at

a charging tank, which was so close that the shell had taken its turret clean off. The tank burst into flames and carried on out of control to crash into the gun, and Jack had died beneath its tracks.

The survivors of the Battle of Knightsbridge caught short moments of sleep in the cold winter air, wrapped in their greatcoats and blankets, brewing hot, sweet tea for some comfort, despite the complete exhaustion and sense of fear. After three days of constant fighting, it was believed that the Germans had withdrawn.

The Eighth Army took up position to attack the German line, but the Germans had been prepared, withdrawing their forces behind the edge of a depression, and luring the 107th South Notts Hussars into the 'Knightsbridge cauldron' – a deadly trap. They were ordered to fight to the last, to act as a shield while the Eighth Army retreated. There was little hope of coming out of this alive. Ray Ellis's gun team held back the Germans, and as soldiers were killed by the blasts, new men stepped in to take their position on the gun.

Ray remembered vividly one injured man from the Royal Corps of Signals:

> He was terrified. I crouched down trying to console him, 'You're all right lad, you're all right. Don't worry, you're not badly wounded, we'll soon have you away, I reckon you've got a Blighty.' Trying to ease his fear, I noticed sand settling on his eyes. He died in my arms.

Eventually he was left with just one man, 'a complete stranger; he wasn't even a South Notts Hussar'. He felt the rattle of machine gun, and this last man was shot to pieces. Ray turned to see a tank behind him, and as he braced to be hit, the German tank, for whatever reason, held its fire and spared him. All around him was carnage.

Ray walked over to the tank where his friend Jim Hardy's body lay, having been sliced in half:

> His water bottle was still attached to his webbing equipment and I took my knife and cut it free because I was desperately thirsty. I drank the tepid water and then, as I looked down at my old friend's lifeless face, the tears ran down my face. All my friends had been killed. Then I made my way over to my own gun, where my gun crew lay as they had fallen. I could still make out the name painted on the shield in the regimental colours, but the little figure with the halo was upside down. 'The Saint' had fought its last battle and it would fight no more. Most of my kit had gone, blown up with the

limber on which it had rested, but I did find my haversack containing the essentials, and I also rescued my greatcoat.

Ray was instructed to climb aboard a German tank and pulled himself up next to its commander:

We stood for a moment eye to eye, two men who had fought each other hard and long, and then we both raised our eyes to heaven and inclined our heads in mutual agreement as to the futility of it all ... We drove away from the battlefield together, two enemies who felt no hatred for each other, only a shared sense of loss and bitterness.

The South Notts Hussars were not the only division to be wiped out in June 1942 by the Germans. The 1st Battalion of the Durham Light Infantry were decimated on 27 June 1942 and one of the only survivors, Lance Corporal Joseph 'Chelsea' Lamb, blamed these losses on their lack of equipment:

When we got back and congregated with the rest of the company that is where the reaction set in. One of the lads started crying. I started laughing like hell. We lost half our battalion, and we lost half the company, out of about ninety men only forty-six got out. That was one of the worst dos we were ever in. If we'd only had the right kit.

Tank battles could be hot and deadly – if a tank was hit, there was no easy way to escape, and the German 88mm guns pulverised the tanks from the inside. Captain Peter Vaux was an officer in the 4th Royal Tank Regiment, and he experienced how hot it could get inside, particularly when the engine was running. Like the airmen who chose not to wear goggles, those in the tanks made the decision to ditch protective wear in favour of comfort:

We didn't wear overalls, just shorts and shirts. There was controversy: some people said overalls would protect you against fire. Others said you would be worse off if the overalls caught fire. We were all issued with topees, as were the Italians and the Germans. We all threw them away. On our feet we wore ammunition boots, but officers had desert boots made of suede.

The first British and American joint operation, known as Operation Torch, was launched in November 1942 with the aim of conquering French North Africa. The winter of 1942 was harsh, and the Eighth Army only had their khaki drill shorts, shirt and pullovers as they prepared for battle to push the Germans and Italians west. Lieutenant 'Scotty' White of the Durham Light Infantry recalled being told to pair up and keep warm as they were only in 'khaki drill shorts and jerseys', and were supplied with a big Thermos of rum and hot cocoa. 'Then it was "On your feet". I drank lots of it. I'd never drunk rum before.'

As the battle broke out with screaming shells and bullets, it was a symphony of noise – pipers from the Highlanders, the Maori cry as they did the *Haka*, and the hunting horn of the Durham Light Infantry. As captured Germans gathered on the sand, they were issued cigarettes by the Allied soldiers. Sergeant Eric Watts of the Royal Australian Artillery recalled that, even in defeat, the young Germans refused to back down from their idolatry of Hitler:

> One of our blokes said to this German, 'Why don't you realise that the tide of war has turned, don't you realise that? Hitler has led you up the garden path'. The young German officer jumped to his feet and he was seething: 'If that's what you think about Hitler, I'll tell you this, I was educated at Eton, and I heard your King stutter his way through his coronation speech.'

To offer a moment of respite, trucks came to supply the Durham Light Infantry with warm clothing and food. Major Bill Miskin, an officer of the Queen's Own Royal West Kent Regiment, remembered, 'The nights were cold; it was very uncomfortable without our greatcoats', but when the trucks were destroyed by a German 88, killing the drivers, 'some of the companies had to go without their greatcoats and evening meal,' recalled Lieutenant Colonel William Watson.

The First Army was formed in November 1942 to command American and British land forces for Operation Torch, the plan to invade French-occupied North Africa. Rifleman Douglas Waller, an anti-tank gunner in the 2nd Battalion Rifle Brigade, remembered meeting Americans in the desert who were part of the First Army, and who were mostly interested in the souvenirs from Germans. The uniform of the Afrika Corps was regularly sought after by opposing and Axis forces – including their soft caps, insignia and the roll-neck sweaters worn under their tunics:

> We joined up with First Army, who took a very poor view of us. Everything was chucked on, and we were in scruff order with dirty old cans, black with smoke, for brewing up hung on the vehicle. They were all trotting around in blancoed belts and gaiters, and they looked down their noses at us. We

began to come across Americans. When we laagered up they would come round asking us if we had any souvenirs, they wanted Berettas and Lügers and belts with *Gott Mit Uns* on them and would offer packs of cigarettes for them. They were the rear-echelon troops. We thought it a bit odd that they would give cigarettes for this stuff: we had masses of it.

Following the success of Operation Torch, the Coldstream Guards fought in the final battle in Tunisia, at Hammam Lif, taking the Bey of Tunis's palace. Second Lieutenant Mark Philips was sent into the palace's harem to seize the Bey, who had supported the Germans:

I thought this is a bit of a lark, and so did my chaps. We rounded up the Bey's guards and the band, and went to the harem; an extraordinary sight. They were a pathetic lot, guarded by eunuchs, nasty fat smiley men, bowing to us. While we were interviewing a few of the French-speaking girls, a rather London sort of voice came from the corner of the room. It was a girl from Hackney Wick, and she had been put into the slave trade in about 1939, and had been in a brothel in Tunis for a time and then put in the harem. She was a very attractive, charming girl so we used her as an interpreter. It was an extraordinary day in the life of a soldier.

The Axis was finally defeated in North Africa, but the Western Desert and Tunisian campaigns cost the British and Commonwealth 20,500 dead. However, it was a turning point in the conflict and brought hope that the war might go in the Allies' favour.

'Suddenly everything came to an end,' said Rifleman Douglas Waller:

Then they opened a cinema, so we went along, and they showed *Desert Victory*, which didn't go down very well. The next night the lads went out with petrol cans and set light to the cinema. The film was all right, but having spent the last two and a half years in the desert the last thing you wanted for amusement was to see *Desert Victory*.

9

Women in North Africa

The recruitment posters, with beautifully tailored uniforms against an azure sea backdrop, had promised Wrens they would see the world, and those who signed up waited in the hope of receiving the much sought-after posting overseas. At the beginning of 1942, Sheila Mills, now a commissioned officer, was given orders to board a ship for the perilous three-month journey to Alexandria.

In preparation, she ordered her tropical kit from Austin Reed, because once on board they were permitted to wear their pristine white uniform, or their 'bluette overalls in warm weather to save the washing of white dresses'. The tropical kit for Wrens included desirable white cotton dresses, white cotton blouses to be worn with white drill skirts, white canvas shoes, stockings, ankle socks, a white tropical hat which came with white hat covers, and navy-blue tropical overalls.

Ship life followed a pattern, 'though it's still a trifle boring,' wrote Sheila. 'Rising, eating, boat drill, drinking, eating, deck games, tea, drinking, eating, drinking then a spell on the deck, and so to bed.' Once in Alexandria, there were strict rules on what Wrens could wear, even down to their underwear. They could dress in civilian clothing when on leave of twenty-four hours or more, if doing sport, or for 'private dances outside any Naval, Military or RAF establishment'. White knee-length knickers were to be worn with the white uniform, along with petticoats. They were given a grant for their tropical underclothing, because the sweltering heat required frequent changes. This would cover a brassiere, four pairs of white knickers and four tropical vests. Wrens were supposed to wear white stockings, but to Sheila's relief, she heard, 'we may be probably allowed to wear ordinary stockings, or none at all. White are too grim.'

Keeping their white tropical dresses clean was an arduous task. As an officer, Sheila was entitled to a batman, who would clean her shoes and brush down her clothes, generally making life more pleasant when it was incredibly hot. 'You have no conception of how hot it is, the sweat just pours off me when I am sitting still. The flies are "appalling" as are the bugs.'

Joan Bawden had also longed to travel, and as a WAAF she was excited to find she was to be sent overseas. In preparation, she went shopping for all the items she need, 'like lots of soap and toothpaste and dungarees for deck and glucose for when I'm sick and a lock for my kitbag and a new suitcase and a key ring, also I've sent off lots of telegrams: to my friends and to my tailor about tropical kit.'

Women sent overseas were warned by the Air Ministry that shoes were often a tempting hiding place for scorpions, and to stock up on insect repellent to ward against mosquitoes. When she received her uniform, Joan tried on her tropical topee, which she thought might be something of a man-repellant:

> However many surplus men there may be in the desert and on the troopship I don't think I, in my topee, tropical kit (khaki is not my colour), smothered in mosquito bites and fifty million freckles and smelling vilely of my anti-everything ointment, am going to be much of a hit with anyone.

Joan reported to Liverpool on 7 January 1942 to set sail on the SS *Otranto*, feeling in awe that her dream of travelling was finally coming true. However, the first days were spent in port, and those on board were ordered to sleep in their clothes in case of a raid, and with their slacks and jumpers, rugs and water bottles, it felt 'just like the days of the Blitz again. I do so detest sleeping in my clothes, but I see their point most clearly and obey without protest.' Once they set sail, the WAAFs wrapped up in warm clothing to stand on deck and began mingling with the RAF and army. 'Diana and I already know the majority of 221 Squadron,' she wrote.

As they sailed into the Azores the weather got warmer, and they set aside their layers of warm clothing to play tennis on deck in Aertex shirts and slacks. 'I have shed practically all my woollies and the day when I can appear in my glamorous blue sunglasses and my dashing boiler suit and Aertex shirt becomes a possibility,' she said.

When they were finally able to dress in their tropical kit, the WAAFs, who had been issued with men's whites due to shortages, found they were far too big. They spent hours cutting and sewing the shirts to tailor them to fit, in the hope that they might be more flattering. As they arrived in Freetown, the heat immediately sapped their energy, with most on board never having experienced a tropical climate before.

The dangers at sea during wartime meant that the traditional ceremony for crossing the equator had to be paired back. But in the evening, they danced to the gentle hum of gramophones under moonlight. During one officers' party aboard, where they knocked back the drinks and leapt over furniture, one of the sergeants gave a rendition of his Hitler impression, 'to which we cheered and booed and *sieg heiled* and *heil Hitlered* and sang "*Deutschland Über Alles*" with every gusto. Then unfortunately the unpleasant adjutant in a Jaeger dressing gown and a very sour expression, entered, and quite soon after that the party broke up.'

Joan and her fellow Wrens arrived in Egypt via the Suez Canal, and from there took an uncomfortable train to Cairo, where they checked into the Continental Hotel. They met an old friend, Squadron Leader Glyn Daniel, who took them on a tour of the best spots in Cairo; to Groppi's for coffee, to Marconi's and the Heliopolis, and for dinner, 'where there was dancing and a very bad cabaret'.

After arriving in Alexandria, Sheila was posted to Ismailia, staying in a converted convent surrounded by tropical gardens. As a 21-year-old officer, overseas for the first time, she was experiencing the time of her life. She relished the chance to bronze in the sun. She wrote home:

> I have turned a marvellous brown – my legs and arms at least – I just can't imagine what it's like at home now – I suppose you are still wearing thick overcoats and not even thinking of spring clothes at all – I feel quite ashamed of the amount of food there is to eat.

Also serving in North Africa were the QA nurses, who put themselves on the front line to treat the men of the Eighth Army. They slept in the same nomadic conditions as the men, yet brought feminine touches to their wards by decorating them with desert flowers. They continued to style their hair by sleeping in curlers, which could cause issues when trying to get their tin hats on during a night raid. They worked with the water rationing for strip washes, and shared techniques on how to get rid of the sand engrained in their skin (the make-up remover carried by ENSA entertainers seemed to be the only thing that worked).

Before leaving on ships that took them to North Africa and the Far East, QAs were issued with their tropical uniform consisting of white overalls with epaulettes and pearl buttons, white stockings, white shoes, a white felt hat with ribbon and a very old-fashioned parasol. Audrey Hayward, a QA who had been at a hospital in Shaftesbury for five months before sailing from Liverpool, said:

> Just to complete the feeling that you had strayed into an earlier century the whole thing had to be topped off by a white parasol with a red lining! We scoured the shops of Lowestoft for a red-lined parasol. In the end we managed to find a green-lined one which I decided would have to do. Needless to say it was never used.

Molly Budge was a QA nurse caring for the 7th Armoured Division of the Eighth Army. At their camp in El Tahag, in Egypt, the nurses were given 'Beatrice' stoves to heat their cold tents and to make hot drinks. Water was rationed, and with only 2 pints to be used for washing and drinking, they would boil up the water after strip-washing. However, this made it difficult to wash their white veils, which were expected to be pristine. What they could wear was limited to their grey cotton dresses or drill trousers with bush shirts. Stockings were were hard to come by, but they could pick up bits and pieces from bazaars.

The weather in North Africa was one of extremes, where it could be so cold in winter and sticky and hot in summer, when three clothing changes a day would be necessary, yet the matron-in-chief at Philippeville preferred her nurses to continue wearing the grey cotton dresses rather than battledress. It was deemed important to the war effort that nurses would maintain their appearances, and that they would wear the white veils that brought comfort to injured men and reapply lipstick despite the uncomfortable conditions. Meta Kelly reported that her matron told the nurses, 'I'm tired of seeing you going round looking so tired all the time. These men have been in battle and they are wounded. They don't want to be looking at tired wan faces. Go to your tents and put some lipstick on.'

Mary English, who grew up on a farm in Northern Ireland, arrived in Algiers before Christmas 1942, freezing in her cotton QA dress. Mary and her fellow QAs asked the quartermaster for warmer clothes, and they were eventually issued with khaki battledress. 'Of course it didn't fit. The trousers were too big … but we were delighted to be warm at last.'

January 1943 in Egypt was bitterly cold, even for those who had been billeted in grand colonial villas, like Wren Sheila Mills:

> We are all in greatcoats, have extra blankets and hot water bottles and just shiver. These houses are so vast and airy, with no central heating and we only have one fire – you can't imagine how chilly it is. I am thankful for my winter dressing gown and wish I had brought more warm clothes.

Life in the desert was hard, but for welcome relief they went for swims and picnics with officers, or they piled into the back of army trucks to be taken to evening dances. Mary English remembered bumping along in the back of a jeep to be taken to a British Army nightclub in Philippeville. They were also pleased to meet up with the Americans, who had better food, such as fresh meat, to dish out. Mary said, 'The Americans had everything – not just stockings, but plenty of beer. We even used to watch films with them … The poor old British Army couldn't keep up.'

The American nurses attached to the 93rd even had a far superior uniform. 'Their working dresses were all made of non-creasing cotton so that they never needed ironing, and they had very smart going-out frocks, designed purposely for a hot climate,' said Sylvia Skimming, a Red Cross nurse, in her memoir, *Sand in My Shoes*.

The Wrens had the sense of being the most exclusive of the services, and Sheila was certainly a snob when it came to the thousands of men who outnumbered the servicewomen and nurses in North Africa. She and her select group of friends, who went for dances at naval bases, picnics and swims:

> [were] terribly tired of a lot of these men, who are so obviously out for a good time, whoever they are with, and you have to be careful in sorting the chaff from the oats. We just can't think how some of these girls are out with different people each night and seem to enjoy it! We thoroughly enjoy life, all the same.

She dated a Scottish commander, John Pritty, who was stationed in the Western Desert as part of the Eighth Army. 'He is so nice, Scotch, wears nice tartan trousers and sensible to talk to and be with – unusual out here, with all the naval fly-abouts.' He impressed Sheila by collecting a pair of 'glamorous undies' she was having made in Alexandria.

As well as having underwear and gowns made cheaply at the local tailors, the Wrens would shop in the Indian bazaar for jewellery and slippers made from gazelle or leopard skin, cotton dressing gowns and nightgowns, or search out Revlon lipsticks and nail varnish. 'I have bought no winter clothes at all, but must really get down to it soon,' wrote Sheila. 'They will always be useful when the war is over. I have had a nice pair of grey gabardine jodhpurs made which are really quite good. I do love riding and hope one day to become good.'

North Africa was full of exotic delights, and the servicewomen went crazy for mangoes, unheard of in Britain at the time. Sheila thought them marvellous, 'but terribly messy … In the end you finish up by being juiced all over.' Nurses in the desert lived on a diet of dates and figs, army biscuits and Maconochie stew, or could sometimes barter with the locals to swap cigarettes for oranges.

After having moved to Alexandria in August 1942, Sheila was posted to Cairo to assist Admiral Ramsay in the invasion of Sicily, and she was proud to be issued a 'second stripe'. Life for officers in Cairo followed a similar pattern. Sheila described how work began at 9 a.m., breaking for lunch at the Gezira or Turf Club, followed by swimming or tennis. They worked again from 4 p.m. to 9 p.m., after which they would go for dinner or dancing. Only officers were admitted to the nightclubs like the Continental and Shepheard's.

'Life in Cairo is very gay,' Sheila wrote in March 1943. 'Dancing at Shepheard's every night, full evening dress, lots of cinemas and good places to dine, but the food is really better in Alex. I like Cairo, but oh it is awfully expensive.'

At the Musky, the bazaar in Cairo, Sheila described:

> … narrow, narrow streets with little shops open to the street, and inside men and boys sorting cotton, beating copper into pans, making minute and intricate silver bracelets in filigree. It's full of shrieking children, beggars, guides, merchants and people buying … we then proceeded on to a silk shop, because the Egyptian brocade is heavenly and I have an evening gown made of it. Well, I bought a glorious bit – a deep royal blue, with gold flowers all down it, and shot so that it shines gold when worn. Already I have given it to the dressmaker and she is making an evening dress for me.

Joan Bawden explored Cairo by *ghari*, searching out fabrics for new summer dresses:

Life out here is certainly less supplied with shop-made commodities than London but I am finding it fun – this doing things for yourself – and I am enjoying the fascination of Cairo: the dirty, colourful streets, the Arabs on the trams trying to sell you fly whisks and roses and trying to clean your shoes.

In April 1942, Joan met a tall, dashing officer called Major Hugh Rice. They spent the day exploring the pyramids, and then drank orangeade on the porch at his hotel. 'We discovered that we had both dabbled in journalism pre-war and all the day, with all these wonders of the world and the banks of the Nile as background, we discussed books and plays and personal ambitions,' she said.

As a young woman who had tasted adventure and had experiences that would not have existed if there hadn't been a war, she felt torn between what she wanted in life, knowing that a husband might try to curtail her activities:

I want freedom, I want to travel, I want to write … Then there comes the complication of sex. To be logical I should be able to say marriage will interfere beyond adjustment with the way I want to live, therefore I must take love as it comes to me without ties and go free after that. But all my deepest instincts know that that way of life is shoddy and cheap and second-rate and unworthy of me. So here I am, torn between two ways of living, unable to see any compromise which will reconcile them.

Rice wrote in his diary of their first meeting while training in Cairo, and his impressions of Joan and her WAAF friends, 'they are quite at ease in over-whelmingly male surroundings, and in this particular case they showed us all up by getting the first three places [on the course]'.

Joan remembered their dinner on the Continental roof restaurant:

It was one of the best places I've been to in Cairo, cool and dimly lit, with multicoloured fairy lights, with the dark star-crammed sky above. We sat in an alcove talking as we'd talked before of life and loving and journalism and the arts, and danced at intervals to the satisfactory band playing old memories like 'Begin the Beguine' and the latest hit in Cairo, though already in England before I left it, 'Sand in My Shoes'.

In summer 1942, the Axis forces were threateningly close to taking Egypt, and plans were made to evacuate to British Palestine for safety. There, Joan enjoyed Tel Aviv, 'a somewhat shoddy little seaside town', where they met with RAF friends, and sat:

… in a café by the shore drinking iced coffee, eating strawberries and cream and laughing a lot. Then we went on to the bar of a hotel called the Gatz Rimon, where we sat on high stools drinking shandies while a pianist played all our dear tunes, like 'Fools Rush In' and 'Begin the Beguine'.

As part of the evacuation, Sheila set off from Alexandria towards the end of July, going by train to Port Said and on to Lydda in Palestine. The train was crammed, and Sheila ended up sleeping on the floor, 'lying on half my rug and with my shoes, handbag and towel as an assortment of pillows'.

In Palestine, Sheila also discovered the delights of shopping:

I collected my beautiful nightie I have had made in pale gray blue crepe de Chine with natural coloured lace trimming it (it really is so lovely I don't think I shall ever dare wear it!). Then Mollie Rendell and I did a grand tour of the shops, when I fell for some very dark gray flannel to have a skirt made, and two lengths of Chinese silk in scarlet and a bright purple-gentian blue for blouses. Somehow, if you are clever, you can buy almost anything you want in the shops here, and I simply love pottering about the quaint little streets. Some of the shops are really tiny, just little square holes in the wall, with shelves and shelves packed with bales and bales of materials.

By August, the Eighth Army had defended El Alamein and the campaign swung back in their favour. Back in Cairo, Joan and Hugh Rice took a taxi to 'the Continental roof garden where we ate ices, drank coffees, danced, watched the cabaret and laughed a lot'. They had fallen in love, and married on 23 December 1942 in Cairo, with war making it seem more imperative that they tie the knot.

Love in North Africa meant snatched moments and enjoying the romance of a far-away city. 'We were all on edge because people were young and falling in love, and yet death was an everyday occurrence,' said QA, Mary English. 'You'd ask after an SAS man you usually saw and they'd say, "Jack? He didn't make it." It was the same with the Spitfire pilots. You'd ask after someone who was missing from the table and his friend would say lightly, "Roger? I'm afraid he bought it".'

10

Female Flyers

When Argentinean pilot Maureen Dunlop was photographed climbing out of a Fairey Barracuda in 1944, she had no idea of the impact her picture would have. Wearing a white shirt with the sleeves rolled up and a dark tie, her parachute slung over her shoulder and the harness clips hanging down, she took off her helmet and ran her hand through her hair to shake it out. The photo was glamorous and cool, and when it was splashed on the cover of *Picture Post* in September of that year, it propelled Maureen and the women of the ATA to fame.

Sometimes known as 'Attagirls', the ATA were a transfixing sight when seen in their blue and gold uniforms. Flying without radio and facing the dangers of barrage balloons, enemy planes and overenthusiastic Ack-Ack units on a daily basis, it was one of the most lethal services for women in the war.

The photo of Maureen Dunlop gave the impression that the ATA was an all-woman outfit, but in fact it originally had been conceived for men. It was formed in September 1939 by British Airways director, Gerard d'Erlanger, utilising a motley crew of skilled pilots who were too old or injured to fight, but could effectively deliver planes from factory to aerodrome. They referred to each other as the 'Ancient and Tattered Airmen'.

Also in the ATA was Prince Suprabhat Chirasakti of Siam, the nephew of Rama VII Prajadhipok, King of Siam, who Diana Barnato described as a 'neat, small, smiling, twinkly-eyed, quiet young man'. He was posted after training to Kirkbride, near Carlisle, known as an incredibly tough pool to fly from. Not long after his posting, 'Chira' was caught by low cloud and flew into the side of the valley and was killed, on 12 September 1942. 'Keen type, pressed on too long. He shouldn't have been sent there so early in his flying career. I shed a tear,' said Diana.

Because women also held flying licences and the ATA needed all the help they could get, it was agreed, after some consideration, that women could be accepted into the service too. 'We were called the lesbians' pool, of course,' said Rosemary Rees, because often these women were more focused on their job than flirting with RAF officers.

The first women of the ATA were a close-knit group with cut-glass accents, who came from wealthy backgrounds, having trained in expensive and exclusive flying clubs in the thirties, where one hour's instruction cost roughly what the average shop worker could expect to earn in a fortnight. They were considered 'It' girls, equally at home at a Chelsea party or West End nightclub as they were in the sky.

At 20 Jackie Sorour was the youngest ATA, and at first she found that her age and lack of sophistication set her apart from the other members, 'who still regarded it in its early days as an exclusive flying club'.

There was a scheme in 1938 to train up a reserve of women for the country's civil airlines, such as for ambulances. At Romford, 300 young women who worked as typists or telephone operators received air training in their spare time as part of the National Women's Air Reserve. They wore high-waisted white jumpsuits, black berets and boots, and two stars on their tunics marked them as a flight leader. Once they passed ground training, they were taken flying by Gabrielle Patterson, the first British woman to earn an instructor's licence. 'The plan is that they will be able to teach themselves without men, and that there will be scholarships,' wrote *Picture Post*.

Aviation was the wonder technology of the late twenties and early thirties, offering endless possibilities in exploration, communications and engineering. Women over the age of 21 had only recently got the vote in 1928, but the new breed of woman flyer was captivating to the public, seeming to defy societal restrictions and expectations.

Amy Johnson was one of the most celebrated aviators in the 1930s, and resplendent in her leather helmet and sheepskin flying jacket, she demolished the old rules for women. The hit song 'Amy, Wonderful Amy' celebrated her achievement as the first woman to fly solo to Australia in 1932. She was a woman so devoted to flying that she had a hysterectomy to solve her debilitating period pains which got in the way of her first love.

Born in Hull in 1903, Amy was considered a tomboy – the only girl who could bowl overarm – and led a protest against the hard straw boater hats at her school, in favour of much more comfortable soft panamas. She studied economics at Sheffield University and worked as a secretary in a solicitor's office in London, but all the time her passion was for flying.

Her groundbreaking journey to Australia took twenty days in challenging conditions, where she wore leathers in the cockpit when cold, and flew only in cottons when it was hot. The trip took her through the terrifying passages of the Taurus Mountains, she crash-landed in a field in Burma, and went missing for twenty-four hours near Bali. Amy continued her record-breaking in 1932 with a return flight from London to Cape Town in a De Havilland Puss Moth and she was the first person to fly non-stop from England to North America. As a celebrity, she advertised a short-lived venture called Air Cruises, where she was dressed in Schiaparelli-designed wool suit and newsprint scarf as she embarked on a flight to Cape Town.

Amy met Glasgow-born flyer Jim Mollison in 1932, and after marrying, they became known as 'the Flying Sweethearts' as they competed in daring flying competitions together. However, he was both a philanderer and jealous of her success, and they divorced in 1936.

In June 1939, she took on work as a pilot for Solent Air Ferry, carrying passengers between Southampton and the Isle of Wight. With her achievements and fame, Amy Johnson had expected a unique role in the war, but it was Pauline Gower who was given the most senior woman's position in the ATA.

In January 1940, the first eight women were recruited to the ATA, soon to be joined by many others. However, there were restrictions on what a woman could do. At first, they were limited to single engines. They were not taught with instruments because they were not allowed to fly above cloud, so they ran the real risk of running out of fuel – and they were definitely not allowed to fly to the Continent. They were expected to be guided only by the instructions in their 'Ferry Pilot's Notes', an A6 ring binder that fitted into their shirt pockets.

The first eight members of the ATA were Joan Hughes, Britain's youngest pilot at the age of 17; Gabrielle Patterson; Marion Wilberforce, an Oxford graduate, mountaineer and expert in jiu-jitsu; Margaret Cunnison, the daughter of a Glasgow University professor who got her private licence at 18; Rosemary Rees; Winifred Crossley-Fair; Margot Gore and Margaret Fairweather, who was the only one of the eight not to survive the war.

A photocall was arranged by d'Erlanger on 9 January 1940, and news desks were promised action and aeroplanes and women in uniform at Hatfield. First, they modelled their greatcoats, Sidcot flying suits and fur-lined boots. Next the photographers instructed them to sling their 30lb parachutes over their shoulders and run to their Tiger Moth planes.

They then changed into what would become their instantly recognisable navy blue and gold suits and forage caps. This outfit was designed to look like that of a flight attendant: stylish, sleek and sharp. It consisted of a single-breasted dark blue jacket, gold trimmings, skirt, white shirt, black tie and black silk stockings, which d'Erlanger had envisioned them flying in. He had old-fashioned views of women in trousers, but Gower argued that wearing a skirt while clambering in and out of planes would be immodest, and so he agreed that trousers and Sidcot suits could be worn while flying, as long as they switched into their jacket and skirt on landing. This rule was gradually relaxed, although they were still expected to wear the suit when on leave in London, with pilots carrying them in their overnight bags.

Women pilots were paid less than their male counterparts, but this was just accepted as the way it was. 'At least we were eventually allowed to wear trousers with our uniforms,' said Diana Barnato. 'Women were still considered second-class material, even though they were doing exactly the same flying job and taking similar risks. We didn't mind at all. All we wanted to do was to fly.'

Jackie Sorour described the nomadic life in the ATA, reporting to the pool at 8 a.m., collecting the ferry-chits, boarding the milk-run aircraft to drop pilots at the collecting points. They would then transport planes between aerodromes. After their last delivery, they would have 'one-night stops in hotels or fitful sleep in the luggage racks of all-night trains with a disreputable macintosh to disguise my uniform when I subjected it to the indignity of climbing into the luggage rack'.

Because of the civilian nature of the ATA, their uniform was measured and cut at Austin Reed's, which would allow them to incorporate unique and individual touches. The navy and gold, imbued with a sense of dynamism, was their access to first-class service. They were sure to attract attention when marching into hotels and restaurants in their suits and, considered to be the daring women of the sky, they were regularly given the best tables and rooms. As Veronica Volkersz said, 'it would even get you a seat on the bus'.

Veronica was a woman who knew all about style. She drove an Aston Martin sports car with the top down, her hair kept in place by a white leather helmet, and while working as an ambulance driver during the Blitz, she would change out of her uniform and into an evening dress for parties at the Brasserie Universelle. She was thrilled to hear that the ATA was now accepting women.

When Jackie Sorour tried on her uniform from Moss Bros, she thought it was 'magnificent'. It was, as she described it:

Navy blue, severely cut, black buttons, a crisp gold stripe on each epaulette, rich gold-embroidered wings on the left breast and an absurd little forage cap that seemed to transform my face. Quite suddenly I realised that I was not bad looking. The nice little thing from Pretoria looked as cute as a button. Twinkling with this remarkable discovery I walked along the Strand through the lunch-time bustle of office workers and servicemen. For the first time in my life heads turned as I walked along the street. The greatest compliment of all came when women also turned. It was a wonderful day.

Like the men of the RAF, they also adapted their uniform to be more effective. Some female pilots refused to wear helmet and goggles, instead tying a silk scarf around their head. Rosemary Rees, who often suffered from the cold, always ensured she had layers of shawls, blankets and furs. Jackie Sorour once flew in her tennis whites and plimsolls, having just finished a game when she was ordered to deliver a Tempest to New Church as a priority.

Other women in the ATA included Lettice Curtis, the first woman allowed to fly a four-engine bomber, and Mary de Bunsen, daughter of the British Ambassador to Vienna, who had one leg shorter than the other, due to contracting polio as a child. She worked as an Auxiliary Fire Service Volunteer, in dungarees and a tin hat, dishing out hot chocolate to survivors, but with her orthopaedic shoes, was unable to drive the fire truck.

Twenty-eight different nationalities flew with ATA. Poles Anna Leska, Barbara Wojtulanis and Jadwiga Pilsudska all escaped their homeland following the German invasion. Anna Leska and a friend stole an aircraft from a Polish aerodrome under lockdown, flew to Romania, and eventually made it to England via France.

Margot Duhalde, the first Chilean woman to hold a commercial pilot's licence, arrived in Britain at the age of 19 to take part in the war and was nicknamed 'Chile' because of the distinctive shoulder flash on her uniform. She could hardly speak a word of English, which Pauline Gower believed made it impossible for her to be a ferry pilot. However, the chief instructor took pity and allowed her three months' training to brush up on her English. The engineers amused themselves by teaching her swear words, which she innocently repeated without knowing what they meant.

Despite having been passed over for the top job, in May 1940 Amy Johnson agreed to take a box-ticking flying test for the ATA, even though she was dismissive of the other female pilots. She described one in a letter:

> … all dolled up in full Sidcot suit, fur-lined helmet and goggles, fluffing up her hair etc. – the typical Lyons waitress type … I suddenly realised I could

not go in and sit in line with these girls (who all more or less look up to me as God!), so I turned tail and ran.

Amy was known for wearing Astrakhan-collared flying coats, but as a ferry pilot she was expected to wear her navy suit and cap like the others. Despite her initial reluctance, she accepted the idolisation as part of the job when RAF pilots all came into the mess to glimpse her while she was having tea.

Jackie Sorour, who joined the ATA in Hatfield in July 1940, spotted Amy Johnson in the mess:

> I looked at her dumbfounded as I recognized the face that had inspired me during my brief flying career and had flitted on the world's headlines for a decade. Idiotically I rushed to her and gushed: 'Miss Johnson, may I have your autograph?' She stared at me, astonished. There was a painful silence. Oh God, I wished the floor would open up and devour me. How could I have behaved so inanely. Suddenly she grinned: 'My dear child, I'll swap it for yours.'

Amy's life ended tragically in January 1941, partly as a result of the no-instrument rule for female pilots. She was caught in thick cloud, and after taking the risk to try to get on top of it, she ran out of fuel and made the difficult decision to bail out. She landed in the murky waters of the Thames, and despite a huge effort from a nearby ship to save her, it's believed she was sucked under the propellers of the boat that was part of her rescue. Her body was never recovered.

Flying in war conditions, without instruments and radio, could be incredibly dangerous, and during the course of the war, out of 164 female ATA, sixteen were killed, equating to nearly one in ten. Bridget Hill and Betty Sayer were the first to die, killed as passengers in a taxi plane that crashed into a house on 18 March 1942.

Diana Barnato was one of the most glamorous of the ATA, and also one of the deftest. She was the daughter of Woolf Barnato, a motor-racing champion with stakes in Bentley, and the granddaughter of a South African diamond tycoon who founded De Beers. After her time as a Bentley-driving debutante, at the outbreak of war Diana volunteered as a Red Cross nurse, driving around Belgravia in a green ambulance, collecting patients and making deliveries.

She had learnt to fly at Brooklands Flying Club in 1938, going solo after only six hours' instruction, and in 1941 she joined the ATA after just ten hours of solo flying. Almost as soon as she was accepted into the ATA, she was seriously injured in a horse-riding accident, breaking her jaw and smashing her face. Six months later, once she had recovered, she re-took her test flight, making an impression in a leopard-skin coat that belonged to her stepmother. The aptly named Captain A.D. Pickup, who was doing her test flight, told her she 'looked far too attractive to know anything about flying'.

Diana had many tales of escaping from perilous situations. She was flying a Typhoon in April 1945 when the undercarriage blew off mid-flight. She looked down to see nothing but sky and the Wiltshire countryside 2,000ft below her. Her uniform was flapping against her skin from the rush of wind and her teeth chattered from the cold. But, keeping a cool head, she tightened her safety straps and managed to land safely at Kemble. Other pilots who suffered the same failure weren't so lucky, yet Diana wasn't offered so much as a cup of tea. Instead, she was lectured for only bringing half a plane back.

During one encounter with thick cloud in January 1943, Diana wrestled with the decision to bail out, but because she was wearing a skirt, with a pair of knickers made from old parachute silk, she felt 'it will really look so silly floating down in a hitched-up and very tight navy serge uniform skirt. We were very modest in those days.' She managed to bring the plane down, landing in huge puddles of muddy water, which soaked her through. She also discovered a downside to the navy blue flying overalls on a particularly hot day, when wearing only a shirt underneath. At 5,000ft and upside down in a Spitfire, her silver powder compact slipped from her overall pocket, spilling face powder everywhere, and covering the window of the craft with dust.

Diana had the energy and ability to party all night in London and turn up for work the next day on only a few hours' sleep. She would regularly take the Tube into London to meet her pilot friends, many of whom were in 601 Squadron. After changing into a long evening gown, she would go for dinner before ending up at the 400 Club in Leicester Square, or the Orchid Room, spending all night chatting about their flying experiences and sketching flight techniques on the pink tablecloths.

In the early hours of the morning she would change back into her uniform for her next assignment. She recalled in her memoirs:

There were two taxi-driver brothers, Bert and Ozzie Jenkins. They ranked at Hyde Park Corner and I had a weekly arrangement with them to get me to the 04.20 train from Waterloo to the railway station at Eastleigh, by Southampton, where I used to leave my car so that I could drive back to Hamble. They never let me down … I would curl up in the train under my thick flying coat for a couple of hours' nap. Arriving at Eastleigh, I just had time to drive fast to the cottage to tidy up and have breakfast. I had no breakfast if the train was late, maybe delayed by air-raids, before going to Hamble to fly all day. I never felt tired …

The presence of women ferry pilots on an RAF airbase charged up the sexual energy. After flying her Magister to Debden RAF base one day, and stopping for lunch, Diana later found that the plane wouldn't start up again. The ground crew took another look at it, but still she had no joy. She spent an evening with Squadron Leader Tony Bartley, who she had known back in their private school days, and one of his closest friends, Humphrey Gilbert, the commander of 65 Fighter Squadron and a Battle of Britain hero. After being grounded for three days, during which time she and Humphrey had fallen head over heels in love, the Magister finally started up and she could continue with her delivery. Diana much later discovered that Humphrey had asked the ground crew to take the spark plugs out, so that she would stay longer at Debden.

They married after only a few months of knowing each other, yet Humphrey died soon after, in a preventable flying accident. He was killed after an afternoon spent drinking, and in a hurry to get to another party, he and another airman squeezed into a Spitfire together and, overburdened, it crashed. Not that long before, a pilot named Gordon Brettell had narrowly escaped a court martial when he had flown a Spitfire with a WAAF on his lap in order to take her to a dance. Tony Bartley had acted as witness for the defence and would later blame himself for Humphrey's death.

In June 1943, Diana was permanently posted to No. 15 Ferry Pool, in Hamble. Not long after her arrival, a well-liked pilot called Honor Salmon was killed when her plane crashed in bad weather. Diana was devastated. Honor's parents instructed her belongings to be shared out at the pool, and Diana was handed a beautiful pale blue shirt. Honor's death had hit home to Diana about the fragility of life, and she hadn't wanted her belongings to remind her of the tragedy. 'It was made from a lovely soft wool, yet looked enough like our ordinary-issue shirts to be able to be worn with our ATA uniform. As clothes were rationed and could only be bought with coupons, I accepted it.' After that, she said, 'when someone had an accident or was killed, I scarcely talked about it at all. Getting bumped off, for whatever reason, was one of the normal hazards of the life. It could happen any time, like stubbing your toe.'

At Hamble, Diana shared a cottage with two other ATA pilots, Anne Walker and Faith Bennett, and they tried to create a cosy home life, despite the hectic nature of their work, and with RAF officers regularly dropping in. They had some simple house rules – whoever arrived home first should light the boiler for the others to get a hot bath after a day of flying. They were then supposed to lay the table for dinner. 'Often the latter didn't happen, as we were usually taken out to "The Bugle" at Hamble, or the "Polygon" in Southampton, or a dark little dive called the "Clausentium Club", an eating haunt with a scratchy gramophone playing in the background,' said Diana.

In December 1944, Margot Gore received a request from an RAF squadron who had suffered serious losses and needed a batch of new Mosquito XXXs urgently. Margot instructed the female ATA pilots, including Diana Barnato, to look as attractive as possible when they made their deliveries, and to spend as long as they wanted in the officers' mess. Because of the losses the men had suffered, the women had been sent as morale-boosters.

'Oh, you pretty girls get all the nice jobs to squadrons,' a pilot called Joy Ferguson told Diana Barnato on her return. Joy wore her hair in a messy bob and, unlike the others, rarely wore make-up. As Diana recounted in her memoirs:

> Joy was often teasing me about painting my nails, putting on lipstick and generally surveying my face in my powder-compact mirror, but always said it in a gentle way. She never did anything to make herself look more feminine or attractive, whilst the rest of us always tried to look as beautiful as possible whilst doing what was then called a man's job. So some of us turned on her, saying, 'Well, if you'd only do something about yourself, we'd be able to make quite a good-looking dish out of you! Take out your kirby grips, fluff up your hair, let your nails grow long; add some lipstick and nail polish, too.'

After the war, Joy Ferguson underwent a sex change, and became known as Jonathon Ferguson. He had been given the green light for an operation at the very moment he had been accepted into the ATA, but not wishing to go through such a procedure with the possibility of being killed while flying, he postponed it.

'She had made a very ordinary-looking woman but, as has been said, she didn't really try,' said Diana:

> Later on we all understood why. He turned into a much better-looking man, confiding to me one day that it was sad that he couldn't have children. He was now hoping to marry a girl who had some of her own. I saw him

once in a while, then one day I rang up his office to be told that he had been shot dead in Hyde Park while driving along in his sports car. No-one knew why. What a waste of an extremely brave and kind person.

In May 1942 the first five of twenty-five American female flyers arrived at Liverpool docks to join the ATA. The arrangement was the brainchild of American Jacqueline 'Jackie' Cochran, who had landed in a twin-engine Lockheed Hudson bomber in summer 1941.

Cochran was born Bessie Lee Pittman and was from a dirt-poor background. Instead of attending school, she worked from the age of 8 at a Pensacola sawmill, then became a hairdresser in Montgomery, Alabama, where she selected her new name from the phone book. Her Nestle perms gained a reputation in town, and from there she found work at a salon in Saks Fifth Avenue. Jackie, with the help of the head of RKO studios, Floyd Bostwick Odlum, who she would later marry, took up flying in the 1930s and, excelling in air-race competitions, she set a new women's world speed record in 1937.

Wanting to create an American ATA, Cochran appealed to President Roosevelt himself, and it was agreed that American women pilots could travel to Britain to assist the ATA. Unfortunately, Cochran rubbed the Brits up the wrong way with her extravagant lifestyle and the head-turning mink coat she insisted on wearing, thinking it would impress the Air Ministry.

In the first group of five to sail to Britain were Ann Wood; ski-champion Audrey Sale-Barker, who would become the Countess of Selkirk; ice hockey international Mona Friedlander, nicknamed in papers 'the Mayfair Minx'; Lois Butler, wife of the chairman of the de Havilland Aircraft Company, and former captain of the Canadian women's ski team; and Dorothy Furey. Dorothy was the only one to pack an evening gown with her flying kit; a red dress she referred to as her *Gone with the Wind* dress, and which always made an impact. Dorothy was the daughter of a New Orleans banana importer who lost his fortune in the Great Depression.

The flyers were whisked from Liverpool to London to be measured for their uniforms at Austin Reed on Regent Street. Audrey Sale-Barker was known for her style, and instead chose her own Savile Row tailor, who incorporated a scarlet satin lining for her jacket. They were also equipped with leather helmets, brown suede leather flying boots and leather gauntlets with silk liners.

The others arrived soon after. Roberta Sandoz had been keen to use her flying skills to help the war effort, having spent childhood summers in British Columbia:

I suddenly began wanting to go and help them win their war. I made myself ridiculous writing to the Royal Air Force and the Royal Canadian Air Force and the British Air Ministry, and got no useful response until someone in Canada said get in touch with Jacqueline Cochran.

After Sandoz's pilot fiancé was killed, she married a British officer, Peter Leveaux, who she met in a Mayfair pub. Instead of a honeymoon, she flew home via Iceland, wrapped in a large US Army Air Corps sheepskin coat borrowed from a sergeant from the Atlantic Ferry Command. Suzanne Ford, from New York, was considered a 'flying socialite' and asked to be posted to Prestwick to be with the Atlantic Ferry Command. She once took beer up in her plane to cool it down at 10,000ft.

The American women travelled down to White Waltham, arriving to find all the men at the aerodrome had gathered to gawp at them. Ann Wood wasn't always impressed with life in Britain, especially the class system, and she didn't like the way the RAF officers treated the WAAFs, feeling that American officers gave their female colleagues their due respect.

In 1944 Jackie Sorour joined the first all-female ferry pool at Hatfield. Jackie was dating an army officer, Reg Moggridge, who she had met at a dance in 1940, but Jackie had doubts about marriage. She was concerned it would get in the way of flying. But when Reg asked if she would agree to an engagement, she said yes, and they went shopping for rings small enough to fit under her flying gauntlets.

After the death of Humphrey Gilbert, Diana Barnato fell in love with another pilot, Wing Commander Derek Walker, who had served in North Africa. They married on 6 May 1944. Diana was in white silk and Derek wore his RAF uniform, and most of No. 15 Ferry Pool was in attendance at their wedding. By coincidence, it took place exactly two years after Humphrey's funeral was held. 'Many of my admirers had, by then, been killed in the war, so I thought I should hook him quick, in case one or the other of us got bumped off whilst flying,' she said, in her matter-of-fact way. Tragically, Derek was buried just eighteen months after they were married, her second love to die in a flying accident during the war.

11

American Culture Before the War

The generation born at the end of the First World War had been young children during the Roaring Twenties, and as teenagers in the 1930s they had suffered the hardships of the Depression. They knew what it was like to feel hunger, to see their parents out of work and to not have enough clothes to wear or bedding to keep them warm at night.

With the progressive recovery measures put in place by President Franklin D. Roosevelt to tackle the Depression from 1933, young people had ambitions to go to college or to find a decent job. They searched for escapism in movies and music, they visited the drug store and milk bar, socialising over Coca-Cola and malted milkshakes. But when it came to signing up and putting on a uniform, their patriotism shone through.

Following the Stock Market Crash in 1929, the Great Depression of the thirties brought mass unemployment, poverty and food shortages to millions of Americans. When Roosevelt came into power in March 1933, he introduced the New Deal, a government response to the need for short- and long-term economic relief. This included programmes focused on providing support to the unemployed, poor and elderly, and initiatives to help young people.

The National Youth Administration (NYA) was dedicated to finding work for 16–25-year-olds, while the Civilian Conservation Corps (CCC) was a precursor to the militarisation of the country during the war. It provided jobs for young, single men, as well as building on America's natural resources. Over the course of the programme, from 1933 to 1942, 2.4 million young men donned khaki army uniforms to plant 2.3 billion trees, lay miles of trails and roads, and build bridges. Once they had completed their day's work, they would relax in their dress uniform of khaki shirts, trousers and ties for study and recreation time.

These initiatives earned Roosevelt much respect amongst young people and, for 1941, $400 million funding was given by Congress to the CCC and the NYA. 'Since 1933 in the CCC, 2.4m unemployed young men have found jobs, health and peace of mind in the out-of-doors, from Maine forests to the craggy badlands of Arizona,' wrote *Life* magazine in April 1940:

> [They have] toned spirits and muscles, put an average of ten extra pounds on their bodies. In their barracks, under supervision of US Army officers, they have acquired solid habits of work and deportment. After-hour classes have taught 80,000 illiterate CCC boys to read and write, and trained thousands more in occupational skills.

Born to a poor Kentucky farming family, Henry Giles joined the CCC and then the army in peacetime to escape the struggles of finding food and work in the poverty-stricken dustbowl states. He left school in 1931, at the end of the eighth grade, as he was needed to work on the family farm to help grow tobacco and corn. He wrote, 'Since I've been old enough I've supported most of the family, besides what we grew on the farm which never was so much.'

Jobs in the Depression were hard to come by and so he signed up to the CCC, working to build roads with the Works Progress Administration (WPA). When Giles found that his mother was pregnant yet again, meaning he would have increased responsibility, he joined the army. 'I enlisted for a good many reasons,' he wrote. 'For one, the depression hadn't ended down our way and I was sick and tired of the scrabbling and the shame of the commodity lines and no jobs but the WPA. You couldn't find a day's work in a month of Sundays.'

Girls were mostly left out of the CCC, and instead they were provided for by organisations like the Girl Scouts and the Camp Fire Girls. For girls from needy families, the NYA offered skilled labour and vocational courses such as home economics and domestic training, where they could learn the etiquette of setting a table and seating guests for a luncheon party.

Despite increased emancipation, women in the 1930s were still very much in traditional roles, yet more and more were going into the workplace. From 1930 to 1940, the number of working women rose from 10.5 million to 13 million. Yet, the typical woman worker was single and under the age of 25, and once she was married she was unlikely to work again.

In the period of economic uncertainty of the early thirties, some scholars argue that Americans retreated from the social revolution of the decade before, when the flapper was a controversial, liberated figure who demanded new freedoms. Margaret Sanger's American Birth Control League may have sought to introduce women to new birth control technologies, but during the Depression these were seen to oppose family values as the country clung to traditional ideals.

Conservatism was also reflected in fashion. The thigh-skimming gowns and bound chests of the Jazz Age gave way to floor-length dresses and promoted femininity in the thirties. Movies offered hope and entertainment for many during the Depression, especially for young women. They watched dreamily the romance and drama of Norma Shearer, Jean Harlow or Greta Garbo on the silver screen. As costume designer Edith Head said:

> The early motion pictures were pure escapism and quite unreal. Sometimes the clothes were pretty ridiculous. You know, the poor working girls going to work wearing sable, fantastically dressed … In that period there was something called the matinee audience. Women would stand in line, come rain or come shine, to see what their favourite stars were wearing.

To dress like their heroines on screen, Butterick offered patterns for running up movie costumes at home, as buying ready-made clothing was a luxury only for those who could afford it. Magazines like *Photoplay* offered advice on how to realistically adapt Hollywood gowns with a limited budget by using less material or substituting cheaper fabrics. Department stores also offered affordable versions of the dresses, and one of the most popular was a frothy, layered organdie gown worn by Joan Crawford in *Letty Lynton*. *Screen* magazine wrote in 1932, 'Paris may decree this and Paris may decree that, but when that Crawford girl pops up in puffed sleeves, then it's puffed sleeves for us before tea-time.'

The 1930s was also marked by the latest in dance fads. The Depression had sparked extreme dance contests like the 'Walkathon', where desperate contestants would be guaranteed three meals a day and the chance of winning money, if they were the last ones standing. These contests were endurance tests, with couples expected to continually keep moving over a period of weeks, with only fifteen-minute breaks every couple of hours. 'A converted garage in Long Island is the venue for the 24 hour spectacle, drawing record crowds,' reported *Picture Post* in December 1938:

> They walk till they have to be dragged round the room by their partners. The only rule is that they must not stop. They get three meals a day. Each lasts for fifteen minutes. They have to stand up, even while they are eating them. The only sleep they get is in 15 minute spells; a quarter of an hour in every hour … about three minutes of the fifteen is spent getting on or off

the floor. More precious time is wasted having sore feet bandaged; having a shower bath once a day and shaving. And the winners, the couple still walking when the rest have dropped, get 1,000 dollars between them.

By 1937, as America came out of the Depression, young people took advantage of increased leisure time and mass entertainment. American teens rose up as a consumerist force who spent money on socialising, music and clothing, and who took part in sports and went to dances. The baby-boom children also stayed in school longer than before, and because of this, new cliques developed in high schools. Affluent high school girls were given the nickname 'sub-debutantes'.

Realising that young women loved to read magazines and were voracious spenders, *The Ladies' Home Journal* ran a column dedicated to sub-debs, which offered advice on dating and make-up. These columns guided young women on how to be virtuous while going steady, and to 'revel in the swish of their party dresses before rushing off to dates and dances'. In February 1938, the column was relaunched as 'Shaggin' on Down' as an attempt to appeal to teenage slang and to reflect an interest in new dance moves.

In the late 1930s and early 1940s the sweater girl became a sub-deb archetype, as defined by Lana Turner. The term came from her debut film, *They Won't Forget*, in which Turner played a sexually promiscuous girl in a sweater, who is punished with rape. Tight-fitting sweaters caught on with teenagers as they implied a combination of innocence and sexuality, buoyed by the push for masculinity as a result of rearmament. 'Bob, why are men so crazy about sweater girls?' Judy Garland asked Bob Hope in a November 1943 newsreel by the *Army-Navy Screen* magazine.

'I don't know Judy, that's one mystery I'd like to unravel.'

By 1940, every fashionable girl wore ankle socks, or 'bobby socks', with her saddle shoes or moccasins. The 'bobby soxer' was a fan of swing music, the hot new craze that had been taking teenagers by storm and sending them into a frenzy, and was personified by big band leaders like Benny Goodman.

In January 1941, *Life* magazine ran a feature on the sub-debs, now using it as a term for girls who liked swing music, bought cosmetics and adored Judy Garland, Mickey Rooney and Benny Goodman. They live in a 'Jolly World of Gangs, Games, Gadding, Movies, Malted and Music' and they 'speak a curious lingo … adore chocolate milkshakes … wear moccasins everywhere … and drive like bats out of hell'.

Swing was influenced by the African-American music and dance moves that came out of Harlem in the twenties and thirties. In 1937 in New York, the Benny Goodman Orchestra made their debut at the Paramount Theatre, in Times Square, and throughout their five performances a day, young swing fans built themselves up into a state of ecstasy as they danced into the aisles to the strains of 'Let's Dance'. The dance was energetic, high-powered and innovative, suiting the frenetic hot jazz sound. The improvisation of the Lindy Hop and the Suzy Q were first explored in Harlem in the late 1920s, and the energy replaced the grace of more traditional waltzes and foxtrots, which still played out on British dance floors.

Tommy Dorsey could only liken swing music to 'love', while the *New York Times*, when trying to search for its definition in 1937, described it 'as authentic an expression of human feeling as folksong, and as difficult to describe'. Swing was an American musical phenomenon that would be the soundtrack to the Second World War, offering hope to those overseas when they heard Glenn Miller or Artie Shaw. The improvisational sound was a welcome break from the regimental order of army life and uniform – no wonder it was so popular during wartime.

The swing movement had its own style and language codes, heavily borrowed from its African-American roots and appropriated by the white community. Male swing fans wore a softened version of the zoot suit, an audacious style that came from Harlem and the Mexican-American urban communities, with baggy trousers, long jackets, pork-pie hats and chains connecting their belts to their pockets. Swing musicians like Duke Ellington and Cab Calloway, who were role models for young black men, were also worshipped by the white crowds who appropriated the culture of the Harlem Renaissance, despite many of the venues being for whites only.

Jive talk travelled into the mainstream, with Cab Calloway publishing his *Hepster's Dictionary* in 1938, to translate the lexicography of Lenox Avenue musicians in Harlem. 'Cats' were the band musicians, fans were 'alligators' or 'rug-cutters', 'hep' meant cool, and a 'square' was someone who was 'unhep'.

Life magazine, on 21 February 1938, in an article entitled 'Swing Music Produces These', wrote:

… an ickey is a cat who is affected only emotionally by swing. Ickeys generally contort their faces into ecstatic expressions, emit low expressive noises … A sizeable portion of American youth is either jitterbug or ickey, giving vent to its passion for hot music at almost any time and place – at home or school, in theatre or trolley car. Its favourite dances are swing dances like shag, truckin', Big Apple, Little Peach.

'Hep-Jills' were young women at the forefront of the swing and Lindy Hop craze and wore flat shoes, white bobby socks and short pleated dresses that flared when they swung around. In January 1938, the Benny Goodman Orchestra played Carnegie Hall to a wild audience, and the first strains of the climactic 'Sing, Sing, Sing' became a trigger for inventing energetic moves. The Goodman Orchestra vocalist Helen Ward recalled how girls had initially dressed up in high heels and stockings, 'but when the lindy really caught on, the gals began wearing saddle shoes'.

At an October 1939 Carnegie Hall celebration of the American Society of Composers, Authors and Publishers, the public were invited to listen to Paul Whiteman, Benny Goodman and Glenn Miller in the plush auditorium. Young girls were so desperate to dance to Glenn Miller's 'Little Brown Jug', their 'shoulders were shaking … arms were waving … hands were pounding'. But they were frustratingly prevented from up from their seats. At the Philadelphia Armory however, 10,000 'boys and girls leaped into the aisles, and many couples rose from the ground floor, dancing the jittery steps in wild abandon until forced to take their seats by the Armory's staff of uniformed ushers'.

It was mass adulation, one of the first examples of the 'teenager' in action – independent and passionate. Swing could be delivered directly into bedrooms by radio stations like NBC's 'Let's Dance'. Their fandom was expressed through new language, fashions and idolisation of musicians, and they also spent their money buying the latest records, with swing musicians Glenn Miller, Tommy Dorsey and Benny Goodman topping the charts in 1939. Phonograph records were big business by the end of the decade, with sales in 1939 up 50 per cent compared with 1938, while sales in 1938 were three times greater than in 1933.

At the end of August 1938, almost 100,000 racially mixed fans packed into Chicago's Soldier Field for a mass swing jamboree. It was described as an 'orgy of joyous emotions' as the crowd rushed the stage when the Jimmy Dorsey band played the 'Flat Foot Floogie'. The non-segregated audience was considered a shocking cultural moment, as hinted at in countless articles. 'The melting pot boils over, and now we have the hoarse and jitterbuggy days. No longer prim, we've all gone primitive,' wrote the *Chicago Daily Tribune* the day after, on 26 August 1938.

The jitterbug led to a moral panic, with concern over the lack of self-control caused by swing music. That the sound originated amongst the black musicians of New Orleans led to racist concern that it was from 'the rhythmic jungle chants of descendants of Africans'.

An American professor, Harry D. Gideonse, in November 1938 declared swing 'musical Hitlerism', because 'there is a mass sense of "letting one's self go"'. On the other side of the Atlantic, in Nazi Germany, the government sought to ban swing as it was considered 'forbidden music' because of the black and Jewish musicians who created it.

The swing kids in 1938 were very different from the teenagers of the early 1930s, who had been driven by the Depression to join unions or had worked as part of the CCC. Now in their twenties, Roosevelt's young people looked down on the teenage swing fans with their hysterical adulation, faddish fashion sense and lack of understanding of what it had been like in the early thirties.

Jack McNulty discovered swing in 1937, while at junior high school. He said, 'Every aspect of my life and that of my friends, revolved around big bands, jazz, dancing, jitterbugging, in my formative teens' and the bands they listened to shaped 'our heroes, our dress, look, styles, morals, sex lives'.

By 1940, America's rearmament had helped boost the country out of the Depression as jobs were created and men voluntarily signed up. However, when war broke out in Europe, America was in a strong position economically, and its citizens were reluctant to be involved in another war. In a 1939 American poll, 67 per cent believed that America should stay neutral, only 12 per cent were prepared to give aid to the UK, and just 2 per cent were in favour of declaring war.

When a peacetime Selective Service draft was introduced in 1940 to ensure the country was prepared for any eventuality, 10 million men were delivered to the armed forces. *Life* magazine reported in May 1941, 'A prime story of the week in war-jittery Washington is the recognition that prospective American soldiers are in no shape to fight Hitler's tough, unpampered blitzkriegers.'

Weapon Sergeant Henry Giles joined the army and signed up to the 291st Engineer Battalion in 1939, but it wasn't clear at that time that he would be expected to fight in a new world war. The army meant:

… security and pride and something fine and good … for the first time in my life I had clothes I wasn't ashamed of, for the first time in my life I was somebody. That uniform stood for something to me … something pretty grand and fine, for I chose it, it didn't choose me.

His journey was captured in letters to his girlfriend and wife, Janice Holt Moore, who later became a celebrated writer. He wrote to her:

So you wonder what kind of civilian clothes I like. Well, I like sport clothes mostly. I very seldom wore a tie before I came into the Army. I guess the only reason I had for enlisting in the Army was that I just wanted to try something different. It was a few months before Selective Service.

On 7 December 1941, Japan staged a surprise attack on American military bases in the Pacific. At Pearl Harbor, the Hawaiian naval base for the US Pacific Fleet, Japanese warplanes sank or damaged eighteen warships, destroyed 164 aircraft and killed over 2,400 servicemen and civilians.

The next day President Roosevelt declared war on Japan and, three days later, Germany and Italy, in support of Japan, declared war on the United States. America was no longer just an observer in this global war. The pressure was on to train and kit out a powerful military force, and this would require the building of new factories, switching industry to wartime production, and massively increasing government spending on rearmament.

The road to war solved the problem of unemployment, and the economic output greatly increased. It also offered new opportunities for women, African Americans and Latinos. The need for workers led manufacturers to hire women, teenagers, older people and minorities who had previously been excluded from some sectors.

The *New York Times* reported in June 1941:

This metropolis is a city in uniform. Its days revolve around 'the service', and civilians readily defer to the khaki the navy or the gray which indicates active affiliation with some phase of the war effort … there is one uniform which rates no special salute, which women wear as effectively as men … 800 of these girls in a plant manufacturing machine guns and aircraft weapons … Described as being 'trousered and turned', 'with goggles safeguarding their eyes', they carried out the task of acetylene welding.

As men were called up for active duty overseas, women were instructed that it was their patriotic duty to do their part, whether that was planting 'victory gardens' or working in munitions and factories, like 'Rosie the Riveter', the inspirational illustration of a female factory worker in blue overalls and headscarf, flexing her muscles, as she 'freed a man for war work'. Yet, despite these huge changes in society, there would be a pervasive notion that women in uniform were loose and immoral.

(Above left) Jessica Mitford with husband Esmond Romilly in 1939. (The Mitford Society)

(Above right) Diana Mitford, who was interned with husband Oswald Mosley during the war. (The Mitford Society)

(Left) Unity Mitford wearing a Nazi emblem. (The Mitford Society)

Flight Officer Colin Pinckney of 603 Squadron in his flying suit. (Battle of Britain Memorial)

'AGGY'

F/O. N. L&C. AGAZARIAN   609 SQUADRON.

ORDE
7 NOV 1940

A portrait of RAF hero Noel Agazarian by Cuthbert Orde, 1940. (Battle of Britain Memorial)

Pilot Officer Peter Howes, one of the 'long-haired boys'. (Battle of Britain Memorial)

Wing Commander Guy Gibson VC, in 1944.

Guy Gibson in July 1943, wearing his tunic in the 'fighter boy' style, with the top button undone.

Battle of Britain hero Richard Hillary, author of *The Last Enemy*.

Mary Ellen Morris, a nurse in the Queen Alexandra Imperial Nursing Service Reserve.

Members of the Women's Auxiliary Air Force (WAAF) enjoy a meal at an RAF base in 1942. (Imperial War Museum)

A WAAF wireless operator receiving a message in morse code. (Imperial War Museum)

(Above) Members of the British Women's Land Army harvesting beets as part of vital war work.

(Left) Land Girls and WAAFs at a dance in Suffolk with men of the US Eight Army Air Force in 1943. (Imperial War Museum)

(Left) Ray Ellis of the 107th Regiment of South Nottinghamshire Hussars in North Africa.

(Below) Shepheard's Hotel, Cairo, was one of the most popular drinking spots during the North Africa campaign.

(Left) Sheila Mills in her Wren uniform. (Vicky Unwin)

(Below) Pauline Gower, far left, with the founding female pilots of The Air Transport Auxiliary. (Imperial War Museum)

Violet Hill Gordon of the Women's Army Corps. (Library of Congress)

Rosie the Riveter inspired American women with the slogan 'We Can Do It!'

An aircraft worker at the Vega Aircraft Corporation in Burbank, California, in June 1942. (Library of Congress)

African American members of the Women's Army Corps at Staten Island Terminal, New York Port of Embarkation. (The New York Public Library Digital Collections)

The cover of *Overseas Women*,
April 1945. (The New York Public
Library Digital Collections)

Elizabeth Richardson of the American
Red Cross in 1944.

The American Red Cross Clubmobile served up coffee and doughnuts to American GIs in Britain. (*Life* Magazine)

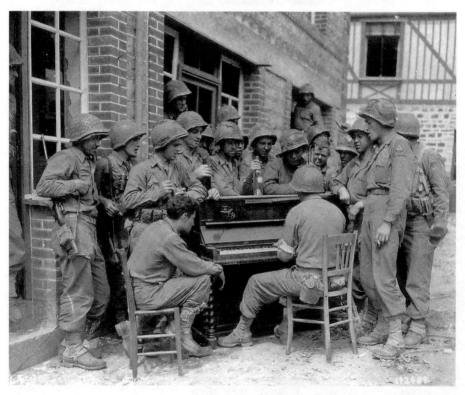

Men of the US 2nd Armoured Division in Normandy.

American GIS in France in 1944, posing with local girls. (*Life* Magazine)

US medics with a local French woman in 1944. (US National Archives)

Soldiers of the US 2nd Armoured Division in France receiving a supply of new boots.

Soldiers of the 8th Infantry Division in France, July 1944.

Lance Corporal J.W. Curtis of the Royal Canadian Army Medical Corp treating a child in Normandy in June 1944.

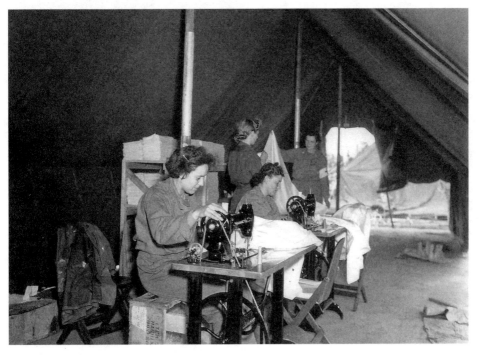

Members of the Women's Army Corps at a field hospital in Normandy, July 1944.

Irving Berlin entertaining the Women's Army Corps in New Guinea. (The New York Public Library Digital Collections)

Women showcasing their style in Cherbourg, after the liberation of France in 1944.

A tondue (shaved woman) punished for collaborating with the Germans and Vichy French imprisoned in the former hotel of Mesnildot de la Grille. (*Life* Magazine)

Swing youth in Hamburg worshipped the sounds of hot jazz and its fashions.

Rebellious German swing youth wearing fashions that were forbidden under Nazi Germany.

(Above) Sophie Scholl, one of the founders of the White Rose resistance group, in 1942.

(Left) British spy Noor Inayat Khan, who served in the Special Operations Executive, wearing her WAAF uniform.

12

Government Issue and Olive Drab

A train pulled out of Macon, Georgia, on the afternoon of 17 December 1941 carrying 188 fresh naval recruits enlisted from the Georgia–Florida district on their way to the navy training school in Norfolk, Virginia. On board, according to *Life* magazine, were:

> … students from the University of Florida, a group of CCC boys, six cab-drivers who joined up as a unit, farm boys, several sophisticates, a Miami bellhop. A handful wanted to learn a trade, one frankly wanted 'Uncle Sam to pay my board', but most of them wanted to beat the Japs.

In their cheap civilian clothes, they looked raw and unmilitary. Lonnie Thomas, dressed like James Cagney in his loose-fitting suit, said goodbye on the platform to his tearful college girlfriend, Agnes Scott.

After the train had pulled out from the station, they relaxed into the journey, playing musical instruments, chatting, writing letters and reading comic books. Yet, once they arrived at training school, their life would now belong to the armed forces. What they could wear was dictated to them, and their former lives as farmworkers or college students were now meaningless. Their buddies would become their new family and they were reshaped to become a part of a mass fighting machine.

In a poll in July 1940, 70.7 per cent of American respondents were in favour of the immediate adoption of compulsory military training for all young men as the threat of war loomed; 88 per cent also believed that if Germany and Italy should win the war, America should 'arm to the teeth at any expense to be prepared for any trouble'. Despite this sense of moral duty, many Americans believed their country should, for the moment, stay out of

European conflicts – particularly with memories of the First World War and the experiences of their parents' generation.

College student Elizabeth Richardson, from Milwaukee, believed 'the US will be suckers if they enter it'. But after the navy suffered such huge losses at Pearl Harbor, she realised the necessity of going to war, even it would be painful. 'Like a toothache, I hope it ends quickly,' she wrote to her aunt. Like other patriotic young women, she wanted to do her bit, and signed up to the American Red Cross.

Due to the growing threat of war, in September 1940 Congress had approved the nation's first peacetime military draft of men between 19 and 57 years of age. By December 1941 there were 2.2 million people enlisted in the armed forces. American youths, raised on the stars and stripes, were patriotic and idealistic, and when the draft was extended to all men between 18 and 64, once America was at war, young people were keen to do their duty.

The honour of wearing a military uniform was something to be proud of, and because of the attack on Pearl Harbor, the navy was one of the most popular services to join up to, although the army was the biggest recruiter. Boys had also been affected by the propaganda of movies like *Flying Tigers*, about the American Volunteer Group delivering planes to Europe, bringing a sense of excitement and glamour to war.

Weapons Sergeant Henry Giles had volunteered for the 291st Engineer Combat Battalion in 1939 and when America entered the war, training at Camp Swift in Texas became more intense. Giles was tough on the younger draftees, who moaned about the food and the sleeping arrangements. He felt they hadn't suffered the Depression as he had:

> If they had gone as lean as I had, army food would have tasted good to them. If they had gone cold as often as I had, warm barracks would have felt wonderful. If they had slept on a cornshuck mattress in an attic where snow drifted in on your bed, they would have felt fine.

By summer 1942, 14,000 recruits a day were registering at reception centres and training camps across America. As soon as they arrived at barracks, their identity was stripped with physical training, identical short haircuts and government-issue equipment, with the abbreviation leading to their common nickname, 'GI', as if they were manufactured like the rest of their kit. The US Government took these young men, trained them into soldiers and placed dog-tag identifications around their neck.

Many of these new GIs were the sons of 'doughboys', the nickname for the US infantry in the First World War, and many had played war games as children pretending to fight in France, never imagining they would experience it for real. David Kenyon Webster remembered his own childhood make-believe, pretending to be doughboys:

> But we never seriously thought that we would ever have to do it. The stories we heard later; the Depression veterans with their apple stands on sleety New York street corners; the horrible photographs of dead bodies and mutilated survivors; *Johnny Got His Gun* and the shrill college cries of the Veterans of Future Wars drove the small-boy craving for war so far from our minds that when it finally happened, it seemed absolutely unbelievable.

They were kitted out in uniforms, some of which dated back to the First World War. If they were lucky, the GIs could be fitted with the army's new 'olive drab' uniforms. Men who complained about the clothes they were assigned were told by their sergeants there were only two types of uniform – too big or too small. On parade, their jacket was designed to fit snugly, with shoulders emphasised by straps or epaulettes and pleatless trousers worn straight. It created the silhouette of an athletic, obedient, self-controlled soldier. Army officers wore 'pinks and greens' – the name given to their winter service uniform of dark olive-drab gabardine wool coat with a cloth belt, light olive-drab trousers (the pinks), russet-brown shoes and matching brim on their service cap.

Some of the new terms for military clothing which came into common use included 'jumpsuits' and 'flight suits', for the all-in-one outfits for paratroopers and pilots, sheepskin 'bomber' jackets, and later in the war, the M-1944 jacket, later known as the Eisenhower or (or Ike) jacket, which was influenced by the British Army battledress.

Living in London, as the commander-in-chief of Allied forces, Dwight D. Eisenhower observed the battle jackets of the British troops, and noted it was more innovative than the American dress jacket. His naval aide, Harry C. Butcher, wrote in May 1943:

> Ike has been impressed by the virtual impossibility of American officers and soldiers appearing neat and snappy in their field uniforms … He thought the material should be rough wool because it wouldn't show the dirt and is more easily kept presentable. He liked the appearance of the British battle dress, but thought Americans should design something distinctive themselves.

Instead of the rough, unfinished khaki of the British battle jacket, the Ike jacket was smooth, made from higher quality wool, and it became a choice item of the dress uniform, despite its lack of gilt buttons. It was a favourite for wearing in combat, along with the dark green cotton field jacket with extra-large pockets for K rations.

General Eisenhower also chose to wear a service cap with leather visor, which was ineffective for fighting but became almost a style statement. Air Corps officers wore these caps when flying, removing the grommet so that earphones could be used. This was known as the 'Fifty Mission crush', and with its air of cavalier rebellion, ground troops tried to copy the look too. However, it was quickly banned by the authorities.

The US Army Air Corps also wore the A-2 leather flying jackets, made from seal brown horse-hide leather, and with a modern zip. The jacket, issued to every officer who passed training, was considered incredibly virile, and men custom-made it with patches that matched the nose art of their planes. Some even had a navigation map sewn into the lining, in case of having to land in occupied territory.

Once in the air, the bomber crews found the temperature was so cold that the jacket wasn't much use. Instead, they wore their fleece-lined sheepskin jackets and flying suits. But, much like the RAF crews, men of the US Air Force would work out their own individual style.

The armed forces colours were visible in every town and city across the United States, and images of men and women in uniform were emblazoned on the front pages of magazines and newspapers, or in recruitment posters, cementing their authority and bravery.

Paul Fussell had enrolled in the Junior Reserve Officers' Training Corps in high school, where he got the chance to wear the uniform of olive-drab trousers, wool shirt and black tie and a 'real US Army jacket'. He wrote in the summer of 1943 that he was finally able to trade them for proper fatigues when he was enrolled in the army and sent to basic training at Camp Roberts, California:

When I moved on to the Infantry School at Fort Benning, Georgia, the daily uniform changed to light green cotton overalls and helmet liners. These remained the fatigue uniforms when, commissioned, I joined an actual infantry division. Shipped to France, we wore uniforms still, but in combat we removed all shiny insignia, secretly pleased to imagine that, as identifiable officers, we were the special targets of German snipers.

David Webster, born to a wealthy family in New York City in 1922, was a Harvard English literature student when he volunteered for the elite parachute infantry in 1942, only two years into his studies. He recalled his first weeks in the army, 'clumsy and foolish', as he dragged 'around an overnight bag with Harvard stickers on it'. His decision to join the 101st Airborne Division, rather than taking the easier option of an officer's commission, was borne from a writerly desire to record his experiences as a 'grunt'. Having attended the exclusive Taft School in Connecticut, he wished to meet a wider circle of people than those he grew up with.

He wrote in his memoirs:

I had grown up with Republicans and gone to school and college with them, and sickened by their selfishness, their cold avarice and lofty contempt for the common people, had early sworn to vote for the Democrats, who, for all their rotten political faults, were more concerned with the welfare of the country as a whole.

Those who signed up to the 101st Airborne were all volunteers, and they came from very different backgrounds. There were farmers and coal miners, Harvard and Yale students like Webster, some from California, some from the Deep South, the Midwest or from Appalachia.

While Webster trained and landed in Normandy with Fox Company, he later joined Easy Company, the subject of the TV series, *Band of Brothers*. Following the Allied invasion of Europe, the company destroyed a German battery that was firing onto Utah Beach, fought their way into Holland, led the attack in the Battle of the Bulge, and celebrated victory at Hitler's Eagle's Nest at Berchtesgaden.

The 101st Airborne Division had its own unique eagle insignia on patches and shoulder sleeves, which invoked pride and a sense of belonging and led to the name 'The Screaming Eagles'. After completing jump school, the recruits received silver wings for the left pocket of their jackets, and a patch for their left shoulder and hat. They could now also wear the much-desired paratrooper boots, with their trousers tucked into them, known as to 'blouse'. These boots were sought after by those outside of the parachute regiments, as they represented the elite – the aggressive, tough paratroopers who had been trained at Camp Toccoa and Fort Benning. 'We were all ready to trade our lives in order to wear these accoutrements of the Airborne,' said Walter Gordon of Easy Company.

They felt proud and confident when arriving back home in their boots and branded uniform. Yet, such was the discipline that those who returned late back after furlough in January 1943 suffered the ultimate humiliation – losing their patches and their boots. Called to parade in their dress uniform, the lieutenant singled out the latecomers and ripped the 506th patches from their uniform, ordered them to remove the boots and to wear their trousers as 'straight legs' rather than 'bloused'. Their barrack bags were dumped in front of them, and they were marched away, where their fate was to become a lowly infantryman.

In January 1942 sportswriter Robert Leckie left his home to join the United States Marines. Like the parachute regiments, the Marine Corps was an elite, voluntary group defined by their green and blue uniforms, which, to Leckie, seemed 'an odd combination of colors ... the gaudy dark and light blue of Marine dress sheathed in sedate and soothing green'.

Leckie and the other raw recruits arrived in South Carolina for their training and were immediately marched to the quartermaster's, where they were ordered to discard their vestiges of civilian life:

It is the quartermasters who make soldiers, sailors and marines. In their presence, one strips down. With each divestment, a trait is lost; the discard of a garment marks the quiet death of an idiosyncrasy. I take off my socks; gone is a propensity for stripes, or clocks, or checks, or even solids; ended is a tendency to combine purple socks with brown tie. My socks henceforth will be tan. They will neither be soiled, nor rolled, nor gaudy, nor restrained, nor holey. They will be tan. The only other thing they may be is clean.

Leckie described how he and the other recruits stood naked as the quartermaster measured them up and threw a cascade of clothes at them, 'washing you clean of personality'. They were given marine-issue caps, gloves, socks, shoes, underwear, shirts, belts, pants and coats, and once they emerged in their uniform and were given their number to be printed on dog tags, their civilian identity was now gone, except for their hair:

The color and cut of our hair still saved us. But in a minute these too would fall ... the barber had sheared me. I think he needed four, perhaps five, strokes with his electric clipper. The last stroke completed the circle. I was now a number encased in khaki and encompassed by chaos.

Leckie's memory of initial training was that they were always marching, they were told to always obey orders, even if told to march into the ocean, and there was no privacy, even for washing and shaving. Once they completed their rifle training, they felt like veterans in the marines, part of the 'Old Breed', the nickname for the 1st Division Marines. They spoke disparagingly of infantry men as 'dog-faces' and sailors as 'swab-jockeys':

> No one could forget that he was a marine. It came out in the forest green of the uniform or the hour-long spit-polishing of the dark brown shoes. It was in the jaunty angle of the campaign hats worn by the gunnery sergeants. It was in the mark of the rifleman, the fingers of the gun hand longer than those of the other. It characterized every lecture, every drill or instruction circle.

Robert Leckie was given one last leave home in May of 1942, and it would be three years before he saw his family again. The 1st Marine Regiment:

> … packed our sea bags with all our excess clothing and personal gear. Each bag was carefully stenciled with our company markings. Then all were carried off on trucks. I never saw mine again until I returned to the States. From that day forward – save for brief intervals in Australia – we lived out of our packs, the single combat pack about the size of a portable typewriter case.

Their marching order bags could weigh around 20lb, and the contents varied between men. As Leckie wrote, 'A soldier's pack is like a woman's purse: it is filled with his personality.' Some would carry extra hair oil or soap, tins of food and letters from home. They marched in their dungarees, soaked in sweat, feet rubbing in their boots, helmets clanking against rifles, canteens swinging and straps cutting into their shoulders.

In an all-male society, away from the constraints of home, these 19- and 20-year-old men expressed their pent-up aggression through male bonding rituals. Their training camps were filled with sexualised images. Soldiers were taught map reading using a grid placed on top of Betty Grable, the walls were covered with images of Varga girls or Rita Hayworth, and women were encouraged to send their own pin-ups to soldiers to boost morale.

Leckie and his fellow marines bonded over beer, endless griping against the food and the officers, and talking about sex. Their excess of energy and aggression was relieved through drinking and fighting at the highway honky-tonk bars near their base, plastered with Coca-Cola and cigarette ads.

Morehead City and New Bern were marine towns, and the streets on a Saturday night thronged with the green of the marine dungarees. Jukeboxes blared out of smoky cafés, and local girls waited to be approached by marines. 'We lived for thrills,' said Leckie. 'Not the thrills of the battlefield, but of the speeding auto, the dimly lighted café, the drink racing the blood, the texture of a cheek, the sheen of a silken calf.'

Watching movie screenings was a way for troops to relax, with temporary theatres set up outside for night-time screenings wherever they were in the world. They spread out their ponchos or sat on top of wooden crates. To relieve the tension, they shouted at the screen and wolf whistled any time Bette Grable and Rita Hayworth came into view.

'We do have lots of fun when some of us guys are together, and sometimes it definitely wouldn't be the right place for ladies to be,' Henry Giles wrote to Janice Holt, in 1944. His life in the army, along with his love of Popeye and Baby Ruth bars, was captured in the love letters he wrote to girlfriend Janice. They had met on a forty-hour Greyhound bus ride from Louiseville to El Paso in Texas in July 1943, when he sat down next to her. She couldn't help but notice the 'very neat, trim, nice-looking soldier' and, keeping in touch, they shared memories of their Greyhound bus ride, eating a steak dinner together in Nashville and falling in love in the pages of their letters.

Women were to be found in new spaces during the war – travelling across country, or in train stations. And there was an expectation that they were willing to be picked up. Giles later confessed to Janice, 'when I was riding a bus or train, I made it my business to ride with a woman. Of course I wasn't looking for a wife, but I'm glad and will always be thankful that I found you.'

He shipped for England on 8 October 1943, and they didn't see each other again for two years, when he returned to the United States. She was eleven years older than him, and after the war became a celebrated historical fiction writer.

For those holding down a long-distance relationship, the emblem of their battalion offered a keepsake and a reminder to their girlfriend or wife. 'The Engineer insignia is a castle. History says that the engineers captured a castle that all other branches of service had failed to do, hence the castle insignia,' Henry Giles wrote to Janice. He found a locket with the insignia on it and sent it to her as a keepsake.

'I have something new to wear, darling. It's your locket – with an inset of mother of pearl, a tiny silver castle is fastened directly in the center. It's quite perfect,' she wrote back.

At the end of May 1943, the 101st Division was transported to Fort Bragg, North Carolina, where they prepared to be sent overseas. They were let loose in Fayetteville for beer and whisky drinking before being shipped out. Loaded up with new clothes and weapons, and a new bucket-style helmet to replace the First World War brimmed helmets, they were instructed to remove the 101st patch, 'the Screaming Eagle', from their shoulders, in case enemy spies saw them and knew that an airborne division was being sent to prepare for invasion.

As they waited at the port to be shipped out, Red Cross girls served coffee and doughnuts, offering the last bit of comfort for some time. On boarding the ships, they tried to guess where they might be heading by the equipment they had been given. Maybe the tropics, as they had been given a yellow fever shot, or West Africa because they received mosquito nets. However, the great-coats, overshoes, woollen coats and thick socks offered the clue that it would be Ireland or Britain.

13

WACs, WAVES and Rosie the Riveter

Five months into the war, opportunities opened up for women to work as emergency workers, in the auxiliary corps of the army and the navy and assisting with supportive duties in the coastguard and the marines. While there had been a retreat to feminine roles and domesticity in the 1930s, American women could take up work during the war unapologetically.

The posters made it clear what their public duty should be, but it was also important to persuade the public of the merits of working women. As Leisa Meyer, in *Creating GI Jane*, wrote, there were concerns that 'the creation of a corps of "female soldiers" would lead women to abdicate their responsibilities within the home and usurp the male duty of protecting and defending home and country'. When American women first donned uniform for the war effort in 1940, they were reminded by magazines such as *Vogue*, 'Don't wear uniform unless you absolutely have to' because 'men don't like you to wear them', and they should always keep up morale by continuing to do their hair and wear make-up.

In the first summer after America entered the war, the debutante was considered a thing of the past. Miss Lucy Aldrich, daughter of Winthrop W. Aldrich, of the British War Relief Society, told the *New York Times*:

I don't know anyone today who can bear being called a debutante. And I often wonder why fashion shops go on using a term that is so completely out of fashion. Last summer I would have gone straight up to Maine to sail and play tennis. This summer I'm taking a course in stenography and getting ready to go to Bernard in the fall.

She said that none of her friends craved possessions or were concerned about glamour:

They do not want to be tied down by belongings. We know that we may be on the move. We don't mind it. The boys we know are stationed at camps all over the country and writing letters back. They've started us thinking about the country outside of New York.

With a desire to travel, they looked for clothes that would last, 'The chief horror is to look dressed up, they stay away from fattening foods like ice-cream sundaes'. The article noted that young college-age woman still thought of marriage as a chief concern, but they wanted 'simple, practical, durable clothes ... they are eager to do their war jobs as efficiently as possible'.

The *New York Times*, in August 1941, had described a new preppy style for women on campus, of houndstooth tweed, pleated skirts, Argyle socks and moccasins, which they called 'the typically 1941–1942 collegiate look'. The look was inspired not only by an increasing number of women going into education, but by the possibility of war. The article wrote:

> Just as her best beau does, the girl will wear her checked jacket with gray flannels, skirt, shorts or slacks, or with a tweed skirt and a sweater having the new high-rolled neck. By way of being her feminine self she'll hang a string of pearls around her neck.

Bettina Ballard was *Vogue*'s Paris editor during the 1930s, but on the outbreak of war and the threat of a German invasion of France, she moved back to New York where she squeezed into the *Vogue* offices. She wrote in her memoirs, 'Fashion was hideous in 1940, although I can't remember thinking so at the time. Shoulders were padded out to ridiculous shapes, jackets were long, skirts short, shoes stubby, hats fancy and over-shaped.' But, following Pearl Harbor, 'we talked war instead of fashion' and 'our pages in *Vogue* reflected a new austerity ... straight up-and-down fashions with little fabric to them the smart patriotic thing to wear'.

Attitudes to women in uniform soon shifted when it was realised that women would be required for vital war work, and *Vogue*'s editorial team became cheerleaders, naming women in uniform as *Vogue*'s 'Best Dressed Women in the World Today' in 1943:

> The uniform stands for our new spine of purpose, our initiative in getting women working, splayed out into hundreds of different jobs, to find talents which have been mossed over. It means that we know that it is time to stop all the useless little gestures, to stop being the Little Woman and be women.

The American Women's Voluntary Services (AWVS), the largest of the women's services, was established in January 1940, almost two years before America entered the war. It was founded by wealthy women with links to Britain, and they modelled it on that country's WVS. The aim of the group was to prepare for war and the possibility of American cities being bombed. Women volunteers carried out vital services to support the war effort, such as ambulance driving, couriering, aerial photography, fire-fighting and selling war bonds.

A *Life* magazine article in June 1942 described how:

Sub-debs in the US have found a new mission in life. Their earnestness and exuberance have been put to useful war work through junior auxiliaries of American Women's Voluntary Services. Nearly 10,000 eager young girls between 14 and 18 are now enrolled in 110 junior AWVS units throughout the country. Under the auspices of senior AWVS they learn first aid, air-raid precautions, how to work a switchboard. Their services include running errands, clerical work, hospital and settlement work, salvage collections.

The article profiled 18-year-old Betty Van Rensselaer and her friends, holding a 'stagless party at home', dancing the rumba to records on their gramophone. The juniors were pictured at a lunch counter in their caps and khaki shirts, enjoying hamburgers and glasses of milk.

Other services open to women were the Women's Army Corps (WAC), which had been created as an auxiliary unit (WAAC) in May 1942 and converted to active-duty status in the Army of the United States in July 1943. The women's branch of the navy was the United States Naval Reserve, commonly known as the WAVES (Women Accepted for Volunteer Emergency Service).

It had been hard to get hold of new clothes during the Depression, with old sacking sometimes having to be used in place of fabric, so for many women, the uniform was considered a luxury and it offered a sense of glamour as it was tailored to fit and looked authoritative and high quality.

A popular theme in romantic 1930s movies was of the Midwest girl who took the train to New York City in search of love and riches, and one of the reasons women wished to join was escape from the boredom of their small towns. They wanted new experiences in life, to do something different, and to escape the struggles they had seen their parents face during the Depression. 'When I was growing up, the subculture I grew up in the only thing girls could be was a mother with a dozen kids and probably a drunken husband, at least that's how it looked to me, a teacher, a nurse or a nun. That was it,' said Josette Dermody, who was signed up to the WAVES. Margaret Anderson, also a WAVE said:

> I was an adventurist. I wanted to do something different. I wanted to excel … In those days, if you wanted to become a lawyer, like a friend of mine really aspired to be a lawyer, everybody was against her. Thought it was a masculine trade. It didn't matter what she wanted.

There were rumours that WAACs only signed up in order to chase men, and because of these supposed loose morals they were given contraceptives during basic training. As a result, there was reluctance amongst men in allowing women to join the armed forces. After a draft for women was introduced in 1943, Henry Giles wasn't keen on the idea of his fiancée, Janice, joining one of the armed forces while he was overseas. On 29 October 1943 he wrote, 'If the bill you spoke of should pass, try hard to stay where you are. Make the WACs or WAVES your last resort. I detest the thought of you having to be in either of those.'

To change the mindset, recruitment posters attempted to drive home the message that joining the services would enhance their femininity and their respectability, despite wearing a uniform.

Around 150,000 women ultimately served in the WAAC, and later the WAC, during the war. Colonel Paul Betters told *Vogue* magazine:

> … of the six hundred types of Army jobs, about four hundred could be done by trained women. What an eye-opener to those of us who thought the WAACs were just secretaries in uniform. Already they are doing jobs that range from blackout convoy driving and cryptography to manning radio control towers on airfields.

In January 1943, *Vogue* writer Toni Frissell visited Fort Custer with Colonel Oveta Culp Hobby, Director of the WAACs, to encourage more women to sign up without worrying that they would lose their looks. To illustrate their point, they described Colonel Hobby as reapplying her make-up 'with a moderate amount of lipstick', and resetting her cap 'squarely on her prematurely grey hair' before driving the jeep into Fort Custer. Colonel Hobby told Toni, 'it's a job for every woman in good health with no physical dependents under the age of fourteen. And, they don't need to worry about losing their looks, their femininity, or their individuality, by being in uniform.'

When choosing a uniform for the WAACs, Hobby had wished for something conservative yet stylish, and while fashion designers submitted sketches, ultimately the Quartermaster Corps declared them to be wasteful of material and opted for a simple khaki design. The WAAC uniform was showcased in Washington on 12 May 1942. Photographers took pictures of models wearing the summer and winter uniforms with different shades of olive drab, created by Israel L. Freedman of New York, a designer for the army:

> Uniforms for the Women's Army Auxiliary Corps will be trim olive drab outfits, closely patterned after the official dress of their brothers in arms but neatly styled for the feminine figure by an expert designer of the Army Quartermaster Corps. The identifying insignia for WAAC members will be a cut-out of the head of Pallas Athene, the Goddess of Victory.

With the aim of 'eliminating waste material', they were designed with plastic buttons and consisted of single-breasted belted jacket, knee-length skirt and blouse, stockings and lace-up shoes. Rank was shown with braid on the cuff of the officer's jacket and with the placing of the eagle insignia on their hats and shoulder markings. They were also issued with 'a combination handbag and utility bag of golden brown, made of water-repellent cotton rayon'.

The WAAC officer's winter cap was a stiff hat made from olive drab barathea, similar to those worn by French army officers, which was nicknamed the 'cheese box' or the 'Hobby hat', after Oveta Culp Hobby. It was emblazoned with a gold eagle, sometimes referred to as the 'buzzard'.

Captain Hobby was the first woman to receive the uniform, in June 1942. She disclosed that every servicewoman 'will get six pairs each of rayon and cotton stockings, plus two pairs of anklets, as well as their undergarments. The corps will wear six-eyelet brown Oxfords with a medium heel.'

Despite the attempt to be economical, a further criticism of women in the armed forces was the expense of their uniform. 'For what it costs to clothe one member of the Women's Army Auxiliary Corps, the United States could provide the uniform for an Army officer and have almost sufficient left over to purchase a sailor's outfit,' wrote the *New York Times*:

> Similarly, the country could finance the tailoring of a new Naval Reserve officer, and still have a little remaining before exceeding one WAAC's clothing bill. In short, the Army is learning something long known to

husbands and fathers – namely, that women's garments, however skimpy, run into money.

Violet Hill Gordon, from Chicago, was one of the first African-American women to join the WAACs and undergo officer training. She graduated as second commanding officer from Des Moines and was assigned to Fort Huachuca, Arizona and then to Fort Lewis, in Washington. She recalled:

> The Army, of course, outfitted us from the skin on out: underwear, stockings, the shirts, the skirts, the pants, jackets, and caps. Then when we were going to the cold weather areas, ski pants, boots. There you were always struggling to get something that really fit you properly … I remember how excited I was when I realized that the Army was supplying a Bali bra, which is what I had worn as a civilian.

After finishing high school, Violet worked as a clerk for A. Philip Randolph, who organised the Brotherhood of Sleeping Car Porters, the first black labour union, which had formed her political views and encouraged her to pursue an interest in group activism. This was, she said, supported by her time in the army, as joining the WAAC 'kind of enabled me to move away from a bucolic, somewhat shy, introspective person. So that I would say that the Army influence was like the final push in a very positive direction.'

Violet had been encouraged to join by a friend of hers who was excited to hear there was going to be a Women's Army Corps. 'At that time I was working in State Civil Service; I was supervising a stenographic pool. I was not bored, but restless. Kind of stuck, I guess. But I wasn't that excited about entering into anything that sounded as regimented as the Army.'

She had never been in an army camp before, and sleeping in one long room with bunk beds and footlockers was a shock, but no matter the discomfort, there was a pervading sense of duty. 'I think that the thing that really sustained and enabled all of us was that underneath the adventurous aspect of it was a sense of duty; it was our country, that we were at war and that there was a purpose to all of this.'

On arrival at Fort Huachuca, the enlisted men were curious enough to gather outside and gawp at the first group of female officers. Violet recalled:

> There was a lot of controversy about women in the Service … It was a little frightening in one sense in that we were like engulfed and surrounded by all these men … They had set up a whole area for the women so that we had

our own headquarters building, our own barracks, officer's quarters, mess hall, and the whole shebang.

Whether they wore uniform off duty was at the discretion of individual commanders. At Fort Custer, because the WAACs were vastly outnumbered by the men, it was thought that feminine dress would bolster morale. But at a WAAC post like Fort Des Moines, they were expected to be in uniform, even when off duty.

In Toni Frissell's feature in *Vogue*, she described the WAAC temporary living quarters to highlight to readers how feminine they still could be:

> They had made some cretonne curtains, bright and flowered, and hung them at the windows. On their dressing-tables, in the neatest ranks, were face creams, lotions, and of course, powder. And on the mirrors and walls were pin-ups − not movie stars, but beaux, husbands, even sons, most of them wearing uniforms. Lined up side by side were highly polished GI shoes and satin sandals, olive-drab overcoat and black 'date' dresses. The girls are allowed as many clothes, including uniforms and mufti, as can be hung in the space equivalent to the width of their bed.

Jeanne M. Holm, from Oregon, was one of the first women in America to enlist in the military. She began as an army truck driver in the WAC, was promoted to an officer, and eventually Director of Women in the air force. She grew up in Oregon during the Depression with her widowed mother raising three children. Before the war, Jeanne trained in silversmithing and metal work, working for the only woman silversmith in the United States. With two brothers in the navy, she joined the army in July 1942, as it was the first service to take women. She had just turned 21 years old. 'My mother and my grandmother were very enthusiastic for it, as a matter of fact, had they been young enough, they would have loved to have done it themselves.'

Travelling to Fort Des Moines in Iowa for basic training was the first time she had been out of the Pacific Northwest. Sharing huge dorms in Fort Des Moines with 200 women, they felt like trailblazers as they were doing something so unique for women at the time:

> We felt like pioneers, we really did. And which is very interesting when I look back on it, I realize we knew we were breaking new ground. Oveta Culp Hobby, who was the Director of WAACs at the time, came down and

spoke to us. And she was a goddess. And she told us that we were making history, and this was very moving.

From there, Jeanne trained at a motor transport school, as she considered it the most interesting of the options available to women:

> There were only three options that you were given as a woman at that time, unless you were a nurse, of course … you could be a clerk typist, and I had no interest in learning to type. You could either be a cook or baker. And I … didn't visualize myself spending my military service behind a stove, but I did know how to drive trucks.

The khaki of the WAC uniform was considered rather dowdy, and in order to make the WAVES more palatable for women, Chicago-born designer 'Mainbocher', who had a pre-war Paris salon, was hired to create the uniform. While women in the WAVES and WAC had limited power within the armed forces, the clothes they wore still gave them respect and social power over other non-uniformed women. The WAVES, with their designer wardrobe, possessed an even greater sense of superiority, and they felt that they were in the same class as movie stars and royalty.

Elizabeth Reynard is credited for coming up with the acronym WAVES, as it was 'something nautical, suitable, fool-proof, and attractive'. In early August 1942, female officer Naval Reserve Lieutenant Commander Mildred McAfee, president of Wellesley College, was commissioned into the US Navy to lead the organisation. She recounted in 1969:

> They had decided to try to get a college president on the principle that the Navy knew enough about the Navy, but they didn't know much about girls, and that somebody who had been working with young women would be the kind of person they'd look for … they wanted to assure the parents and boyfriends of girls that they would be looked after in the Navy. That this was not going to be a wild show, but it would be respectable.

While their First World War 'yeomanette' counterparts served as nurses and secretaries, thousands of WAVES worked as aviation mechanics, photographers, control tower operators and intelligence personnel. The jobs considered most glamorous were those outside the normal roles for women, such as radio operators, control tower operators and coders and signallers at naval stations.

McAfee advised the navy on how it could attract women of high calibre. The minimum age to volunteer was 20, and officers were required to have a minimum of two years of college and two years of professional work, while enlisted women needed some college and work experience.

The uniform of the WAVES communicated their identity, and it was central to the recruitment drive. McAfee told the press, 'one thing we have kept in mind is that there should be no effort to dress the women up to look like men. Their uniform will be becoming and functional.'

The first uniform sample was dark navy blue, with patriotic red, white and blue shoulder braiding, which, to McAfee's horror, 'looked just like a chorus girl'. The braid was switched to blue, and McAfee also insisted that the women wear nude stockings rather than black, and that the blouse would be easy to wash and iron.

The final version of the uniform consisted of a tailored jacket with round collar and the insignia of the Women's Reserve – an anchor over a propeller. Instead of shoulder boards, rank was shown by stripes on the sleeves in reserve blue, which was a 'bright medium blue adopted by the navy as an official colour of the WAVES'.

While the WAC underwear was much ridiculed, the WAVES were given attractive slips and brassieres under the uniform, and even had short pyjamas to wear at night. This underwear added extra individuality and femininity, making it even more appealing. WAVES were also issued with plain black-laced Oxfords, regulation black or white gloves, a shoulder-strap bag, an envelope 'pocket book' (purse) worn over the shoulder and a winter overcoat with belted back. The hat, based on an eighteenth-century sailor hat, was described as 'an all-round feminine chapeau', but some recruits would refer to them as 'go to hell hats'.

Because the WACs had been tarnished with a reputation that they were either lesbians or prostitutes, McAfee wished to protect the reputation of the WAVES. She described how she asked for a recruitment film to be withdrawn as it depicted women joining up solely to flirt with men. She said it was 'a little bit cheap in the way that it was going to appeal to these girls. When I saw it, I was simply bewildered and baffled.' Ali McLaughlin, who was a WAVE, said, 'To tell the truth, I never considered joining the Army, the WACs. You know, the women in the Army did not have a good name … The Navy turned down a lot of people … the women I met in the Navy … were more refined.'

The uniform further established the WAVES as elegant and of high calibre, and for many of the recruits it was their first opportunity to wear designer clothing. Virginia Gillmore recalled that the uniform 'fit beautifully. And you felt so comfortable. It was probably the most expensive thing any of us had ever had. Well made. Beautiful material. And besides, it had two pockets just inside where you could put Kleenex...'.

Joan Angel wrote of the uniform in her memoirs, *Angel of the Navy: The Story of a WAVE*:

> I looked at myself in the long mirror. By heavens, I did look impressive. The suit was beautifully cut, trim and efficient-looking without being stiff and masculine. It was the kind of tailored outfit I might have bought in civilian life – but in navy blue, with the fouled-anchor embroidery on the collar and black regulation buttons, it gave me the bearing of a woman in whom great responsibilities were vested. Unconsciously, I straightened and got a look of fire in my eyes.

New recruits were instructed to meet at train stations across the country, where they would be transported to boot camp for six weeks training and for being measured up for their uniform. Margaret Anderson recalled meeting at Union Station in Los Angeles:

> There must have been about 80 people, women. Women dressed differently then, so everybody came dressed up ready like they were going to a tea party, not for the train. Well, you traveled on trains in those times too. You dressed up. So we really weren't dressed that comfortably for a long trip. I think I had on a skirt and sweater, but I still wore my heels. And the train took about four days to get to New York.

Marie Brand Voltzke, a West Virginia girl born in 1918, joined the WAVES because both her brothers were in the navy. She entered active duty in February 1943 at Stillwater, Oklahoma:

> The day we were issued our uniforms, we were given our clothing allowance in cash. Moving down the line, we paid for each item, with no cash remaining at the end. We never questioned the procedure. The raincoat issued to me was two sizes too large. Upon request for a smaller size, I was told to move on. Fortunately, at drill inspection by a male commanding officer, he stopped and wrote a note to the supply office to give me a

raincoat that fit my size. I could have kissed him but a salute and thank you were in order.

After a crash course to learn the ropes, Marie arrived in Washington, D.C., and was assigned to the Naval Communication Annex where she lived in huge, temporary barracks along with 4,000 others:

> To compensate for having the lower bunk, I permitted my bunk mate to hang her weekly washed hose by hangers from the springs of her bunk ... . Rita, from the Bronx, patiently taught me to knit. I learned to roll my hair in pin curls, and was told to wear a girdle. Oh, they were all helpful, teaching me not to 'catch a streetcar' and many other proper phrases that corrected a West Virginia 'hillbilly'. I made many dear friends and continue to correspond with them at Christmas.

The Women's Reserve division of the US Coast Guard (USCG) was known as the SPARS. They at first trained with the WAVES, but later were given their own bootcamp in Palm Beach, Florida, and then Manhattan Beach, New York. The recruitment slogan was 'Train under the Florida sun', and it was considered one of the most glamorous postings as those who signed up would be trained at a hotel resort alongside the male coastguard recruits.

The name SPAR was the brainchild of its director, Dorothy C. Stratton, who combined the first letter of the motto of the USCG, *Semper Paratus*, with the English translation, 'Always Ready'. If the ideal WAVE was an elite college girl in the recruitment posters, the ideal SPAR women was the pin-up girl of the services. She was like the wartime Varga girl, the sexy girl next door in her form-fitting, almost transparent suit, on the arms of a chiselled-jawed man.

Despite the dreamy recruitment posters, the WAVES and SPARS were banned from overseas duty. It wasn't until 1945 that they were permitted to serve 'abroad' in Alaska, Hawaii, the West Indies and Panama; with the largest number of women serving in Hawaii.

Due to the surge in women requiring regulation shirts for their uniforms, Saks Fifth Avenue opened up a 'uniform clearing house', which gathered together the uniforms and accessories for all the volunteer organisations. Mannequins were dressed in the winter and summer issue for the WAACs, the American Women's Hospital Reserve Corps, the Red Cross, the army and navy nurses,

Bundles for America and the WAVES. It was ideal for the fashion-conscious woman who wished to buy her service pieces from a department store.

If they didn't want to join one of the services, women could sign up to the American Red Cross. With her male friends enlisting in services, *Vogue* editor Bettina Ballard wanted to discover what she could be capable of in wartime. She volunteered at the Soldiers and Sailors Club, where she gave away tickets to Broadway shows, but after wishing to contribute further, she left *Vogue* to work for the Red Cross. Edna Woolman Chase, *Vogue*'s editor-in-chief, tried to persuade her to stay because she believed, 'It is very important to keep fashion magazines going during wartime'.

However, Bettina may have been lured by the patriotic articles in the very women's magazines that she helped to write. 'Most of us can do little for our men when they are far away and on the edge of battle,' said an editorial in *Harper's Bazaar* in March 1945:

> One American woman, long since dead, still serves them best – Clara Barton, the found of the American Red Cross. Her Red Cross today serves in ways she never thought of since it serves in a modern, complex world, half vision, half nightmare. The women who wear her scarlet and white badge in the battle zones furnish the humanity, the woman's hand, the woman's voice, which give comfort and help to our soldiers, fresh from agony and noise of mechanized war.

After being accepted by the Red Cross, Bettina moved to Washington for training, where she arrived at camp looking 'very, very *Vogue*', with a lavish wardrobe in suitcases that she could barely fit into her dorm. She was dismayed at the other girls who used the shared bathroom to wash their underwear and then hung the garments up from the wall, making the room smell like a 'cheap beauty parlour'.

For Bettina, the day she was issued her uniform 'was the most depressing day of our training. The dark-grey winter one reminded me of what mother always called "that good serviceable tailored suit". The summer ones were a pretty shade of blue-grey and rather becomingly Chanel in their loose shape.' In order to give her uniforms a 'little *Vogue* personality of their own', she took them to Garfinckel's to have them re-tailored, and purchased 'pretty, soft, shirred-neck, small-collared blouses from Clare Potter in New York in a lovely shade of blue'.

When it came time to be assigned overseas, Bettina remembered that 'there was quite a scene in our crowded room with footlockers on every bed being suffered over by conscientious Red Cross girls'. With an eye on being posted to North Africa, Bettina planned what to pack in her footlocker with a hot climate in mind, although its contents were not perhaps the most practical. She wrapped her bottles of nail polish and hand lotion in a black jersey Norell dress, packed 'jars of Botany Lanolin Cream' to protect her skin from the sun, and bottles of russet Clairol dye to upkeep her favoured hair colour. She also included 'a plaid cashmere rug that Ben Zuckerman had given me, having bought a lot of them in Scotland to make coats'.

She and her fellow Red Cross recruits travelled back to New York in preparation for being shipped out. They were given inoculations and issued with dog tags, steel helmets, canteens and gas masks, and then ushered up the gang plank of ships. Bettina's duffel bag was stuffed with high heels and civilian clothes, and so heavy that she had to drag it, until a GI snapped at her, 'Give it to me. We'll never get this rowboat loaded with a bunch of dumb broads gumming the works.'

Bettina travelled with the American Red Cross to follow the Allied campaigns, from North Africa into Italy and then the South of France, always adding a sense of glamour to her Red Cross uniform, as befitted a *Vogue* editor:

> As I moved through North Africa, the footlocker was a Pandora's box. A pailletted scarf over my head, worn with the black sleeveless Traina-Norell dress, seemed like the most daring Mata Hari type of costume in the Casino of Constantine on the edge of the desert in Algeria. But when I arrived in Rome the summer of its liberation and saw the lovely, warm-skinned Roman women in their gay pretty print dresses, their long, aristocratic feet smartly clad in Roman sandals, the contents of my footlocker lost their glamour. I took the parachute silk a soldier had brought me, quickly had it dyed in gay shades, and found a little dressmaker to bring my civilian clothes up to Roman standards of fashion.

One of the major recruiters for wartime women were munitions, where over 600,000 women in America took on roles as real-life Rosie the Riveters. In July 1942, *Life* magazine wrote:

> At Vultee and Lockheed and Vega, at General Motors and Martin and Wright, at Douglas and Brewster and Boeing, in arsenals and ammunition plants, in motor works and assembly plants, girls in uniform are welding

and wiring, riveting and loading, assembling and inspecting man's weapons for war.

The woman worker in a war industry in the US has acquired some of the glamor of the man in uniform. In labor's social scale, she belongs to the elite. At the very top is the girl who works in an airplane factory. She is the glamor girl of 1942.

The article highlighted Marguerite Kershner, who worked at the Boeing airplane factory:

This is her first factory job, she has worked as a salesgirl, usherette, elevator operator – all jobs which call for meticulous grooming. Now, at day's end, her hands may be bruised, there's grease under her nails, her make-up is smudged and her curls out of place. When she checks in the next morning at 6.30 a.m., her hands will be smooth, her nails polished, her make-up and curls in order, for Marguerite is neither drudge nor slavery but the heroine of a new order.

Despite the emphasis on women always maintaining their looks to boost morale, there were conflicts with safety. Veronica Lake's long blonde waved hairstyle was one of the most popular of the time, but it was banned in factories because of the dangers of hair being caught in machinery. Instead, women wrapped turbans around their heads to keep their hair back and wore slacks instead of skirts. While these women undertook dangerous work dressed in regulation overalls, the media insisted on maintaining the idea of these workers still being feminine, wearing silk underwear beneath their masculine work clothes.

There were mixed messages on how women should behave during the war in order to fulfil their patriotic duty. On one hand, they weren't to be complacent around their looks and on the other, victory would be better achieved in practical clothing. An advert for slacks read:

Who said 'weaker sex'? – All over the land, America's women are in the drive for Victory! They're helping to build planes and tanks, making munitions, aiding civilian defense, conduction canteens, working in Victory gardens. Not only these, but all active women and girls choose the freedom and practical comfort of slacks.

There were also plenty of reports about women rebelling against the regulation clothing, reinforcing the idea that women should be primarily invested in their looks. Women at a United Aircraft Corporation in Stratford, Connecticut, went on strike because of a company ban on 'sweater girls'. Sweaters were considered a safety hazard as the threads could be caught in machinery, and girls were sent home by the management for wearing sweaters in violation of company rules. The *New York Times* reported in April 1943 that an agreement with union leaders was reached, and 'girls who were not employed on moving machinery or on jobs requiring safety clothing might wear sweaters' and the company would 'buy standard two-piece work clothes in a choice of two styles and colors, of cotton twills, for women workers'.

14

Coca-Cola and Pints of Bitter

'All my life I wanted to go to England' was the opening line of David Webster's memoirs:

> Finally, in September, 1943, I did go to England. I was a little boy no longer. The toy soldiers had come to life. Instead of a Black Watch cap with ribbons, I wore a steel helmet with a parachutist's chin strap. Jump boots were my leggings now, an M-1 rifle my steamer basket.

The first US soldier to officially set foot in Britain during the Second World War was Minnesota-born Private 1st-Class Milburn Henke. Henke had enlisted in the army in September 1940, in order to beat the draft, and joined B Company, 135th Infantry Regiment of the 34th 'Red Bull' Division. Arriving in Belfast on 26 January 1942, he was encouraged to be the first to step down the gangplank and talk to the press.

The waiting crowd roared in approval at the handsome soldier in an army greatcoat, M1918 helmet and rifle, and with his photo splashed in the papers, he became a minor celebrity, meeting Queen Elizabeth and President Roosevelt. Even his girlfriend back in Minnesota, Iola Christensen, was persuaded to do a press conference to profess she would wait for him. 'I was just sort of picked out of a hat,' he later said. 'But I never tried to downgrade what it meant: the symbol of America sending its boys to Europe to help win the war.'

Americans had unofficially supported Britain before they entered the war, with pilots acting as mercenaries to deliver much-needed planes across the Atlantic. The US Eagle Squadron had a wild reputation for their maverick behaviour as 'Fortune of War' flyers to support the UK. Represented by Tyrone Power in *A Yank in the RAF*, they assisted in ferrying Lockheed Hudson bombers to Britain from Canada, so as not to compromise American neutrality. In lieu of wool-lined flying suits, they dressed to their own tastes in business suits, tweed sports jackets, ski parkas or beaver hats. 'We looked as though we were heading for a costume ball instead of a transatlantic hop,' commented one pilot.

For the troops being sent to fight in Europe, the journey over the Atlantic was rough. On 15 September 1943, the *Samaria*, carrying the first half of 101st Airborne Division, docked in Liverpool to begin training for the invasion of Europe. They had spent the uncomfortable, overcrowded journey sleeping in their clothes, two people rotating each bunk bed, and with life jackets on at all times. From Liverpool, they were transported south and marched the final stretch to their barracks in Aldbourne, Wiltshire in blackout, which was their first experience of being in a conflict zone. Their freezing, damp Nissen huts were heated with twin pot-bellied stoves, and they slept on straw-stuffed mattresses with thick wool blankets. It would be home for almost nine months.

On arrival, the Americans were met by WVS and Red Cross girls, who provided coffee and doughnuts for the hungry troops, and they were cheered by waiting crowds who considered their presence an overwhelmingly positive turn in the war. Henry Giles recalled being greeted in Greenock by a kilted pipe band from the Scottish Highlanders:

> Even the weight of a full pack and the crammed barracks bag didn't seem too heavy as we came ashore to be gloriously serenaded by a band of Scottish Highlanders playing shrill tunes on their ancient bagpipes, music which sounded like a one-night jazz-session right out of the dim of Harlem.

For the GIs, the first impression of Britain was that it was quaint but cold and drab. They were struck by how small Britain seemed, how green it was, and how, as one infantry officer on his way to Hampshire noted, 'occasionally the train ground to a halt at station platforms, dimly lit by blackout lamps, where ladies in dark uniform poked trays of vaguely sweet buns and mugs of hot tea at us.'

The troops received a booklet to help them adjust to British customs by Eric Knight, called *A Short Guide to Great Britain*. The guide noted:

> If British civilians look dowdy or badly dressed it is not because they do not like good clothes or know how to wear them. All clothes are rationed, and

the British know they help war production by wearing an old suit or dress until it cannot be patched any longer. Old clothes are 'good form'.

It also advised, 'You will be interested in getting to know the British Tommy. Two actions on your part will slow up friendship – swiping his girl and not appreciating what his Army has been up against.' British women were also praised for 'proving themselves in this war. They have stuck to their posts near burning ammunition dumps, pulled aviators from burning planes, died at the gun posts.'

In January 1940, *Life* magazine reported the peculiarities of Britain to its American readers:

English people eat oily little fish, kidney stew, lukewarm mush and other such stuff for breakfast. This suits them perfectly. They also consume strange drinks such as gin and tonic, which serve to keep the swamp fever out of their bones ... Just as it is conventional in England to dress for dinner when there is no war, it is conventional not to dress for dinner when there is war. Englishmen like military uniforms but now call them 'battle dress'.

In Britain, American popular culture and the democracy of consumerism offered an exotic escape from the constraints of wartime austerity. After watching American films, young British people hankered for the things they had never seen or experienced – drugstores with milkshakes and soda fountains, skyscrapers and the bright lights of Broadway. Everything in Britain seemed smaller compared to this utopia.

Those who watched the GIs disembark had been impressed by the silent shuffle of their march because of the rubber-soled shoes. They seemed looser in procession than the Brits, they were broader and taller, and carried themselves with more confidence. Resembling film stars in beautifully cut uniforms, they made the British seem positively weedy in comparison.

As a boy watching the build-up to D-Day around his home in the West Country, the military historian John Keegan was disappointed that the British soldiers he saw 'wore khaki from top to toe ... so ill-cut, shapeless and hairy that I could find almost nothing in its wearers to admire'. When the Americans arrived, he and his school friends were amazed at 'how different they looked from our own jumble-sale champions, beautifully clothed in smooth khaki ...'.

Children were won over by the Americans, who gave them treats from their PX canteens, such as chewing gum, chocolate and cigarettes; items that soon made it onto the black market. The Americans were effortlessly cool with their charm and wisecracks and unique expressions.

As a 15-year-old, Betty Curtis remembered when she and her friend Rosemary met their first GIs on the beach one day. 'There were about 10 of them,' she recalled. 'They seemed so tall. We started talking and these two chaps, they asked us if we had any tinned fruit. We said no, and the next day they came over with a basketful.'

In comparison to drab Britain, America was a dreamland offering glamour and excitement, and there was something incredibly exciting about dancing the jitterbug with an American in uniform. It offered the promise of a whole world out there waiting to be experienced. By 1945, British youth were completely Americanised. 'Britain seemed so dull and corny; the Yanks gave us cigarettes and chewing gum and the music was fantastic,' said one Sussex schoolgirl:

We used to make these dresses with short, pleated skirts and when we danced they'd flare up right around our waists, so we couldn't stop the leg make-up (or the eye-brow penciled 'seams') at our knees. Who wants to listen to some schmaltzy sentimental music when they're young and can dance to the A-Train with the Yanks?

Land girl Amelia 'Mitzi' Edeson was impressed by the American soldiers when they were stationed near Leominster and described how they 'brightened our lives' with their gifts of chocolate Hershey bars and salted peanuts, and the jitterbug at local dances. She said:

The first time we saw them we thought they were all officers. Their uniforms were gabardine and they wore collar and ties … so different to our soldiers in their rough khaki uniforms. They were like film stars and had badges for everything, 'gee honey this one is for sharp shooting' and so on. Our lads would say they get a medal for the one who can spit furthest, a bit of jealousy there I think, although they could have been right.

One I met came from Chicago, he said, 'Honey when I get back I'm going to be mayor of Chicago'. When they left we went to the pictures, it was a Deanna Durbin, she sang, 'say a prayer for the boys over there', there was a lot of sobbing in that cinema, there were a few broken or 'bent hearts'. They liked girls and were polite, it was 'honey you look like a million dollars in that dress' or 'baby when this war is over I'm taking you back to the States'.

Americans earned seven times the pay of the British troops, and their brag-
ging led to conflict in cinemas, train stations, dance halls and pubs, where they
got drunk on rounds and rounds of bitter. The GIs should have heeded the
words of the *Short Guide to Great Britain*:

> The British dislike bragging and showing off. American wages and soldiers'
> pay are highest in the world. When pay day comes it would be sound prac-
> tice to spend your money according to British standards.

A Mass Observation survey after the first troops arrived found that 48 per
cent of those polled disliked American boastfulness the most, and that their
Fort Bragg seemed suited in its name.

George Orwell commented in December 1943, 'I rarely see American and
British soldiers together. Quite obviously the major cause of this is difference
in pay. You can't have really close and friendly relations with someone whose
income is five times your own. Financially the whole American Army is in
the middle class.'

The men enjoyed the attention they received from British women, who
were impressed by their charms and their relative wealth. But they suffered
the consequences, with one-third of all babies born illegitimate during this
time. Condoms, known as 'French letters', were often found abandoned in
street corners the morning after a military dance. When they were told, 'The
trouble with you Yanks is that you are overpaid, oversexed, and over here',
they would reply, 'The trouble with you Limeys is that you are underpaid,
undersexed, and under Eisenhower.'

'It's true that some girls would go with the Americans just to get nylon
stockings,' said Laura Hardwick, who worked at ROF Swynnerton. 'And our
lads definitely didn't like the Americans, but that was pure envy – they had
lovely uniforms. And more money. Our lads just had the rough khaki.'

In May 1942 the first group of USAAF arrived in Britain to join the
Eighth Air Force, and by August 1942, 8th Bomber Command began strategic bombing of Germany to knock out the Luftwaffe in preparation for
the invasion of Europe. The American bomber crews were stationed at bases
across Britain.

In their leaky huts, with only a scratchy blanket to put over themselves
at night, the flying crew could at least use their warm sheepskin jackets as
coverings. They improvised their grim space with Varga girl pin-ups on the
wall, and turned the bomb cluster crates and flare boxes into foot lockers. An
Eighth Air Force gunner remembered, 'The huts were dark, their concrete

floors were usually littered with traced-in mud, and their mingled odors of cigarettes and cigars both past and present, damp woollen clothing and socks too long unlaundered gave them the heady aroma of a goat barn.'

Like many of the bombers, the nose of the Eighth Air Force bomber *Memphis Belle* was painted with a pin-up 'Petty girl' motif, reflecting the 1940s pop culture influence on the war. American Red Cross worker Anne Haywood, who was half-English and half-Austrian, had plans to study art in Paris, but this was halted when war broke out. She served up coffee and doughnuts in the Aero Club at Great Ashfield, the base of the 385th Bomb Group. Her artistic talents were first appreciated when she created wall murals for the club, and soon she found a new calling as a sign writer. The American troops all asked for her to decorate the aircraft noses of B-17 Flying Fortresses and embellish their A-2 leather jackets with images such as 'Madame Shoo Shoo'.

Swing music burst into mainstream America at the end of the 1930s, but it was slower to arrive on British shores. Yet, once the GIs introduced British girls to the jitterbug, the foxtrot seemed quite dull to some. They wished to be thrown over shoulders and under knees, to feel like Rita Hayworth under the magic of the swing band in a throbbing dance hall.

Glenn Miller toured internationally with his US Air Force Orchestra, playing seventy-one concerts to a quarter of a million guests in the UK in 1944, with regular broadcasts reaching out further. In December 1943, *Picture Post* illustrated swing style for British readers, demonstrating the lingo, the dance moves and the history of the dance.

Stephanie Batstone recalled:

We went to a Yank dance in Warrington. Once in the arms of a real live Yank, you forgot the prohibitions and disapprovals and succumbed to the magic. They could dance properly, even a slow foxtrot … your hand was on that smooth pale, beautiful cloth, your eye was level with the US shoulder flash … They had proper shoes, not hobnail boots, and they never trod on your feet.

Betty Nettle, a munitions girl who worked at ROF Bridgend, said:

One time, the Americans organised a huge 'do', a social 'thank you' to everyone. The dance was such a big deal; I even went to the hairdressers after my day shift. I had it hanging down in ringlets, rather than the usual swept-up style. When I got to the social, everyone ignored me. So I ran to the loo, combed it out and when I came back, everyone clapped and cheered. So I didn't bother with the hairdressers again. But at these dances there was never a chance for any of us to really talk about what we were doing. You'd just dance and enjoy the evening. But suddenly, after that social, all the Americans had gone from the area. Where we lived, no one knew about D-Day, the Normandy landings.

For the 101st Airborne, evening entertainment in Aldbourne was limited to quiet beers in the local pub. They were eventually given passes to go to a local dance in Swindon but were instructed to keep on all their layers of clothing when dancing. When Private Thomas Burgess found himself sweating from dancing, he stripped off the blouse worn over his shirt so he could cool down. Word got back to their captain, Herbert Sobel, and Burgess was ordered to wear his blouse over his fatigues all week, even while sleeping.

The US Army policy was that there should be racial segregation, even when overseas, and black troops who volunteered or were drafted were denied a combat role in the war. Instead, they were kept as labourers, kitchen staff and transporters.

In Britain, women found African-American men fascinating. A 1943 Mass Observation poll found Britain 'overwhelmingly opposed to racial discrimination'. Many thought black GIs were less boastful and more charming than their white counterparts, and many Brits chose to defy the segregation by serving drinks to all customers at pubs, or by dancing with African-American soldiers. In October 1942, *Picture Post* dubiously announced, 'Negro troops are already a familiar sight in dozens of towns in Britain. They fitted into our grey, unexotic background with surprising ease.'

Many American women were also sent to Britain to aid in the war effort, including 2,000 volunteer WACs. Violet Gordon was stationed in Birmingham before being transferred to France after D-Day. She remembered seeing Cab Calloway, who was performing with the USO (United Service Organisations) on an overseas tour. She said:

The towns' people in Birmingham particularly were so warm and receiving. When we had free time and went into town. One of the things that I remember is that…the churches would have twelve o'clock or one o'clock concerts. If you had free time on that particular day you could go into town to the concerts. That was just like a wonderful reward. And of course we had free time to travel.

The aim of the American Red Cross was to lift the spirits of American soldiers far from home by offering comforts and reminders. At the Red Cross clubs located in major cities across the country, a taste of America was brought to the troops. 'Meals cost about thirty cents each and are uniformly terrible, but you can eat at a snack bar in between and buy Coca-Colas,' wrote David Webster. 'Beds are two shillings a night – sheets changed every day. Through the Red Cross you can get tickets to shows, visit local citizens, go on tours, or find friends. The only things free are individual cigarettes.'

Elizabeth (Liz) Richardson from Wisconsin was stationed in England and France in 1944 and 1945. Working in advertising in Milwaukee in the first years of the war, she signed up to the American Red Cross with two college friends at the beginning of 1944, as she wanted to do something to support her male friends who were enlisted. Once in England, Elizabeth worked as a 'Clubmobiler', serving up coffee and doughnuts to troops going to and from combat.

The Clubmobile was a service club on wheels, fitted with coffee and doughnut equipment, as well as carrying chewing gum, cigarettes, magazines and newspapers, and a Victrola record player and speakers to blast out the latest records. Three glamorous American Red Cross women worked from each van and were taken to a location close to American forces bases by a British driver.

In 1943 there were almost 500 American girls working for the American Red Cross, supported by more than 6,000 British volunteers. Always offering a cheery welcome and conversation, they were dressed in a blue wool skirt and jacket with Red Cross insignia, or when near a conflict zone in France, they wore a military-style uniform of boots, belted shirt and calottes, jacket and cap. It was hard work lifting the coffee urns and deep-frying the doughnuts in the van, with the smell permeating their hair, but they always tried to keep up their appearances with lipstick and a smile.

Liz was tall, athletic and striking looking, and she liked perfume and make-up, going to dances, and speaking fondly of home with American soldiers. The girls had all been selected by the Red Cross for their ability to banter, to have the right All-American look, to be hip to popular culture and to know the latest slang and music. Clubmobiler Eleanor Stevenson recalled how they'd yell out to a truckload of GIs, 'Hi, soldier. What's cooking?'

An article in the *Milwaukee Journal* from 21 September 1943 described the training of the Clubmobile girls:

In the Basement of one of London's Ancestral homes, in the heart of Mayfair, a doughnut school has been set up. Here pretty girls newly arrived from the States learn how to turn out doughnuts for the troops at the rate of 840 an hour. They wear white overalls and are easily the loveliest Army that has ever visited England ... There are no beauty bans in this service, and all the girls look glamorous with their silk stockings, varnished nails and elegant footwear.

The British ATS, WAAFS and WRENS, look drab in comparison, with their Khaki, Air Force blue uniforms and black Lisle stockings, heavy shoes, little make-up and no nail varnish. These American girls have caused a great impression on what is left of the British men in England ... American girls with their alluring accents, trim well cut uniforms, lovable natures and untiring zest for work and play have caused the English 'Tommy' a terrific heart throb.

For many GIs in England, meeting an American woman was a rare treat. Liz wrote home soon after she had arrived:

You feel sort of like a museum piece – 'Hey, look, fellows! A real, live American girl!' and that 'If you have a club foot, buck teeth, crossed eyes, and a cleft palette, you can still be Miss Popularity'. The main thing is that you're female and speak English.

These women stayed in the minds of the homesick GI's they had flirted with. Liz wrote to her parents from France in spring 1945, that she was passing some resting troops in France when she heard them shout, 'Hey Liz! Hey, Milwaukee!' She said:

It was a whole unit that we had known in England and we had a wonderful reunion right there on the road. And yesterday I met one of the cooks who had helped us brew our coffee during that week of the invasion of Holland. It's funny how they remember you and stranger yet how we can remember them after seeing thousands and thousands of faces.

At Le Havre airport on the morning of 25 July 1945, Liz jumped into a two-seat military plane to fly to Paris. Near Rouen the plane crashed. Liz and the pilot, Sergeant William R. Miller of the Ninth Air Force, died instantly. She was 27 years old.

The American Forces Network (AFN) provided entertainment for the GIs in Britain, providing round-the-clock swing music, Bob Hope broadcasts and hourly BBC new bulletins. For David Webster, 'with the exception of "Music While You Work", the BBC was no equal to the entertainments of the US Army'. Despite his childhood longing to visit Britain, David realised how much he missed American culture, such as milk bars on every corner. And the repressive, rainy weather in England didn't help:

> I, for one, never realized what a fine place America was until I came over here. America is richer, cleaner, healthier, more progressive, and more stimu-lating. People here are over civilized, too set in their ways. They lack the fluidity, the spontaneity of Americans who, though acting like semi-savages at times, are much more alive than the English ... America has a future; England has a past. The Scotch, though, are more like Americans than the quiet reserved English. They're cleaner, talk more, are more friendly, and will buy you drinks. You can't help liking a Scotchman.

Henry Giles was shipped out overseas from Boston on 8 October 1943 and later that month he sent a letter to girlfriend Janice from 'somewhere in England'. He wrote:

> England is rather a beautiful place ... We have a lot of fun talking about the English money. It seems funny to ask if someone has change for a pound or a shilling or sixpence. Someone told of him weighing thirteen stone, what-ever that means. They call a saloon, a 'Pub'.

On 28 November 1943, the engagement of Janice Holt Moore and Henry E. Giles of Knifley, Kentucky, was announced in a local newspaper. They hadn't met since their Greyhound bus ride, but through writing to one another they realised they had fallen in love. As she began planning the ceremony, he joked, 'Regarding colors – anything but Khaki or OD [Olive Drab]'. He was also looking forward to married life, when he wouldn't have to wash his own clothes, 'be glad when I'm out of the Army, so someone else can do my laundry and pressing'.

Janice wrote to Henry of the culture in America, mentioning a song called 'The Shining Hour', which hadn't been released in Britain, but was one of the big hits in the States. She also mentioned the phenomenon of Frank Sinatra, and he wrote back in a February 1944 letter:

> I've never heard of him (or much of him) but according to newspaper articles, cartoons, etc, every female is supposed to swoon when he croons, I saw a cartoon where a Chicago hotel manager was 'bawling him out' because the women were fainting in every place they saw him.

In March 1944, the American Army began the gruelling preparation for the invasion of France. By the spring of 1944, there were 1.5 million American troops in Britain, who had been trained up over months in order to match the perceived power of the Germans.

On the way to embarking for Normandy, Mary Morris and her fellow QAs stopped at an American Army transit camp set up in a forest outside Southampton, and they were awed by the reception and hospitality that they received. 'The Americans are delighted to entertain us,' she wrote:

> We are the first women to be in transit here, and the generosity of our hosts is amazing. They have showered us with presents from their PX, chocolate, chewing gum and tins of fruit. There is one rather attractive young man called Steve who appears to have taken on the role of my personal batman. He wanted to give me a lovely pair of silk stockings, which I had to refuse reluctantly, mainly because I have a suspicion that they might not be very useful in Normandy.

The next morning they waved goodbye to their new American friends, and 'we girls were all clutching addresses stretching from Maryland to Ohio'.

15

Victory Girls and Zoot Suits

'A girl gets to know medals like the boogie-woogie, but a Purple Heart, that means you were wounded,' says Shirley Temple to Joseph Cotten over dinner in *I'll Be Seeing You* (1944). Later in the film, her mother scolds her, 'Barbara, after dinner you go upstairs and take off some of that lipstick. Looks as if you fell in a pot of red paint.'

Shirley Temple represented the new type of sub-deb. She was now known as a 'Victory Girl', and she was so crazy about men in uniform that she could recognise the medals they had pinned to their chests. While their older sisters actively took part in the war effort through work, teenage girls were confused by the sexualisation of society in wartime, a result of having to grow up too fast. Temple, the popular child star of the thirties, also had to grow up quickly in the spotlight, and during the war years, she played the relatable teenage girl on the Home Front.

The phenomenon of the Victory Girl was considered symptomatic of the problems of a lack of parental supervision for teenagers. On 20 December 1943, *Life* published a long feature on the growing issue, which they called 'one of the most disturbing problems on the US home front today'.

When women were called on to build morale, they inadvertently crossed the line into what was unacceptable, and were defined as 'Khaki-Wackies', 'Patriotutes', 'Good-Time Charlottes' and 'Victory Girls'. It was accepted that men in war required sex, but they also had to be protected from venereal disease. A poster depicting a 'girl next door' suggested, 'She may look clean, but …', and another said, 'Men who KNOW Say no!'

The term 'Patriotutes' was a blend of patriot and prostitute, and was coined by the US Public Health Service physician, Otis Anderson, to describe women who entertained the troops in order to maintain morale. Yet, it was insulting to the women who had obeyed the call to support the war effort, and led to the rumours surrounding the reputation of women in uniform. There was a contradictory campaign by the government which validated masculine sexuality in the military yet denigrated the women who were expected to provide it.

Girls who were under the conscription age of 20 were expected to grow up quicker than the generation before. With a groundswell of men in uniform in cities across America, teenage girls were confronted with the message that women should be available to boost the morale of troops. Instead of playing dolls, many were now cheerleaders for the armed forces and were encouraged to do so even when at high school.

The National Sub-Deb Club Federation was organised by writer Elizabeth Woodward, who wrote a sub-deb page for the *Ladies' Home Journal*. These clubs planned a succession of parties for teenage servicemen, who complained that women in the USO canteens were too old for them. Sub-deb clubs were particularly popular in the Midwest, according to *Life*. At one Indianapolis club, boys from other youth clubs answered questions such as whether boys expect to 'neck' on a first date, and what they thought of a flirt. ('They're kind of fun if there aren't too many people around.')

With heavy make-up to convey a sense of older sophistication, Victory Girls walked in gangs along the street, wearing their recognisable uniform of Sloppy Joe sweaters, bobby socks and saddle shoes, with the aim of pairing up with sailors and soldiers. Figures from the National Association of Hosiery Manufacturers revealed that in 1936, 10.1 million ankle socks were sold. By 1941, sales had increased to 19.9 million, and by 1943 this had risen to 24.9 million. Because thousands more women were working in overalls and slacks during the war, there was a greater requirement for socks rather than stockings. This was also coupled with the fact there was a silk and nylon shortage, and limited rubber for girdles and garter belts following the Japanese occupation of Malaysia and its rubber plantations.

A pamphlet from the National Recreation Association, 'Teen Trouble', described how they:

… walk down city streets, six or seven abreast, breaking as they pass civilians, but holding onto each other's arms as they approach a soldier or sailor, forming a very flattering net around him. As the walk progresses, the line gets shorter and shorter, as girl and boy pair off and leave the group. It's a childish, very effective get-your-man plan used by girls around fourteen and fifteen years old.

Heavily impacted by the changes to society during wartime, the delinquency of young girls increased, with an epidemic of shoplifting and 'crimes against common decency', which included drunkenness, prostitution and vagrancy. *Life* magazine wrote:

> The well-known fact that many girls of their own age are interested only in older boys in uniform has produced a whole crop of juvenile desperadoes, who will try almost anything to impress their girl friends. Girls who would normally be developing a healthy interest in boys of their own ages, seem to mature overnight and become unabashed uniform-chasers. Many of these precocious children give themselves so cheaply to uniformed men that the soldiers and sailors call them 'khaki-wackies' 'cuddle-bunnies,' 'round-heels,' 'patriotutes,' 'chippies,' 'good-time Janes,' and, most commonly, 'Victory Girls.' The Victory Girl is 'different from most girls in that she is promiscuous, careless, sometimes diseased – a sexual delinquent in the literal sense of the words.

Life's correspondent in San Antonio described the girls:

> Dressed in their unmistakable hair ribbons, Sloppy Joe sweater and anklets, the little girls do everything but a strip-tease act when a uniform goes by on Houston Street … after the pickup there is a picture show with popcorn or peanuts, then a walk along the river, then a beer or two. Now comes the girl's chance to reciprocate for the evening's entertainment. If she does, and properly, she's looked on as 'a good sport' by the boy in uniform.

Girls in bobby socks were also known to congregate around Times Square as New York became a 'crowded war-boom town'. The *New York Times* noted that 'a sharp distinction must be made between [Victory Girls] and the ordinary adolescent, high school or college kid who calls her anklets bobby socks and who prefers a wrinkled, sloppy sock. "Sharp" is what the kids around the soda fountain, say … '

The *New Yorker* in March 1944 also reported how three young students at the Columbia School of Journalism disguised themselves in bobby socks and went to Times Square 'to land themselves an exclusive story on the shadowy world of soldiers, sailors, victory girls, and the police department'. The 21-year-old students, Florence Brudney, Betty Lou Moorsteen and Edyth Efro, dressed up in costumes that demonstrated teen patriotism – a red cotton skirt, a blue pea jacket with quartermaster's insignia on it, white bobby socks and red ribbons in their hair. Walking up Broadway, the girls attracted the attention of a group of sailors who followed them, and at 45th Street the girls stopped for the men to catch up with them. They explained to the sailors they were really reporters who wanted to get arrested, and asked them to play along. They eventually managed to get taken by police to the Temporary Juvenile Aid Bureau at 105 West 44th Street, gave false addresses, said they were born in 1926, and kept it up until a policewoman saw their ID.

The behaviour of Victory Girls created a moral panic, and in March 1942 former magistrate Jeannette G. Brill of Brooklyn spoke out against the rise of juvenile delinquency, calling for schools and parents to take action. 'We have got to stop bringing unwanted war babies into the world,' she said. She noted that she had observed young girls in a hotel lobby, dressed as if they were 18 or 20 in order to attract soldiers. 'They label themselves the Victory Girls,' she said. 'They think that the boys are here today but may be dead tomorrow and they reason "we'll give them all they want".'

It wasn't just teenage girls who caused concern. Not conscripted until they turned 20, boys in America often felt restless as they watched their older brothers go to war. *Life* noted that the increase in vandalism, arson, assault and even rape and murder were on the increase among young males, and this could be 'traced directly to war excitement, to misguided desire on the part of underage youngsters to do something as thrilling as their big brother in uniform'. It continued:

Several cities have reported young 'Commando Gangs' that fight vicious little mock battles with real knives and guns. They also use these weapons in raids on isolated gasoline stations to steal money, gas and tires, or invade restaurants and night clubs to terrorize the patrons. In one city a group of these armed kids set upon an old man they found alone in the street and beat him so badly that he died.

The darkness of the movie theatre encouraged kids to destroy seats and cause disruption, and in the Bronx, a 17-year-old girl reported she had been gang-raped in a theatre box. The article reported, 'Child experts are almost unanimously agreed that the overdose of battle news and bloodshed which issues from the radio, movies and newspapers today can be very harmful to young imaginations when it is not counter-balanced by a good home environment.'

The youth bodies of the 1930s, like the CCC and NYA, which had been formed as part of the New Deal, had been put to bed and in their place were groups that helped to train up teenagers for the realities of fighting in a war.

High school children like Raymond Boylston, whose older brother Sam was stationed in the Pacific, signed up to be part of the Victory Corps, where they could wear a uniform once a week, offering them a taste of things to come:

> We drilled and used dummy wooden rifles. This training later helped me when I was drafted during the Korean War. Each day we read about the war in the newspaper, heard about it over the radio and saw pictures in newsreels at the movies on Saturday night. We also discussed the war during classes at school.

Army and navy conscripts who had been shaped into the ideal fighters at camps across America were unleashed in towns and cities when on leave or granted weekend passes. They were at a restless, in-between stage as they waited to be shipped out to some unknown, distant place – foggy, rainy Britain, the desert, or the damp humidity of the tropics. Now that they were on leave, they wanted to let off the anger and aggression that had been harnessed in their training. They went to bars and strip shows, and as they drunkenly roamed cities at night they were angered by seeing migrants in urban areas who were not wearing uniform.

In May 1943 the GIs took out their aggression on zoot-suiters, the young Mexican-Americans who wore exaggerated, ration-flouting suits. The zoot-suiters felt that they were 'in-between', as they were rebelling against their two cultures, Mexico and America, and what they wore was a way of expressing their disaffection. But they were vilified in the media as weed-smokers, unfit for the army because they had delinquent records, and wore suits that required an amount of fabric that was at odds with the war effort.

'Last week the nation's needle nuts and gandydancers (jitterbugs) were cut to the quick by a WPB [War Production Board] official who declared that the wasteful manufacture of "zoot suits" and "juke jackets" was interfering with the US war effort and must stop,' wrote *Life* magazine, on the decision to speak out against zoot suits. 'Spokesmen for hepcats in Washington DC, a hotspot which ranks with Harlem and Hollywood as a style center for the glad rags of solid-diggers, claimed that the WPB edict was a "persecution of a minority".'

Following the 'Sleepy Lagoon' murder of August 1942, when seventeen Mexican-Americans were arrested by Los Angeles police and charged with the murder of José Gallardo Díaz, the media called for action against the perceived threat of the zoot-suiters. This led to a nationwide moral panic and discrimination against any one in a zoot suit.

Over ten days in LA, off-duty GIs attacked the zoot-suiters, pulling them off streetcars, going for them in cinema lines, and stripping them of their clothes and cutting their hair. On 3 June 1943, sailors, armed with rocks, sticks and belts, cruised through *barrios*, and the police arrested the victims. Riots spread to Detroit where there was already simmering racial tensions, and over the summer of 1943 there was violence in New York City, Indianapolis and amongst middle-class children at school events. Vice President Henry Wallace spoke out to try to quell the violence, 'We cannot fight to crush Nazi brutality abroad and condone race riots at home'.

The problem of delinquency was so concerning that a subcommittee of the US Senate launched a congressional investigation into wartime delinquency, health and education. Curfews were put in place in some towns and cities for those under 18. Already suffering from the rationing of gas and sugar, which impacted on the production of Coca-Cola, it was not a popular choice.

Another explanation for the surge in delinquency was a lack of recreational facilities during the war. There were plenty of dances available for those in the armed forces, but facilities for teenagers were lacking. To try to combat it, new types of youth clubs sprung up in cities during the war, supported by both public and private funds, which featured a jukebox and soft drinks bar. Taking their name from the swing phenomenon, they were called 'Teen Town', 'Hi-Nite Club', 'Hep-House', and the 'Flamingo Club'.

Swing music had become the phenomenon in the war years, and it shaped the language of advertising and magazines. The *Ladies' Home Journal* ran a slang guide for parents to understand wartime teenagers, 'Young America is hep to the step and goes merrily on rockin' to the rhythm of sling lingo'. An attractive girl was known as a 'slick chick', 'whistle bat' or a 'dilly', attractive boys were 'drooly' or a 'hunk of heartbreak'. It defined 'khaki whacky' and 'slack happy' as boy crazy, and men who were girl crazy were 'dame dazed'. A good dancer was a 'jive bomber' or a 'pepper shaker'.

Sub-deb swing fans, known as 'Hep Jills', wore the female version of the zoot suits – flared skirts with long droopy coats with shoulder pads. They danced in the aisles, and left lipstick marks on the posters of their idols. Number one on the list by 1943 was Frank Sinatra, who caused complete hysteria when he shared the bill with Benny Goodman at the Paramount Theater in January 1943. It was his youthful looks, his intense blue eyes and his charm that made girls feel like he understood them and talked their language.

Publicist George Evans came to the show to decide if he wanted to represent Sinatra. He was shocked by the crowd in the theatre at 2.30 p.m., where 5,000 teenage girls were squeezed into seats and aisles, close to hysteria and screaming out his name. Evans recalled he could smell 'perfumes, BO, the faint acrid tang of urine', and it was this that persuaded Evans to represent him.

In October 1944, Frank Sinatra put on a series of concerts at New York's Paramount Theater, and such was the demand that hundreds of girls queued up overnight to secure their place. They were dressed in bobby socks, Sinatra-style bow ties, and with his photo pinned to their clothes. When he came on stage the audience greeted him with a pulsating scream and wet themselves because they didn't want to miss a moment by going to the bathroom. It became known as the 'Columbus Day Riot', a phenomenon of mass hysteria compared to the death of Rudolph Valentino. 'It was the war years, and there was a great loneliness. I was the boy in every corner drugstore, the boy who had gone off to war,' Sinatra remembered.

Sinatra was unable to join the army due to an ear defect from a difficult birth, but in the press he was criticised for not wearing uniform. Many GIs were angered at this non-uniformed singer being mobbed by girls, and in one moment captured by photographers, sailors threw tomatoes at his blow-up image outside the theatre. The *New York Times* reported in December 1943, 'Frank Sinatra will not lay that microphone down and take up a gun or a duffle bag. Completing a special engagement with Army physicians this morning at the Newark induction center, the crooner came out rejected and dejected. Another punctured eardrum case, he was classified 4F.'

One way in which he tried to contribute was through presenting a short public-awareness film called *The House I Live In*. Through this film, he aimed to reach out to young people to combat the religious and racial intolerance that was evident in both America and in the Third Reich.

Young men were being killed overseas, but it was in 1944 that the word 'teenager' was first used to define a frivolous, consumerist demographic. In December 1944, *Seventeen* magazine wrote:

You buy loafer moccasins because your friends do … you go to Joe's Grill … or Doc's for cokes, not because those places are charming, or the food is good – but because the crowd goes. Most of your surface habits are picked up from people your own age.

GI David Webster reflected on the sacrifices young men in the army were making, as he watched many of his friends die, while at home young people still had the freedom to have fun:

Back in America the standard of living continued to rise. Back in America the race tracks were booming, the night clubs were making their greatest profits in history, Miami Beach was so crowded you couldn't get a room anywhere. Few people seemed to care …

16

Mae Wests, Tin Hats and the Invasion of Normandy

'There was blood coming out of my mate's mouth,' Captain Wilkens of the Royal Engineers told Irish QA nurse Mary Morris, who wrote of her devastation at the destruction she saw, 'I could cry for all of them, but what use are tears?'

At the end of May 1944, as Britain prepared for the invasion of Europe, known as D-Day, the 101st Airborne travelled south to get ready to jump into occupied France. As David Webster recalled, they were loaded 'with gear and ammunition and sweating terribly in woolen winter uniforms'.

Taking part in the Normandy invasion were the First Allied Airborne Army, which included the 17th, 82nd, and 101st American Airborne Divisions, the Polish 1st Parachute Brigade and the British 1st and 6th Airborne Divisions, along with the 52nd Lowlanders. As they readied to board the army aircraft on 5 June 1944, the American paratroopers were loaded down with equipment. Their vests, long johns, combat jackets and trousers were airless and stank of the anti-chemical coating to protect from gas attacks. In their trouser pockets they kept their K rations, which were cartons of survival foods that included gum, cigarettes, sugar lumps and soya bean meal crackers, along with extra socks, ammunition, grenades and a compass.

Over the uniform they wore webbing belt and braces, a 45mm pistol, water canteen, shovel, first aid kit, bayonet and a gas mask attached to their leg. The parachute harness was layered over this, and the main parachute was packed into a backpack. Finally, the Mae West life jacket and helmet were positioned. A knife was kept in their blouse pocket to cut themselves out of their parachute harness, as they could be strangled by it when their life jacket inflated.

Insignia could not be shown on their uniform, in case of capture, and instead they were given an American flag to sew on to the right sleeve of their jump jackets. Officers painted vertical stripes on the back of their helmets, while non-commissioned officers used horizontal stripes.

During a rousing speech by their corporal, the 101st Airborne Division was instructed not to wear their wool-knit caps on their own, without a helmet. The reason was never clear, except for the obvious protection the helmet gave, but wearing these caps had become something of a fashion within the division. However, the general hated them. 'I don't care what else you do, but for God's sake, don't let the general catch you in a wool-knit cap! Steal a tank, rob a German payroll – anything but a wool-knit cap,' they were told.

As David Webster wrote in his memoirs:

> British commandos might raid Dieppe in sock-like caps and British para-chutists wear red berets to Sicily, but we slept in our helmets and hid our wool-knit caps under their iron lids. This was a source of constant friction, with men continually trying to wear them and the officers, goaded from on high, on the lookout to snatch them off. Wool-knit caps became a command phobia of such proportions.

Waiting for the jump into Normandy was torturous. The 101st Airborne Division tried to calm their nerves by checking over their equipment, cleaning their weapons and chain smoking. Some of the men also shaved their heads into Mohawks, and painted their faces with battle marks, like Apaches. They had reached their ultimate fitness peak, and now it would be put to the test against three German divisions behind Utah Beach.

In the evening they were treated to a last meal of steak, mashed potatoes, peas, coffee and ice cream – their first since arriving in Britain. But then they received the announcement that the invasion was delayed, due to bad weather. The next day, Tuesday, 6 June, the weather cleared and 13,400 Americans were given the command to jump into German-occupied territory. They were bulging with equipment, their boots tramping on the ground, the gas masks and bayonets clanking against their legs, and they battled with their nerves and a sense of nausea. 'I shiver and sweat at the same time. My head is shaved, my face darkened with charcoal, my jumpsuit impregnated for gas. I am carrying over a hundred pounds of equipment. I have two bandoleers and three hand grenades for ten thousand Germans, and yes, I am ready,' wrote Webster.

Webster fell 100ft in three seconds, landing in water, and without the time to begin the procedure of getting out of the chute, reserve and harness. He was relieved to find he was only submerged in 3ft of water, and managed to free himself of gear. 'A lot of men drowned in that swamp; I was lucky to have landed in shallow water,' said Webster.

The survivors of the jump met up behind Utah Beach, and they threw away all their unnecessary equipment, including their gas masks. Webster took the decision to discard his water-soaked woollen shirt and pants:

> I took off my wool underwear, wrung it out, rolled it up, and put it in my musette bag. I cut off the bottoms of my jump pants to keep them from holding water. Then I put my jumpsuit and webbing back on again. I threw away my jump rope and two cartons of cigarettes that I had brought along to trade with the friendly natives.

On landing, Lieutenant Harry Welsh held onto his reserve parachute, storing it in his backpack throughout Normandy, as he wanted to send back the precious length of silk to his girlfriend, Kitty Grogan, 'to make a wedding gown for our marriage after the war.'

Corbin B. Willis, the co-pilot of a B-17 bomber, bailed out over Germany when his plane came under attack:

> I descended quite a distance with my rip cord in my hand before I realized the parachute was still in its pack – I was wearing a chest chute – so I had to peel it open and then it blossomed out above me. I looked up and my combat boots were dangling above me for I didn't take the time to detach them before jumping. We strapped them to our parachutes so we wouldn't leave them in the plane after each mission as we wore heated boots while in flight. These boots were later a 'god' send for the long distances we traveled later in Germany.

As well as by air, American troops landed on the beaches of Normandy from huge ships. War reporter Martha Gellhorn had also made it on to the beaches of Normandy without an official press pass. She had persuaded a British sailor to let her on board a hospital ship for the invasion. She reported:

> Pulling out of the harbor that night, we passed a ship going the same way. The ship was grey against the grey water and grey sky and standing on her decks, packed solidly together, khaki, silent and unmoving, were American troops. No one waved and no one called. The crowded grey ship and the empty white ship sailed slowly out of the harbor toward France.

The next morning, after the first push of the invasion onto the beaches, she saw the bodies of some of these young men, now just 'swollen greyish sacks', floating in the sea.

When she was accepted into the QAs in 1944, Galway nurse Mary Morris went to London to order her indoor uniform from Austin Reed. She wrote, 'It is very attractive – a simple grey dress – scarlet cape and white organdie head-dress – two lovely shining pips on the shoulder and our own QA badge.'

By the time preparations for the D-Day invasion were taking place, she found that wearing her new uniform brought respect and authority. 'There were troops and armoured vehicles everywhere and I was amused to see how quickly the wolf whistle was transformed into a smart salute when the soldiers noted our two pips!'

Both Katherine Jones and General Montgomery believed that the white veil enhanced the femininity of British nurses, which was vital in keeping up the morale of wounded men. However, it was recognised that the dress wasn't very practical when it came to climbing into an army lorry or working in extreme weather conditions. By the time of D-Day, they were issued with tin helmets and battledress with khaki barathea suit, shirt and tie.

To prepare for D-Day, QAs were also required to purchase their active duty kit. Mary wrote, 'There are fascinating pieces of equipment such as a canvas bowl on a tripod, a canvas bucket, a Tilley lamp and even a collapsible canvas bath. We had great fun trying out this latter piece of equipment.'

At the port, where they would board ships to be taken to Normandy, Mary and her fellow QAs were instructed to be fully kitted out in battledress and tin hats. As their ship got closer to Graye-sur-Mer, they were ordered to assemble on deck, wearing their Mae Wests:

> We were told to put all the personal valises together. The sailors would look after them. Our hands must be free … The wearing of a Mae West, although essential in such weather, would increase our girth and make the effort of climbing down the scrambling net very difficult. It might have been easier if we were all eight months pregnant.

Mary Morris was stationed in a ward at the front line in Normandy where she treated international patients, including Canadians, Poles, Free French soldiers, Americans and Germans, who were to be treated exactly the same as the

Allied men. 'This multi-national microcosm of a Europe at war is interesting and sad. A badly wounded cockney says "thanks mate" to Hans as he gives him his tea and fixes his pillows. Why are they all tolerant of each other inside this canvas tent, and killing each other outside?'

Joy Trindle was a QA at the Normandy beach landings, where she came under sniper fire as they set up a front-line hospital in the field. 'Polish men, Germans and Canadians came in – as well as our own troops. I had only the clothes I stood up in so washed my underwear – wrapped them in tissue paper and dried them in the camp oven!'

American nurse Aileen Hogan of the Army Nursing Corps worked with the 2nd General Hospital Unit in Normandy. She wrote in a letter home in October 1944:

> I am having a bad dream. You walk out of your tent and the grounds are being policed by men dressed as you are, in green fatigues, except that PW is printed on various prominent parts. You cut across the field and meet an English soldier in battle dress, beret slanted over one eye. You say 'Good Morning,' and he says, 'Bon Jour' and you realize that he is Free French in English uniform. You pick up a bundle and start for your ward, an English nurse with a perfect Oxford accent says, 'Sister, that is too heavy for you, allow me,' and you turn and you find the grey-blue Nazi uniform behind you. A POW [prisoner of war] of course, but after a while you get mixed up yourself …

After wearing the same battledress for days on end, it was difficult to keep it looking smart. 'The American Sisters are charming,' wrote Mary Morris. 'But I was not too pleased when one extremely smart lady lieutenant described my rather battered battle dress as "cute".'

As they worked their way into occupied France, the American troops picked over the war dead to collect souvenirs. Lugers were favourite bounty, followed by anything branded with a swastika, watches and daggers. It was common to take souvenirs, and rather being opportunistically macabre, it was also a way to think of survival. As Philosopher J. Glenn Gray, who was a soldier in the Second World War, wrote, 'Primarily, souvenirs appeared to give the soldier some assurance of his future beyond the destructive environment of the present. They represented a promise that he might survive.'

German clothing was often considered more efficient so collecting coats and ponchos to keep warm was common among the Allies. Yet it could also place them in danger of friendly fire. One evening, while on watch, Sergeant Floyd Talbert put on a German poncho to keep warm. As he woke his replacement for duty, Private George Smith, by nudging him with his gun, Smith only saw the silhouette in German uniform and immediately drew his bayonet. Despite Talbert pleading with him to stop, he was stabbed by Smith several times, and was wounded severely enough to be taken out of action.

The 101st Division was eventually relieved by the 83rd Infantry Division and they were given the chance to shower and shave, eat hot food and sleep uninterrupted for the first time in two weeks. Sergeant Burton Christenson said of the pristine, war-untouched men in the 83rd, 'Even the paint on their helmets looked as if they had just been unpacked. The impact of seeing such a dishevelled motley group as we were was a shock to them.'

101st Division returned to England on 1 July after thirty-one days in Normandy, where they received a warm reception in Aldbourne. It felt like coming home, and a memorial service was held for those who were killed. Webster wrote:

I closed my eyes and saw the Regiment as it once was, tramping down the shining wet roads in the old, tan jumpsuits, weapons clattering and sergeants shouting cadence. I heard them whistling 'She Wears a Yellow Ribbon' ('for a trooper who is far, far away') and watched them turn off and go cross-country, breaking fences and stealing rutabagas, strongpoint.

One of those killed was a medic, Howard R. Porter, who had been shot despite wearing the Red Cross armband, a red cross on his helmet and the big red cross on his first-aid kit. The Germans were notorious for ignoring the Red Cross markings, in breach of the Geneva Convention. A Midwest boy, known for his 'very short crew cut', he learned how to treat STDs, and 'what proportion of medicinal alcohol to add to a can of pineapple juice to make a socially acceptable cocktail'.

On arrival back in Britain, the survivors were given two complete sets of new uniforms, including green jumpsuits, all their back pay and a seven-day pass. Many of the paratroopers headed straight to London where they were treated as heroes, with drinks and meals bought from them. However, all that aggression and fear came out under the influence of booze, and they fought with infantrymen, who the paratroopers looked down upon and saw as inferior. It was considered one of the wildest weeks in London during the war.

17

London Nightlife

> London in the morning was still the best place in the world. The smell of
> wet streets, of sawdust in the butchers' shops, of tar melted on the blocks,
> was exhilarating ... I loved the capital. The wind on the heath might call for
> a time, but the facile glitter of the city was the stronger.

As he recovered from his serious, life-changing burns, Richard Hillary was
allowed out of the hospital to visit London on occasion. With a pair of dark
glasses to cover up the protective cotton wool under his eyes, and his right
arm in a sling, he thought, 'I looked fairly presentable'. It was inevitable people
would stare at his injuries, but his burns, combined with the silver wings on
his air force blue, also marked him out as a hero.

For anyone in the armed services with leave, London was the place to
come to meet up with friends at hotel bars and to dance with uniformed
strangers at the Café de Paris, the 400 Club or the Ritz. Night-time in
London was transformed during the war, as a symphony of uniforms in
different styles and colours collected together in the city. In the restaurants
were soldiers in brown, sailors in navy and white, the white headdress and
red cross on nurses, pilots on leave in their air force blue, or civil serv-
ants and government workers in suits, relaxing and socialising after a hard
days' work.

All night, the anti-aircraft crews were stationed in parks and streets across
the city. The Auxiliary Fire Service were on standby to deal with the fires
from bomb raids, and air-raid wardens patrolled the streets, directing people
to available bomb shelters and underground stations. Some Tube stations were
equipped with bunk beds and toilets, with 60,000 people taking safety each
night. Underground shelters such as those at Holborn, Knightsbridge and

Notting Hill Gate all had their own first-aid post manned by the Red Cross, who arranged concerts, games and film shows.

Jackie Sorour described walking through London at night during the Blitz:

> A London of darkness shattered by the flash of death, the scream of agony, the sobbing of despair and a reckoning at dawn in the debris of fallen masonry. This was a very different God from the one my grandmother used to talk about with a soft look in her eyes.

Anne Douglas-Scott-Montagu, whose family home held the headquarters for the ARP for the area, began her nursing career with the Red Cross, proudly dressed in its uniform of dark blue coat and skirt, black stockings with flat black shoes, white shirt with black tie and Red Cross insignia on the shoulder. By January 1945 she was working at the Red Cross headquarters in London:

> I used to go round London by bicycle. It was very difficult to get hold of batteries for bicycle lamps then and I managed to find a wonderful little paraffin bicycle lamp. I remember bicycling back past Cadogan Gardens, where a lot of American soldiers were stationed, with a stream of smoke pouring out of my lamp and a trail of wolf whistles following me.

When in London, the RAF fighter pilots would go to the 400 Club in Leicester Square, where steak and champagne was available, or to the Bag O'Nails, where they found there was always queue of women wishing to dance with a pilot in blue. The airmen lapped up the hero worship they received and, as well as the attention of women, their uniform awarded them free drinks. Squadron leader John 'Chips' Carpenter went so far as to have the name of his favourite West End club (Chez Nina) written on the side of his aircraft.

At the 400 Club, Diana Barnato would regularly sketch out flying tips on the napkins with Battle of Britain pilots. As Brian Kingcombe wrote in his memoirs, the 'dimly lit dance floor and seductive music were excellent back-drops for young men in uniform trying their luck with the "I'm off to war tomorrow and may never come back" routine.'

'We always felt safe in the 400, as we saw all our friends,' said Betty Shaughnessy. 'The minute the siren went we would dive into Leicester Square Underground station where everyone was sitting with their blue tin teapots. "Oh, hello Miss, come and have a cup of tea," they'd say. There was such a sense of camaraderie.'

Nightclubs stayed open until dawn, and London's grand hotels were fashionable meeting places. The Landsdown at Hyde Park Corner was popular for dancing, or drinks were taken at the Dorchester and Savoy. The Ritz was the smart choice close to Piccadilly. Fiona Colquhoun said, 'We used to be given drinks at the Ritz bar if we'd driven an officer anywhere. We got them half-price because we were in khaki.'

As the war drew on, the Ritz's downstairs bar became an unofficial meeting place for gay soldiers. With this reputation, the Brigade of Guards eventually banned their officers from going there. The Alhambra Theatre in Leicester Square was dark and romantic, with walls covered in red silk, red velvet curtains and tables lit by candles. Members kept their own bottles of gin or whisky at the club, marked at the level to which they had drunk when they left. It was run by Luigi Rossi and was packed every night with officers and their girlfriends.

Soho was the heart of wartime nightlife in London. This section of the West End, filled with cafés, private clubs, ethnic restaurants and brothels, became a focal point – a place for writers, artists, drunks, prostitutes and drug addicts to converge. After a Mayfair party, Joan Bawden enjoyed people-watching at the Piccadilly Lyons Corner House in April 1941, while tucking into Welsh rarebit, waffles and coffee:

> The people there were more interesting to look at and listen to than the Mayfair bunch: chorus girls with inky black hair, phoney eyelashes, phoney glamour and looking like they needed a wash, with much-smaller-than-themselves boyfriends with bright suits and an equal absence of cleanliness.

The West End was filled with Allied soldiers who all had their own mannerisms and uniforms to mark them apart. 'The city has an air of bustle and excitement,' wrote nurse Mary Morris. During air raids she wrote in her diary how people kept up their spirits by singing 'Run Rabbit Run', and she was surprised 'at the number of noisy Australian soldiers in the West End. They are our allies, over here to train I suppose, but I dislike their uncouth manners and atrocious voices.'

When Diana Barnato was working as an ambulance driver for the Red Cross, before signing up to the ATA, she would regularly call in at the Café de Paris in Leicester Square, to watch 'Snake-hips' Johnson's band. It was here that 'Girls dressed up in beautiful long dresses, not their war work uniforms or, in my case, my Red Cross costume'. Despite the bombs raining down on the city, the Café de Paris's basement location felt safe. After staying out late every night for a whole week, Diana's father scolded her that she was treating his house like a hotel and told her to stay in for once. That one night, 8 March 1941, she did so. The same night, the Café de Paris was hit by a bomb and 'Snake-hips', along with many other guests, was killed in the blast. In the chaos, looters took advantage of the dark and ripped jewellery from the bodies of the victims in the chaos.

Wartime London revealed a criminal underbelly. The 'Spivs' were rakish criminals who ran the black market and were known for their natty dress. They wore pin-striped suits, trilbies, Clark Gable moustaches and 'duck's arse' hair, sourcing bootleg clothing and booze for those who had the cash.

There was an economy based around the needs of soldiers – with prostitutes known as the Piccadilly Commandos, dressed in a uniform of sorts to take advantage of drunk, rich GIs. Such was the concern that the Commissioner of the Metropolitan Police commented, 'Of course the American soldiers are encouraged by these young sluts, many of whom should be serving in the Forces'.

David Webster longed for London when he was suffering in the cold European winter during the invasion:

> The weather had turned damp again; it was a close, drizzly night that made me think of London. I longed for it very much, as I recalled the steaming, wild, wild bars and the girls waiting outside, one pound quick time, three pounds all night. It's been a long time since I got drunk, I mused, wishing that I were back in Piccadilly.

Because of the number of GIs in the city, London was the centre of American culture. Rainbow Corner, a twenty-four-hour recreational club for Americans, opened in November 1942. It replicated the American way of life with a jukebox, pinball machine, pool tables, a snack bar with waffles, hamburgers, doughnuts and cokes, and Glenn Miller even played four nights there. Local teenagers were desperate to get inside the Utopian clubhouse pumping with the sound of swing music, free-flowing Coca-Cola and Yanks in uniform, until the doors had to be closed to ease the pressure.

A Mass Observation study of Paddington and Bermondsey noted that after the Blitz, when 2 million Londoners lost their homes, the lives of teenagers were disrupted, with many taking to roaming the streets with wild gangs. 'Young people,' they noted, are 'always running amok from shelter to shelter, with opportunities for promiscuous sexual relationships, drinking and gambling' and, in the East End, 'a general slackening of moral sense among the young, owing to the complete devastation of life'.

Not only was there the constant threat of their homes being obliterated by bombs, but schools in major cities were closed and there were limited places to go for those who were too young to join the armed services. As a result, reports of teenage delinquency, malicious damage and vandalism increased by 33 per cent. Instead of the bright lights of downtown, the Blitz plunged cities into blackout, and any open theatre venues and cinemas were filled with people in uniform.

'London to me was a magic carpet,' wrote Sergeant Gordon Carson, Easy Company, 101st Airborne Division:

Walk down any of its streets and every uniform of the Free World was to be seen. Their youth and vigor vibrated in every park and pub. To Piccadilly, Hyde Park, Leicester Square, Trafalgar Square, Victoria they came. The uniforms of the Canadians, South Africans, Australians, New Zealanders, the Free French, Polish, Belgium, Holland, and of course the English and Americans were everywhere … Those days were not lost on me because even at twenty years of age, I knew I was seeing and being a part of something that was never to be again. Wartime London was its own world.

Don Malarkey of 101st Airborne was thrilled to be one of six people in his company to see swing band leader Glenn Miller, who was tragically killed in a plane crash in 1945. He could still remember the programme years later, when he thought back to that time.

American ATA pilot Ann Wood found visits to London under black-out thrilling, dining with friends under a sky filled with barrage balloons, spending the night at the Red Cross Club on Charles Street, or supper with friends at the Grosvenor House Hotel. She wrote in her diary, 'Somehow these jaunts to London fill me with utter glee.' At the Red Cross Club she would enjoy the milkshakes and Coke, and she could talk of home with the manager of the club, Mrs Biddle, wife of the former US Ambassador to Poland.

Once she had received her uniform from Austin Reed's, she would attract plenty of attention when her gold USA flash on her shoulder was spotted. On one of these London trips, dining with Colonel Peter Beasley in Mayfair in September 1943, Ann spotted Clark Gable, who was in the Eighth Airforce, and a girlfriend sitting a few tables away. 'Poor guy,' she wrote. 'So stared at that he couldn't take his eyes off his lassie without confronting a hundred other pairs of eyes.'

Servicewomen like Diana Barnato would take advantage of their leave by heading to London for a night out, change from uniform into evening dress and back again, and report for duty the next morning, not worrying about only having had a couple of hours sleep. Upper-class girls were used to getting their own way and would often break the strict rules placed on them.

While staying at a Wren hostel with a curfew, Elizabeth Scott discovered the fire escape key and sneaked out to visit her friends in London:

> I would manage to telephone my friends, say I'd meet them at the 400, and catch the tube at the Finchley Road station straight to Leicester Square. It was more difficult getting back as the tube stopped at midnight, so whoever I was with had to bribe a taxi to take me back. I was in uniform as I didn't have any other clothes there. I did that once or twice and was never found out. I told one or two of the other girls I'd made friends with but nobody else dared do it.

Suzanne Irwin and her friends, who worked as FANYs within the ATS, would hitch a ride to London for a night out:

> We'd stand on the main road that went through Bagshot, outside a pub called the Jolly Farmer. Then we'd go to the 400 or the Florida. We were in the ATS by then but off duty we could wear our FANY uniforms, which were much nicer. Our ATS uniforms were rather nasty – the jacket, the hat and those thick lisle stockings.
>
> We were not allowed to leave barracks other than in uniform, so we had to go to nightclubs in our uniforms. I remember once in Edinburgh putting on an evening dress, with its skirt tucked up, and my greatcoat over the top to hide it. Because I was 'other ranks' I had to report to the sergeant before leaving and she said: 'Irwin, undo your coat.' So I had to, and down fell the skirt of my evening dress. That was the end of my evening out as I was punished by being confined to barracks for twenty-four hours.

The status of the service uniform would also serve as a code amongst those in the armed forces, where WAAFs and ATS officers, particularly, would be treated with respect by RAF and army officers. In October 1940, during the Blitz, when London was hit by the unrelenting bombs of the Luftwaffe, Joan Bawden and friend Molly took a couple of days' leave to visit London, where they saw the desolation of Oxford Street. 'It was dreadful to see the ruins of John Lewis,' wrote Joan. They went for drinks at the American Bar at the

Regent Palace, where they met a party of RAF officers who, on recognising their WAAF uniform, invited them for drinks.

Joan Wyndham had lived as a bohemian in Chelsea before she joined the WAAFs, and she relished a return to London where she could experience her own unregulated life in the city. She had an unconventional relationship with her father, artist and writer Dick Wyndham, and after a drunken evening together at the Café Royal and the Gargoyle, dressed in a 'grey crepe dress with daisies on it and a coral necklace', she met her cousin David Tennant, who owned the Gargoyle, and they spotted novelist Philip Toynbee (and friend of Esmond Romilly) 'being sick on the sofa'.

Her father allowed her to stay at his studio in Bedford Gardens, where she took his supply of Benzedrine, drank Manhattans and went to the party of a Yugoslavian artist:

> Inside were a lot of clever girls in corduroy trousers, a few young artists, an elderly social worker, a tongue-tied young soldier in battledress and a former prime minister of Hungary who appeared to suffer from a cleft palate … there was some talk of war, the attacks on Russian convoys, our raid on Tobruk, the fighting on the outskirts of Stalingrad, but most people seemed more interested in the relation of art to science.

After being posted to Inverness, Joan Wyndham looked forward to being able to take her next leave in London. She managed to get a prescription for 100 Benzedrine when she wrote to her doctor to tell him she wanted to lose weight. It would be perfect for her plan to take London by storm with her friend Oscarine and the two Norwegian sailors they had met in Inverness – Hans and Danny.

In June 1943, they took the train to London, where already the sailors began to get drunk on a lethal concoction of booze. 'Soon we were joined by a Norwegian pongo who had recently escaped from Norway and the Gestapo. We exchanged clothes and sang,' she wrote. After taking Hans on a 'typically English day' to impress him, going to Battersea Park and drinking cider in the pub, they prepared for a night at the Embassy Club:

> Dinner at Scott's, lobsters, strawberries and crepes Suzette. I just couldn't wait to go dancing. I felt as if I had ginger in my heels … We drank whisky and took Benzedrine and our legs felt as if they had springs in them.

Neither Hans nor I had ever enjoyed a night out so much. Mario Barretti was playing Cuban music on drums and reed pipes, and I swayed in his arms to 'Brazil' and 'Black Magic'. At four in the morning, the bright lights came on, and suddenly 'everything was strange and garish in the white glare'.

The next day they went to see *The Merry Widow*, one of the must-see stage productions in London at that time, with Oscarine and Joan dressed to kill in black dresses and with red roses in their hair. Their last night in London before having to return to Inverness proved to be bittersweet, as it marked the end of something special. 'We lay awake all night drinking whisky and talking about death. I cried and cried,' she wrote.

18

Scavenging in Occupied Europe

The next major Allied campaign after Normandy, known as Operation Market Garden, was to land in southern Holland, capture the canal and river bridges, and hold the road open for the tanks of the British Second Army to smash into Germany.

David Webster was satisfied with his 'perfect' jump into Holland and, appreciating that he had survived the drop, he considered taking a souvenir from his parachute. 'I had always wanted a piece of parachute silk for a scarf but had never dared cut a chute on a training jump. Now was my chance. I pulled out my trench knife and went to the canopy ...' But he was interrupted by shell fire, and instead picked up his rifle to run into action.

As the 101st Airborne Division marched through Eindhoven:

> Orange flags and armbands appeared everywhere, and the cheering, clapping crowds soon thickened so much that we could barely move. The civilians wanted to help us, to shake our hands, to pat our backs and thank us for driving away the Germans ... It was the most sincere thanksgiving demonstration that any of us had ever witnessed, and it fixed Holland forever in our hearts.

They felt like heroes as they posed for photographs, signed autographs and drank glasses of cognac and wine to celebrate the victory. 'The girls stared at us in admiration, the small boys fingered our gear, the older civilians mobbed us as if we were movie stars,' wrote Webster. They soaked up the adulation and relief of those freed from Nazi rule, and admired the beauty of the people and the scenery with the meadows and windmills.

However, the sunshine turned to rain as the Germans held ground, and the Allies slept in foxholes in constant slush, with no chance for their clothes to dry out or to wash or shave. Claude Woodring from Ohio was drafted into the army when he was 18, and served in the 1st Division 18th Infantry Regiment:

> The most horrible part of the war that I remember is always being hungry, always being dirty, and always being tired. When I was wounded on September 22nd, or whenever, they cut the same clothes off of me that we went in on D-Day with, we fought in O.D.'s our dress uniform, hot. They issued those clothes with a double flap and a gas-impregnated Vaseline all over them. A horrible uniform to fight in. So if you young people have to go to the military, get in the Navy or the Air Corp. where you got clean sheets at night and a lot of food.

Ultimately, Market Garden was a failure, and of the 10,000-plus men who went in, 8,000 were killed, wounded or captured. The Germans had made a miracle comeback, re-equipped their units and defended their position.

Canadian troops replaced the American paratroopers in November, allowing the 101st to travel to Camp Mourmelon, near Reims, where they enjoyed hot showers and laundered their clothes. On leave in Reims, they drunkenly clashed with the 82nd Airborne who made disparaging quips about their screaming eagle shoulder patch. With violence coming to a head, their passes were cancelled and instead they were subjected to long marches to expend the energy.

New replacements stepped in to take the spots vacated by the originals who had trained together in the summer of 1942, and who had been killed, wounded or captured. These fresh recruits found the veterans, battle-scarred from weeks of action, intimidating. The veterans were casual with their weapons, they kept knives hanging from their belts and mixed their uniform with German souvenirs.

The rain and snow continued as they pushed towards Germany in the latter part of 1944, and it was miserable being constantly soaked through from the cold, wet weather, particularly when underequipped with replacement clothing. David Webster wrote:

> Wiseman and I took our raincoats out of our musette bags and put them on and settled down for the night, each of us sitting in one end of the trench with his head on his knees. Our boots were wet through, and the rain and dirt kept trickling down our necks. We were so cold and miserable that we couldn't sleep.

The looting and raiding of pieces of clothing continued, as soldiers adapted what they could to try to make themselves as comfortable as possible. In the pine forests they discovered piles of abandoned German uniforms and gear, left by young German deserters. Webster described the smell in these clothes, 'a rank body odor that seemed appropriate to their long, oily hair and sweaty uniforms of cheap wool'.

When they came across an abandoned British truck, David Webster described how they found:

> ... hand-knitted Shetland sweaters, thick gray socks (which were always welcome), clean handkerchiefs, an armored corps black beret, and a late captain's jacket, complete with pips and campaign ribbons. Apparently, the Germans had taken all the food and cigarettes, because none was to be had, not even on the dead men. Never able to touch a body or go through the pockets of a corpse, I left that part of the search to less inhibited persons.

The dead lay everywhere, along with the items that they left behind. In the village of St Oedenrode they came across the body of a British dispatch rider in his leather gauntlets, knee-length boots, and round helmet. They met another group of British men, from the Queen's Own Guards Regiment, who 'were the neatest soldiers I had ever seen in action. Crouching in holes as square and precise as the Germans', they were all clean-shaven and in regulation uniform, with their helmets squarely on their heads:

> We knew that the Guards' units were the best in the British Army – every man had to be at least six feet tall and a superior soldier – but we had never realized how well disciplined they were on the field of battle. By comparison, we looked like a rabble in arms, with our beards and muddy uniforms and tattered gear. Our helmets were worn with a jaunty individuality, and most of their tops had been blackened by cooking and shaving fires, for the helmet served as an all-purpose iron pot.

As they crossed the Waal River into the Lower Rhine, they came across British Field Artillery soldiers in fleece-lined leather jerkins. They had hoped to find American fleece-lined flying jacket or gloves in an abandoned Stirling bomber, but the Brits had got there first. Another prize possession was the red beret of the elite British Commando, an item that was hard to come by, but much treasured.

Their feet ached from the continuous marching and they were always hungry – their rations not providing enough sustenance. The men were on a constant lookout for fruit to pick from orchards, cows to milk or goods left in abandoned houses, taking pillowcases and filling them up with coffee, jam, tins of fruit and alcohol.

Surrendering German soldiers, with perfect English, were known to pass themselves off as Polish, but the clothing could always be a giveaway. 'One by one, half a dozen burly Germans in spotted ponchos rose like sprouting flowers with their hands in the air,' wrote David Webster. 'Hard-eyed and almost middle-aged, they bore the double lightning insignia of the S.S. on their collar tabs. "*Polski*," they cried, "*wir sind Polski*," but their German sounded remarkably good to me.'

Germans would also attempt to be Americans in order to infiltrate. Alvin Dickson, an officer in the US Army, from Canton, Ohio, recalled, 'Where'd you come from? They said Canton, Ohio. Where'd you graduate from? The high school there. What was the nickname of the team? They never knew. That's how we captured them.'

During one attack, Webster was shot in the thigh, and he limped across the ground for what seemed like an eternity, until he could reach the lines of safety to be treated by medics. Yet he still found time to take souvenirs. 'A German poncho caught my fancy as I approached a grassy embankment two feet high. Make a good souvenir for my sister's boy, I thought. I scooped it up and ran on.'

As he hobbled to safety, he came across a Dutch farmhouse, and was welcomed in by the family until they could get help. He was given German pancakes and strawberry jam, cups of hot coffee and milk. 'I hadn't shaved for almost a week, my boots were filthy, and one leg of my pants was covered with dry blood. I told them that I was a wounded American paratrooper and asked them to send somebody for help,' he said.

He was then taken to a safe point in the road to be picked up by a medical jeep. He took off his helmet, to relieve his itching scalp, rolled up his pistol in his identification scarf and hid it in his pocket, to ensure a medic wouldn't steel it. The jeep arrived shortly after, taking him on the journey back to England for treatment.

The next campaign in the Bastogne region, known as the Battle of the Bulge, took place from 16 December 1944 to 25 January 1945, in the dense pine forests of the Ardennes. It was a fierce battle on rough mountain terrain in the middle of a hard, desolate winter. Charles B. MacDonald, in his history of *The Battle of the Bulge*, described the mutilated landscapes:

> Everywhere discarded soldier equipment – gas masks, empty rations containers, helmets, rifles, here a field jacket with a sleeve rent, there a muddy overcoat with an ugly clotted dark stain on it. One man kicked a bloody shoe from his path, then shuddered that the shoe still had a foot in it … Here and there bodies of the dead lay about in grotesque positions, weather-soaked, bloated, the stench from them cloying.

Thousands of men from the Twelfth and Sixth US Army Group, and the British Twenty-First Army Group were to take part in this campaign but had not been given adequate clothing to protect from the cold. Winter 1944 was freezing, with snow falling across Europe, and the lack of equipment was felt. The 101st Airborne were without long underwear and extra socks to wear under their jump boots, battledress and trench coats. The burlaps wrapped around their boots got wet from the snow, and as the damp seeped into their boots and socks, trench foot was an extra danger to contend with.

Colonel Ralph Ingersoll, an intelligence officer with the First Army, recalled travelling through the Ardennes, dressed in 'woolen underwear, a woolen uniform, armored force combat overalls, a sweater, an armored force field jacket with elastic cuffs, a muffler, a heavy lined trench coat, two pairs of heavy woolen socks, and combat boots with galoshes over them – and I cannot remember ever being warm.'

Alvin Dickson remembered:

> A lot of our soldiers, including me, got trench foot. Trench foot is when you have your socks on day after day after day and they become soaked and your feet turn blue. And if you don't catch it in time, why you lose your feet. I went to the field hospital. Fortunately, mine were not to that stage yet … they used to take blankets and build little booties to put inside your field boots to keep your feet dry as much as possible … in the cold and in the dampness you absolutely couldn't change your socks every day.

Some of the men of the 101st Airborne went on a scavenging hunt into Bastogne, where they sourced flour sacks and bed sheets to provide extra layers for sleeping in foxholes, or to make their own snow suits.

It was a harsh existence as they fought the toughest Nazi units, those who had been completely indoctrinated in their dangerous ideology. The Germans were also better equipped, having learnt to fight in harsh conditions on the Russian front. They had leopard snow suits, the precursor to the camouflage jacket, and stacked straw boots designed to protect inner shoes from the snow when pushing into Russia.

When one of the new recruits to the 101st Airborne died painfully and in anguish, David Webster thought of the people back home who perhaps gave no consideration to the suffering of these young men, who should have been at college, rather than dying brutally overseas:

He wasn't twenty years old. He hadn't begun to live. Shrieking and moaning, he gave up his life on a stretcher. [...] we wondered if the people would ever know what it cost the soldiers in terror, bloodshed, and hideous, agonizing deaths to win the war.

Back in Mourmelon, after ten weeks on the front, the men were issued with clean clothes and Class A uniform. However, the 17th Airborne had got in first and raided the storage area for equipment for the Bulge. They took all the jumpsuits, shirts, regimental insignia, jump boots, British airborne smocks, panels from Normandy and Holland parachutes and their souvenirs, including Lugers. It was a blow to the 101st, but it demonstrated how in-demand uniform was for morale.

On return to his unit in February 1945, as the snow was melting, David Webster lamented that with the mix of uniforms, the paratroopers had lost their uniqueness when it came to how they dressed. 'Paratroopers wore boots,' he wrote in his memoirs. 'In those dear dead days we had a certain pride, a certain distinctiveness, a certain feeling that as volunteers for a slightly dangerous job, we were a little better than the average soldier.' But, after the Normandy invasion, he noted:

Everybody wears boots and we wear the infantry uniform to battle. Our glider troops were issued jump boots (we can't even get them) and are allowed to wear their pants bloused over them. In the last marshaling area, they were equipped with jump boots, while we had to wear those ugly combat boots. But the gliders aren't the only ones: the Rangers, the engineer beach battalions, and many elements of the S.O.S. are wearing boots now. It's a hell of a note.

When he looked at the grizzled men in his outfit, Webster admired their lack of discipline in both attitude and dress. They wore German black leather belts with the First World War Prussian '*Gott Mit Uns*' buckle and Lugers on their hips. Their jumpsuits were mud-encrusted and well worn:

> They wore a motley array of raincoats and field jackets and German shelter halves. Some of them wore woolen GI overcoats, others truck drivers' mackinaws or tankers' jackets that they had found in the Bulge. Some men had piled little rolled sleeping bags on top of their musette bags and lashed them down with bootlaces, while many more made hobo bedrolls and looped them in a horseshoe over one shoulder with the ends tied, Russian style. There were many German pistols on their belts and no gas masks, and the griping was both universal and profane and yet strangely cheerful, for every move made them talkative. The next place, they hopefully rationalized, couldn't possibly be this bad.

One of the men, Corporal Donald Hoobler, was later killed when he accidentally shot himself in the leg with a scavenged Luger and bled to death. Webster found out when he returned. 'It isn't fair,' thought Webster. 'It just doesn't seem right. They were the old boys who had never been hit before.'

Private Patrick S. O'Keefe was a new recruit who joined the army when he was 17. His first impression of the men at Mourmelon was that 'they were all tough, old and grizzled. I thought, "You have bitten off more than you can chew, O'Keefe".' The journey into the Rhine was O'Keefe's first combat. He said:

> We wore light sweaters under field jackets, trousers bloused over combat boots, trench knife strapped on right leg, pistol belts with attached musette bags, one phosphorus grenade and one regular hand grenade taped onto our chest harness, canteens, first aid kit, K rations stuffed into our pockets, steel helmet and rifle. We carried cloth bandoliers for our rifle clips in place of the old-fashioned cartridge belts. Our musette bags carried a minimum of shorts, socks, shaving gear, sewing kit, cigarettes, etc.

As they entered into Germany, the Americans found that despite being in enemy territory, they loved German food and beer, and found the standards of living as comfortable as that of America. As they made their way through the war-ravaged country, they took what they could as they went along – Lugers, Nazi insignia, watches, first editions of *Mein Kampf*, alcohol and vehicles.

They looted the houses, trying to get there first before any other outfits to collect the bounty, going through drawers and flinging unwanted contents aside. Webster noted a stocky soldier with a Brooklyn accent holding up a tablecloth and saying, 'This'd make a choice scarf.'

> The bureau drawers had all been pulled open, for this was the first act of any invader, drawers often being hiding places for jewelry, watches, cameras, sweaters, and wool socks. Some of the men also liked to fondle women's underwear. It always embarrassed me and made me feel ashamed. I wanted to apologize to the owners for the mess that we made, to tell them that we were only looking for little comforts to make our life more bearable, but I would have been lying, for deep in all our hearts we hoped to find more rewarding treasures than socks or sweaters.

On 19 April, every soldier advancing in Germany was supplied with a clean pair of socks, plus three bottles of Coca-Cola and two bottles of American beer. They were paid their wages in Military Marks in advance of their route into Munich, Innsbruck, and on to Hitler's Eagle's Nest.

As they pushed into southern Germany and Austria, the German soldiers, seeing an elite airborne unit, surrendered in their thousands, many still dripping in pride and only wanting to surrender to an elite airborne unit. 'We relieved them of their watches, pistols, and binoculars and sent them on their way to rear echelon, for we couldn't be bothered with them now; there were just too many of them.' They picked up German stragglers along the autobahn, stripping a Luftwaffe sergeant of his 'soft-leather, fleece-lined flying pants', leaving him only in his long underpants and a sweater.

From the liberated labour camps, survivors poured onto the autobahn, proudly brandishing their home countries' symbols now that the Nazis had been defeated:

> No matter how tattered their clothes, the freed men had all taken pains to fashion tiny ornaments of their national colors for their buttonholes. They wore them as proudly as a medal for bravery: the red star of Russia; the tricolor of France; red and green for Italy; blue, white, and gold for Yugoslavia.

The concentration camps were a shock to everyone, even the most battle-hardened of soldiers. 'The sight, after so many years of propaganda, of those striped uniforms, so like pajamas, that signified endless death on the widest and most coldly methodical scale was very chilling.'

They travelled through a rocky gorge into the Alps, coming across a lone German tankman wearing the black uniform of the SS troops. One of the Jewish paratroopers pulled out his M-1 and shot around his feet, making him dance as if he was in a Hollywood western.

They saw a grizzled French tankman in a clearing of pine forest, with three young German boys in their long Wehrmacht overcoats, and without weapons. They were the victims of Hitler's last desperate recruitment of 16-year-old boys. One of the boys had been shot, the other two knelt beside him, helpless and paralysed with fright. The Frenchman shot them in turn.

Webster observed the youngest-looking boy, appearing as if he hadn't yet reached the age to start shaving:

[with a] fresh, cheerful, pink adolescent face that had never been creased by worry or the awareness of death. All the thoughts that old men have but that he had never had before crowded in an instant into his mind and came out in his eyes and on his forehead and splattered his brains red and yellow and purple on the snow behind him.

Webster turned to a cocky young replacement, eager to fight. '"There's your goddamned war!" I said. "Did you like it, did you like it?" He gulped and shook his head.'

After Corbin B. Willis bailed out over Germany, he was captured and taken to Stalag Luft III and presumed dead by his family. The clothing he wore for the entire time he was a prisoner of war was the same that he had worn when he was shot down. The Germans removed the wires from inside his heated flying suit, but he sewed the jackets and pants together to make a jumpsuit that kept out the draft in his middle. 'We were issued a GI issue overcoat captured from our ground forces – also a scarf and a stocking cap – I had my combat boots, so I was in pretty good shape for the cold,' he said.

Chocolate bars were the currency of the POWs when playing bridge or bartering, and they would come in useful when they were forced to march. 'I was actually offered seven candy bars for my boots, on our long cross country trek, to outrun the Russian advance,' he recalled. 'The chocolate bars were found in the American and Canadian Red Cross food parcels and we would divide one with four others, so we could have a taste of chocolate each night for a week.'

Without enough to eat, Corbin, along with the other POWs, lost weight. He could feel the bones in his hips:

> I had to sacrifice my sweaters warmth to make a doughnut shaped pad under my hip in order to sleep at night. Laying on my back created snores and loud disapproval, so I fashioned the doughnut, so I could sleep at night without a lot of pain and noise.

He remembered an amusing letter to one of the POWs from their mother, which was posted up on the wall to make everyone laugh:

> His mother had sent him a sweater for Christmas and he mentioned, to her, it shrunk when he washed it, so she wrote back and admonished him that sweater had to be 'dry cleaned – not washed'. We all laughed at that remark.

19

Fighting in the Pacific

After the Japanese entered the war, British troops were sent to fight in the Far East. The Long Range Penetration Groups were a special British and Indian army and operated from 1942 to 1945. They were known as the Chindits, named after the protective mythical beasts guarding Burmese temples, and were a guerrilla force, pushing into areas occupied by the Japanese, and fighting with guns and grenades and the Gurkha *kukri* knife.

It was a tough, hard campaign and the men felt like a 'forgotten army' as they went without food and suffered malaria and dysentery. As they trekked through sticky, humid rainforest they were weighed down with 72lb of equipment, and some of those in the grip of illness chose to strip off completely to try to relieve the discomfort.

It took a long time for any new equipment to reach them and instead, those in India and the Far East took to wearing locally produced items, bought cheaply from market traders, such as the cotton *musrey*, in lightweight blue-grey fabric, khaki wool shirts with two pleated breast pockets, or collarless Indian wool shirts in dark brown flannel. The humidity made everything damp and caused their leather identifying wristlets to rot, and so their ID tag cords were replaced with chains.

The official uniform for those fighting in the campaign was similar to the kit for North Africa. The shorts exposed the legs to injury and insect bites, and while beige was camouflage in the desert, it was conspicuous against the deep green of the Burma rainforests. They bought their own 'Bombay bloomers', which were Indian-produced khaki drill shorts which had turn-ups that could be rolled down over the legs for when the temperature dropped and the mosquitoes were biting. By 1942, these shorts were considered dated, and the fashion was to modify the bloomers by cutting off the turn-ups and wrapping puttees around the legs for protection. The tropical pith hat wasn't well suited for hot tropical jungles, but they were worn with an Indian camouflage net, which went over the top to break up the outline.

Later, in 1942, the uniform destined for troops in Indian Far East was dyed dark green, they were given khaki drill trousers instead of shorts, and Indian-made dark green woollen shirts. From 1943, the Indian Army produced a wool battledress in 'jungle green', with a cooler Aertex blouse and cotton drill trousers. Troops were also issued Indian-made V-neck pullovers for night, when it got colder at a higher latitude.

In Japanese-occupied South East Asia, the Women's Auxiliary Service (Burma) (WAS) went into the front lines despite the heavy bombardment, to serve tea to weary, battle-exhausted men. In the rainforests of South East Asia, from Burma to Sumatra, they dressed in khaki slacks, bush shirts and gum boots as they served up tea and smiles. Robert Sawyer, a private in the 2nd Battalion Welsh Regiment, recalled, 'There was always a buzz when word spread that the girls would be coming into our company area – char and wads and those gorgeous tins of fruit, peaches and pears, biscuits.'

The Women's Auxiliary Corps (India) was established in early 1942 for Indian and British women. By 1945 there were around 10,000 enlisted in the WAC(I), with 1,160 officers. As the only women's military service in India it also provided personnel for the air force and navy.

When researching the film *Bhowani Junction*, starring Ava Gardner, producers got in touch with Jean Dodd, a former WAC in Bombay, who lent her WAC photo album, her uniform, badges and lanyards to the studio costume department for research. She also wrote a letter to the director George Cukor:

> WACs did not wear uniforms in the evenings – only during office hours. They either wore the sari – or the bush shirt and skirt or dress – not both. Indian girls only wore the sari. If they worked in shifts and had night duty then only they would wear the uniform of course. We were all so proud of the uniform and I would not like to see the WAC character in a poor light.

Compared to Normandy, India was considered a glamorous posting for women. However, the mosquitoes in places like Madras and Calcutta were a big problem. The uniform rules at the beginning of the war dictated that nurses should have bare legs with their dresses. They used their veils to cover their faces and to protect from breathing in dust during sandstorms. In the evenings, they staved off mosquito bites with their long-sleeved tunics and khaki drill slacks tucked into their shoes.

Mary Davies was posted in December 1943 to join 65th Combined Military Hospital at Asansol, West Bengal:

We knew the officers quite well and they used to invite us over for dances. They were quite a relief as it meant we could put on long dresses. This helped protect us from mosquitoes which always seemed to go for the legs. Sometimes it would be gramophone records, sometimes someone would play the piano. The Americans were not far away and they used to invite us over too. Our NAAFI did not supply things like chocolate and stockings and they tried to shower us with these sought-after luxuries.

Limited in what they could wear to dances, they had dresses made especially for them by local tailors:

The great thing about India is that there is wonderful material to buy – and very clever tailors to make it up. We used to choose our material, draw the design of the dress on a piece of paper and give it to a tailor … They would make it up in next to no time – and charge a very modest fee.

Meg Minshull Fogg decided to join the Red Cross rather than the Wrens when she saw the uniform at a fundraising concert. 'I thought: this uniform looks pretty like a naval uniform, so I thought I'll join. The uniform was navy blue with white shirt and black tie, with gold shoulder tabs giving your unit.' She volunteered for India and served on the Arakan Front as the war raged on the Burma and Indian border. 'We were given the nickname the Blue Roses of the Arakan – the area. It sounds lovely but it was no picnic – it was hard work … We were issued with boots, trousers and bush jackets – everything buttoned up – and mosquito beds and nets, and canvas beds and washbasins.'

After the Japanese were defeated and the prisoners of war released, the WAS would offer a soothing reminder of home to the emaciated men who had been treated so inhumanely and forced into slave labour on the railway lines of South East Asia. The Japanese soldiers were known for their cruelty. When a member of the US 1st Division Marines was reported missing, his body was later discovered covered in bayonet wounds, as if he had been used for practice. His arm tattoo of the marines emblem, with the anchor and the globe, had been cut out and stuffed in his mouth.

Following the attack on Pearl Harbor, American forces fought the Japanese in the Pacific. It was an unrelenting campaign in hot, sticky rainforest where they were constantly under attack from a fervent, unrelenting enemy. A Pacific

War style was developed because of the heat and was inspired by General Douglas MacArthur, a reformed peacock who had been partial to extravagant dress. He arrived in Australia in 1942 and learning something from the casual style of General Eisenhower, he chose to wear an open-collared shirt, khaki trousers and no tie. It was cool, less formal and suited the humidity, and it quickly caught on. But official field dress tended to go out of the window when fighting a war in the tropics, with the discomfort of heat, sweat, mud and rain, and where mosquitoes and disease were rife.

Diarist Victor Klemperer described the way American soldiers in the Pacific had departed from their official uniform:

> They are not soldiers in the Prussian sense at all. They do not wear uniforms, but overalls or overall-like combinations of high trousers and blouse all in gray-green. The steel helmet is worn as comfortably as a hat, pushed forward or back, as it suits them.

On 22 June 1942, Robert Leckie and the 1st Marine Division were shipped out from San Francisco to the South Pacific. Disembarking on Guadalcanal's white palm-lined beaches, they were immediately thrown into battle as enemy aircraft scored across the sky and fired down onto the island.

As they made their way across rivers, clambered up rainforest-clad hills and through fields of kunai grass, their dungarees were soaked with sweat, clinging to their skin, and sweat trickled down their heads from under their helmets. Then the rain fell, and they were 'hunched in our ponchos' eating the rations from their packs, 'each man to himself alone, but all afloat on a dark sea of the night', wrote Leckie.

The 1st Marine Division wore their hot, heavy ponchos over their equipment and weapons, and at night to ward off the mosquitoes. Later, once they were issued with mosquito nets, they slept on their poncho on the ground, or over them if it was raining:

> The mosquito nets were a boon. Now we could use our blankets to sleep on, rather than to guard our head against mosquitoes. The poncho could be rolled up for a pillow; if it rained, it went over us. But the nets really came too late. We were full of malaria.

After a ferocious battle, the marines went back to where the bodies of the Japanese lay in clusters, picking souvenirs from them, such as bayonets and field glasses. One marine used a pair of pliers to remove the gold fillings from their teeth and stored them in a tobacco sack which he wore around his neck like an amulet. He earned the nickname 'Souvenirs'. At night, the Marines could hear the crocodiles crunching on the bodies that lay floating in the river. They covered themselves in their blankets to try to block out the smell of decaying flesh.

Like the British troops in Burma, the marines felt like forgotten orphans. Leckie wrote in his memoirs:

> All of America's millions doing the same things each day: going to movies, getting married, attending college commencements, sales meetings, café fires, newspaper drives against vivisection, political oratory, Broadway hits and Broadway flops, horrible revelations in high places and murders in tenements making tabloid headlines, vandalism in cemeteries and celebrities getting religion; all the same, all, all, all, the changeless, daily America – all of this was going on without a single thought for us. This was how we thought. It seems silly, now.

A marine nicknamed Red protected himself from the heat and humidity and gunfire by withdrawing under his helmet, keeping it pushed down over his eyes. 'He wore it always,' wrote Leckie:

> He wore it for fear of the heat and for fear of the bombs. He slept with it on. He bathed with it on. It was not uncommon to see him, standing in the middle of the stream near E Company's lines to our rear, his body ridiculously white – his helmet on!

Leckie and his friends became fixated with removing it from his head and came up with a plan to knock it off and riddle it with bullets. When Red saw what they had done to it, instead of getting angry, tears came to his eyes. They thought he would laugh, but instead he ran to the aid station in tears, waiting there until a new helmet was found for him. 'When he did, his manner was more distant than ever and his chin strap was never again undone.'

When Leckie's father sent a letter to let his son know his Marine dress blues, worn for formal occasions, had finally arrived and asked if he should send it out him, it caused great amusement amongst Leckie's buddies. As they wolfed down their dinner, they made quips, 'Hi'ya, Lucky – where's yer blues?' or 'Hey, Lucky, yer old man send you the blues yet?' The thought of that marine blue uniform was comical because it was so far removed from the reality of serving in the Pacific. 'I squatted, clothed only in trousers cut off at the knee and a pair of moccasins stolen from an army duffle bag and I contemplated this vision of glory.'

After five months on Guadalcanal, suffering from malaria, depression and dysentery, they were finally given the word they were to be replaced by the 8th Marine Regiment. They had been given the nickname the 'Hollywood Marines', but on arrival looked miserable in their Kelly helmets, 'the kind which our fathers wore in the First World War'.

For Americans like Sam Lionel Boylston, the South Pacific was different from anything ever experienced. As an illustrator, he would send unique letters home with envelopes decorated with amusing cartoons that would make his parents laugh before they even opened the letter. His pictures featured GIs in summer khaki and fantasy native girls in grass skirts. He wrote of the novelty of picking bananas, being entertained by Bob Hope and 'three girl performers!', and watching movies in the outdoor cinema, 'I guess that's one thing to be proud of, for the boys in 1918 didn't have that,' he said.

Sam, his younger brother Raymond and parents lived in Stieffeltown, South Carolina, with his mother running the restaurant and his father the filling station for a textile company called Graniteville Company. Sam graduated from high school in 1940, and attended the University of South Carolina for two years, before having to drop out in 1942 when he was called up to join the Medical Corps in 13th Army Air Force. After training at Camp Grant, he was shipped to Espiritu Santo in the New Hebrides Islands in August 1943. The 13th Army Air Force was known as the 'Jungle Air Force' as it served the Pacific islands and covered hundreds of miles. Sam was then stationed in Guadalcanal, where there was still intermittent fighting despite the Americans taking control from the Japanese.

Around 40 to 45 per cent of those in the Pacific saw no action, and for those servicemen, the time was marked by boredom, loneliness and discomfort. They lived in floorless tents with no electric lights and their main sustenance came from tinned foods. To relieve themselves of the heat and humidity, they stripped off their tops and tanned their skin, or sometimes they would have the chance to change into shorts or swimming trunks to cool off.

Being so far away from home, Sam reminisced about the life back in America that he was forced to put on hold because of the war. He told his little brother, 'Maybe when this is over we can go to school together, college, I mean. I'm going to finish that year and a half if it's the last thing I do.' In a letter to his brother in February 1944, he said, 'Today will be a hot one and I will sit and dream of those good ole days when I was in the Drug Store with all that ice cream and nice cold things to drink. Those were the good ole days and I often think about them.'

While Sam was stationed on Guadalcanal, he had the opportunity to visit Australia for two weeks. After many months in the jungle, it was fantastic to see streets and sidewalks, where women strolled in summer dresses. In Brisbane, they were given admission to the luxurious American Red Cross, which featured all the comforts of home. The GIs bought souvenirs to send to their family back home, including toy kangaroos, koala bears, wool blankets and sheepskins.

When the marines first arrived in Melbourne for rest and relaxation, they were given six months of pay in arrears. Discipline quickly eroded as they spent nights getting drunk and fraternising with girls who acted like groupies, despite the dishevelled appearance of the marines, wearing old dungarees and sunburnt skin. They were outfitted in fresh uniforms, including the new green field jackets, which now bore the nickname 'Ike jackets', after General Eisenhower. They were also given New Zealand Army leather boots but, compared with the soft buckskin marine 'boondockers' with crepe rubber soles, these were stiff and heavy and became instruments of torture as they cut up their feet during a long march.

Robert Leckie described how the marines, without their own song, marched to the Australians' 'Waltzing Matilda' and the British 'I've Got Sixpence'. But their singing couldn't take the pain of their boots away, with deep blisters forming on the soles of their feet. The New Zealand boots were never issued again as 'they had come close to ruining the feet of a quarter of the battalion'.

In late September 1943, Leckie and the 1st Division Marines marched from their camp to the docks where they boarded onto ships to be sent back to the war in the Pacific. They were cheered off by groups of Australian women, who were also waiting for the next boat of GIs to arrive. The men pulled out their leftover condoms from their pockets, inflated them and sent them like balloons from the ship deck towards the shore.

Finschhafen in New Guinea was covered in lush, wet rainforest and the constant rain caused letters and packs of cigarettes to disintegrate, pocket knives to rust, rifle barrels to fill with mould and socks to become unwearable. The damp of the forest eventually reclaimed everything and permeated clothes with the smell of rotting vegetation. The main concern of a soldier living in these conditions was to be dry and out of the rain.

They trekked through the jungle in complete silence so as not to be heard by the enemy. Their canteens, knives and ammunitions were secured so as not to make a noise, not even a cigarette could be lit, and their weapons were carried close to their chests, ready to be deployed in an instant. They were attacked by groups of Japanese soldiers, who were easily defeated by the better-equipped Americans. Again, the marines searched the bodies of the dead, taking their souvenirs – the Japanese insignia from the tunics, any rings on fingers, pistols and the gold teeth.

After battle, the beach was scattered with naked marines as they washed their clothes in the ocean, scrubbing them clean against the sand, wringing them out and drying them in the sun. They put on damp clothes, hoping their body would finish drying them before the rains hit again. 'The war was forgotten,' wrote Leckie:

> The day was but twenty-four hours and the mind had but two or three things to command it, objects like dryness, food – oh, most of all, most unbelievably of all, a cup of hot coffee – a clean, dry pair of pants and a place out of the rain!

When new replacement men arrived, they agreed to swap their shiny new khaki for the sun-bleached, salty uniforms of the veterans, as it had the sense of experience in it:

> An insecure replacement would feel more confident clothed in the faded ensigns of 'the old breed', while the veterans, having no psychological problem of 'belonging' to distort their sense of value, were quick to sense a sucker. Within a few days, the change was so complete that the veteran who could formerly be recognized by his lusterless garb was now identified by its shiny newness.

After falling ill with pains in his abdomen, Leckie was evacuated to the army base at Cape Sudest in New Guinea. The nurse who treated him was the first woman he had seen in six months, and he spent pleasant days in hospital sleeping in pyjamas, reading, watching movies and eating three good meals a day.

American nurses were stationed throughout the Pacific to treat injured men. Sally Hitchcock Pullman arrived in Dutch-owned New Guinea and noted how the Melanesians had modified the army uniform, as they were dressed in 'the most brilliant yellow and purple shirts … we later learned these were GI shirts dyed with the commonly used drugs gentian violet and atabrine'. She also recounted how nurses adapted their standard-issue equipment to suit the equatorial heat, rain, mud and humidity of New Guinea.

They had pillowcases but no pillows, so they improvised by stuffing them with clothing, and instead of showers and sinks, they used their helmets to bathe in. 'The only trouble is that washing shirts and pants in a helmet is a bit difficult. Life here is a real adventure.'

Sally was made all too aware of racism within the US Army when working in the non-segregated hospital:

> Across from the last patient on the left was a black officer. I crossed to him to do his care when his left-hand neighbour (an officer) said: 'Don't touch me after you've done him!' Such terrible racial prejudice! I was shocked. The ward was suddenly silent. I turned to him and said, 'I won't!' I did special care to the black officer and skipped the offending person. I was angry. I could have made a speech but didn't. I went right up the right-hand row of beds and finished. How terribly unfair and unkind and small!! Next afternoon I had the same assignment. There were no comments from anyone and I did everything with no comments. At this time I was unaware that there was so much segregation and discrimination in the Army, I only knew about the Navy.

On Pavuvu, there was no water except for what the soldiers caught in their helmets at night. They washed their naked bodies in the rain and cleaned their clothes by boiling them in cans of rainwater. To prevent their feet from rotting in the wet, they assigned an appointed time each day to take off their shoes and socks and dry out their feet in the sun.

After visiting Banika, the 'Broadway' of the Pacific with sleek sailors, nurses and PX canteens, Leckie had the uneasy feeling that it would be the image of Banika and not Pavuvu that would be presented to America as the Pacific War, '… ah Banika! There was glamor for you. This was war in the Pacific. This was what America would hear'.

The final battle of the 1st Marines Division was devastating to the original veterans of the campaign, wiping many of them out as they struggled to fight in the unrelenting heat, without adequate water. Many were killed, and after being caught in a blast and seriously injured, Leckie was evacuated and hospitalised.

For troops in the Pacific, there were outdoor movie screenings at night, where the men sat on whatever they could – logs, boxes, bomb crates, drums and wooden benches. The movies offered a reminder of home and the chance to relax, and were vital for morale. Bob Hope brought his USO show to Pavuvu in August 1944, and it was one of the fondest memories of the war for those who attended it.

Sometimes the Pacific had moments of wonder. 'Tonight it's another one of those nights when the old moon comes out in all its glory and it's as bright as day outside,' Sam wrote in April 1945:

> From here, I can see the silver lining on the coconut palms and see the moon shining through the leaves ... I can hear the crickets singing their little tunes but over here they sound more like a telegraph operator ... In the distance, I can hear the generator humming away and the music coming from the movie.

Sam's ship landed in San Francisco in December 1945, where they lived aboard the ship for three weeks. Sam painted a large banner that was hung over the side of the ship which stated, 'Members of the 13th Army Air Force – The Jungle Air Force', with a large insignia. Finally, train transportation was arranged for the long journey across the United States to Fort Gordon, Georgia, where he was discharged.

20

Paris Under Occupation

'The Paris spring season in 1939, before the war, was the gayest I had yet seen,' wrote Bettina Ballard, Parisian correspondent for *Vogue*:

> There were garden parties or big cocktail parties every day and balls or some sort of spectacle every night for all of June and well into July … I danced until dawn, slept a few hours, made a token appearance at the office (after all, going out was part of my *Vogue* job), stopped in at the hairdresser's to be combed for the evening or into Suzy's to borrow a feathered head-dress, and then I would start all over again.

In summer 1939 in Paris, war seemed inevitable and there were worries of air raids sending clouds of poison gas onto the city, yet Parisians continued to sit at the sidewalk cafés, dressed up for costume balls and swayed to jazz musicians like Django Reinhardt in the dive bars at Pigalle and Montmartre.

American actress Drue Leyton was in Marseille when war was declared on 3 September 1939. Drue had met husband Jacques Tartière in New York in 1937, where she was working in a musical, and she moved to France with this 'good-looking, tall man … six years younger than I'. Not long after, he would be killed fighting with the Free French in Syria, and she would become an important figure in the Resistance.

On the announcement of war, they headed back to Paris as quickly as possible in a 'train jammed with soldiers who looked pitifully ill-equipped for the ordeal they were going to endure. Many of them wore carpet slippers in place of boots.' The French Army was unprepared and inadequately outfitted, with many dressed in old uniforms from the First World War.

To be prepared, citizens were instructed to pick up their own gas masks from the police station. Just as had happened in Britain, the cases for the masks became an expression of fashion. Some were covered in satin, or made from leather, and Jeanne Lanvin sold her own 180-franc version. Designers also began incorporating military touches such as braid and tassels to coats in response to the war. Fashion magazines offered tips on how to knit balaclavas and jumpers to keep warm over the winter, or to send to soldiers. With shortages of fuel, bicycles became the most popular mode of transport. By 1943, there were 2 million bicycles on the streets of Paris and fashions were shaped around making it easier to cycle.

Elsa Schiaparelli created a stylish cycling costume, with skirts over bloomers, jackets with big pockets and fedora hats. Yet, while some kept going in Paris, the designer Mainbocher returned to America and designed the uniform for the WAVES and Coco Chanel closed down her business, with the exception of her perfume. It continued to be sold at her boutique on Rue Cambon, and would become a souvenir much sought after by the Germans.

Life in Paris initially continued as normally as possible, despite cafés and bars shutting at 11 p.m. every night. Bettina recalled:

> Small dinners in private houses became popular; Maxim's was jammed and had a speakeasy atmosphere with the blackout curtains drawn, holding in the noise and the smoke. Guests checked their gas masks at first and then they gave the whole thing up. I had given up my car and bought a bicycle, on which I rode to and from work, across the Place de la Concorde and up the Champs Élysées.

Edna Chase, American *Vogue*'s editor in chief, instructed Bettina to report back to New York and file stories on how smart women were adapting to air-raid shelters and war work. Bettina said:

> I recorded that slacks had not yet been seen on the Paris streets, but that they were acceptable now in cold country châteaux, that white gloves were worn at night as a practical means of making protective gestures when crossing the blackened streets. I rather frowned on such special war fashions as Hermes leather gas-mask cases.

There were noticeable changes to the city – women driving taxis and buses, at a time in French history when women didn't have the vote and couldn't own property without their father or husband's permission. Sandbags were piled up to protect the city's statues and monuments in the event of an air raid, and men had been called up and sent out of the city to military training camps.

However, this calm feeling came to an end when Paris fell to the Germans on 14 June 1940. The Nazi's daily newspaper, *Völkischer Beobachter*, declared, 'Paris was a city of frivolity and corruption, of democracy and capitalism … That Paris will never rise again.'

The city was deadly quiet, as 2 million people had already escaped the city as the Germans approached. There was a blackout and 9 p.m. curfew, and the bars, cafés and nightclubs were shut down. The city was placed in the same time zone as Berlin and the Reichsmark was introduced, immediately making it cheap for the occupiers but expensive for the locals. German troops acted like tourists, carrying cameras and taking snaps of the sights, like Notre-Dame, the Arc de Triomphe and the Eiffel Tower, and sending home silk stockings and perfume to their families.

Winter 1940, the first of the occupation, was harsh, as the Nazis plundered France of food and warm clothing and sent all furs to Germany to make winter clothes for the troops. The leading ateliers in Paris continued to fulfil the orders for their fashions, and with a textile industry that employed thousands of sewers and cutters and milliners, it was important to keep the industry moving. Couturier-designed clothing was far outside the budget of most women, who took to making their own clothes in imaginative ways and 'only collaborators could afford to dress well,' said Drue Tartière.

At first the frivolity of fashion quietened, but then women once again emerged in even more elaborate hats, turbans and velvet snoods. Turbans may have been fashionable accessory for women throughout the 1930s, but during the Second World War in France they took on a whole new level of meaning for women under Nazi occupation and the Vichy Government. The turban, basically a twisted scarf, was practical for helping women keep their hair back when working, but it also allowed a colourful expression of style within limited means, when clothing during the war was hard to source. Turbans could be made out of scraps of fabric, or built up with other salvaged materials, such as cork, cardboard or feathers. Davis, a popular Parisian milliner, created the 'brown turban', which was a readily formed turban made from brown felt.

These confections would become a symbol of French spirit. Rather than the sense of duty that British and American women felt in following the rules of rationing and austerity, women in France, suffering so much under the Nazis, used fashion to resist and to rebel. 'The Parisian women,' according to Elsa Schiaparelli, 'as if feeling it was their last chance, were particularly chic.'

Three months into the occupation, France had been stripped of its resources – energy supplies, leather, fabrics – as anything with value was being sent to the German front. Even hairdressers were ordered to send all their cuttings to Germany to fill pillows for the army. But, rather than give in, French women believed, as *Vogue* magazine had instructed British women, that 'their duty is in beauty'. Lips were slashed with crimson, and the common fashion for women in Paris was a knee-length, nipped-in dress or skirt in bright colours, high platform shoes built up from wood or cork, stockings if possible or a pencilled leg seam if not, and an elaborate confection balanced precariously on the head. Silk stockings could cost 300 francs on the black market, and so Elizabeth Arden created an iodine dye in three different shades of flesh for the silk stocking effect.

The magazine *L'Officiel de la Mode* showcased even more elaborate hats in 1943 as the war progressed. They were constructed from satin and chenille, covered in ribbons or piled high with fabric daffodils, leaves and berries, or great plumes of ostrich feathers. One of the most prolific hat designers during the war was Madame Agnés, who worked from her salon on Faubourg Saint-Honoré, and 'made do' with string if she ran low on felt, silk or straw, or structured them around pieces of cardboard.

If a parachute was found in a field, abandoned by airmen, it could be collected and used to make blouses or cami-knickers. Warm coats were made from the scraps of old ones, and fabric was wrapped around the head to disguise unwashed hair in the face of soap shortages. Drue Tartière recalled, 'The people on these trains were now looking very shabby and, since there was a great shortage of soap, the smells in the train were almost overpowering.'

Christian Dior lamented Paris's wartime fashions as being clunky and ugly. 'Hats were far too large, skirts far too short, jackets far too long, shoes far too heavy,' he lamented. 'And worst of all there was that dreadful mop of hair raised high above the forehead in front and rippling down the backs of French women on their bicycles.' But what he didn't take into account was that the clothing was acting as a form of resistance.

German propaganda described Parisian women as powdered and painted, with looser morals than the young German women, yet they could never be as chic as the French. Fräuleins in Paris wore a grey uniform with a stripe on the shoulder, which earned them the nickname *Blitzmädchen*, *Blitzweiben* or the 'Grey Mice'.

Some Parisian women found the German soldiers to be polite and cultured, and it could be beneficial to be civil to them, even if it was to acquire food through sex. Micheline Bood began socialising with the Germans in May 1942. She described meeting a German soldier in a white linen jacket, 'like Lohengrin', with a shining eagle emblem, and although the other soldiers saluted him, 'the women, the *Blitzweiben* or little Grey Mice, scowled at us'.

Over the winter of 1943, women in France took to reading *Gone with the Wind*, which had been translated into French and resonated with the theme of hardships during war. With many Parisian women being arrested or executed for challenging the regime or taken away to concentration camps for their Jewish heritage, residents felt completely helpless under this terror. But, as well as joining the French Resistance, there were non-verbal actions for defying the occupation. They could wear the red, white and blue of the tricolor using ceramic buttons or rosettes, or a victory emblazoned in studs on belts, and then cycle around the city to embrace their freedom as much as they could.

The Nazi Party, in response to noticing the defiant meaning in these clothes and hats, tried to control fashion, and one way was to ensure that milliners showed their hats to a review board, as the Germans recognised how these hats had become a 'psychological weapon'. But it was no use – women were making turbans and hats for themselves, from whatever pieces of scraps they could find.

Spring Wind was the July 1942 operation to arrest Jews in Paris, to satisfy the orders of the Germans. In June 1942, all French Jews over the age of 6 were ordered to wear a yellow star, with '*Juif*' written inside it, on their outer clothing. Three cloth badges used a month's worth of textile rations and they had to be collected from police stations. People were desperate to get out the city, crammed into train stations, dressed in big coats over pyjamas, in case they had to escape their homes quickly and hide from the Gestapo.

During the German occupation, the British symbol 'V' for victory began to appear on the walls of Paris. In Paris cafés, on the news of America joining the war, brawls inevitably broke out when young Frenchmen, after a few drinks, went up to German soldiers and shouted, 'Ha, ha! *Kaput!*' At this time, swing was the sound of joyous symbolism, with '*Etes-Vous Swing?*' and '*Mon Heure de Swing*' becoming hit songs. Like the hippies, who would proclaim 'You can't trust anyone over thirty', a group of teenage swing fans, who called themselves 'Ultra Swings' dressed to shock. Swing was a way of cutting loose, listening to Johnny Hess's '*Je Suis Swing*', and embracing American fashions and English slang.

The Ultra Swings enjoyed British and American novels, they collected vinyl, smoked Lucky Strikes and drank beer with grenadine syrup in the cellar bars of the Latin Quarter. They took after Cab Calloway with their pegged pants with baggy knees, oversized check jackets, high English collars covered with hair, a pompadour, pencil moustaches and dark glasses, key chains hanging from their belts. The girls wore short skirts, baggy roll-neck sweaters, boxy jackets, necklaces around their waists, bright red lipstick, long curled hair and stacked soles. Calloway also inspired their new name, the *zazou*, which came from Calloway's '*zah zuh zah*' slang in the 1930s.

With the introduction of the yellow star for Jews, the *zazou* created their own star to show solidarity. In the centre of the star was the word 'swing'. When the French Government announced that hair should be collected from barbers to be made into slippers or to stuff into pillows for German soldiers, the *zazou* grew their hair and refused to have it cut, and as a response to clothes rationing, they wore oversized suits, much like the zoot-suiters. It was provocation, choosing to ignore the rules of the occupying forces in an act of non-violent rebellion.

Mike Zwerin wrote, in *Swing Under the Nazis*:

The *Zazous* were fond of kitsch, which involves unmasking pretentiousness and elevating mediocrity to an art form. Pétain's Vichy was classic kitsch. Hitler's moustache was kitsch. Chamberlain umbrellas and bowler hats were kitsch. Wearing a yellow star was kitsch if you were not Jewish.

Simone de Beauvoir, writing at the Café de Flore in 1942, observed the *zazou* style that she saw on display, and was impressed by the creativity and uniformity:

The young men wore dirty drape suits with 'drainpipe' trousers under their sheep-skinned lined jackets and brillianted liberally their long hair, the girls favored tight roll-collar sweaters with short flared skirts and wooden platform shoes, sported dark glasses with big lenses, put on heavy make-up and went bare-headed to show their dyed hair, set off by a lock of different hue.

A 1942 article by Roger Baschet in *L'Illustration* magazine described their long hair, outrageous suits, the index finger in the air and he called them '*Nouveau Dandy*'. He described how their rebellion was a symptom of troubled times; just like the *Merveilleuses* after the French Revolution.

The jazz scene had flourished in Paris between the wars, and African-American artists found they were welcome in the city, compared with the discrimination they faced at home. There was also a North African community centred around the Latin Quarter, and it was here that the music scene grew.

Django Reinhardt, a Romani traveller who was raised in a caravan and learnt to play the banjo for money, was one of the leading figures in the Paris jazz scene, finding fame in the clubs of Montmartre. He formed the *Quintette du Hot Club de France* in 1934, where he introduced the guitar as the lead instrument. The band was in London the day war broke out and, with searchlights in the sky and air-raid sirens blaring, it felt immediately threatening. Django took a train to Paris that night, 'You're less afraid at home'.

The city was dangerous for Django after the Nazis swept in, as the Romani were sent to concentration camps or forced to work as slave labour. When he tried to escape from occupied France he was captured, and after being saved by a jazz-loving German officer, he was sent back to Paris to entertain German troops.

Belgian saxophonist and bandleader, Fud Candrix described Django:

He loved shiny things. When he was in Brussels during the war, he walked around town wearing a cowboy hat, a red scarf with white polka dots, white leather shoes and a shiny bright blue suit. Obviously everybody stared at him, but he did not do these things to attract attention. He was just like a child wearing a costume. It was a game to him. Life was a game to him.

After America entered the war, the Nazis cracked down on American culture in Paris, closing down the cafés on Boulevard St Michel and banning dance parties, to prevent the *zazous* from gathering. Yet, the more the Vichy Government tried to stifle them, the more they thrived, and they still gathered at the Pam-Pam Café on the Champs-Élysées to show off their style – high-collared shirt, short, straight trousers to show off primary-colour socks and crepe-soled shoes, and slick, long hair.

The Vichy Government encouraged right-wing youth movements to counteract them. In spring 1942 the *Jeunes Populaires Français*, under their leader Jacques Doriot, stormed through Boulevard St Michel in their blue shirts and black ties, attacking those who looked like *zazous* and shaving their heads to the cry of 'Scalp the *Zazous!*' 'You will be hard, you will be strong, you will be violent, but you will be correctly dressed,' said Doriot.

The Nazis introduced forced labour drafts for those over 18 in October 1942, and young men could be sent to Germany if discovered out in public. The police would raid a *zazou* café and round them up for questioning.

They would be forced to have a haircut and could be sent to the countryside to work on the harvest.

Because of the dangerous atmosphere, the *zazous* quietened the way they dressed. Writer and journalist Jean-Louis Bory, who was a *zazou* when living in the Latin Quarter, said, 'We had to regroup amongst ourselves to avoid getting our faces smashed.' Some went underground, joining the Resistance and cutting their hair themselves in order to avoid detection.

Yet, the *zazou* look was being replicated in other occupied cities. Svend Asmussen, the Danish jazz violinist, opened a jazz club in Copenhagen called 'My Blue Heaven', which was popular with swing fans and German officers; and in Germany an underground swing scene was defying the rules of the Nazi Party.

21

Resistance in Nazi Germany

In September 1934, American journalist William L. Shirer, a correspondent in Berlin, wrote in his diaries of the cultural changes under the Third Reich, compared with the experimental, liberal 1920s of the Weimar Republic. 'I miss the old Berlin of the Republic,' he said:

> The care-free, emancipated, civilized air, the snub-nosed young women with short-bobbed hair and the young men with either cropped or long hair – it made no difference – who sat up all night with you and discussed anything with intelligence and passion. The constant Heil Hitler's, clicking of heels, and brown-shirted storm troopers or black-coated S.S. guards marching up and down the street grate me …

Berlin in the 1920s was a decadent, cultured city. Opera, theatre and concerts thrived alongside an underbelly of burlesque and nightclubs playing the latest import from America – hot jazz, which the Weimar Republic considered a bold symbolism of modernity. Despite the freedom of this decade, racism simmered under the surface. While Josephine Baker's performances offered titillation and a sense of exoticism at a safe distance, those from African colonies were treated as second-class citizens.

In 1932, the conservative chancellor Franz von Papen declared that black musicians could not be hired by any venues, and in response British and American musicians began to leave the country due to creeping xenophobia. After Hitler came to power, rights were gradually squeezed from those not considered to be 'pure'. The Blood Laws of 1935 declared Jews, blacks and gypsies to be racially undesirable, and in 1937 mixed race children of French colonials living in the Rhine were forcibly sterilised. In Berlin, in April 1937,

William Shirer wrote, 'The shadow of Nazi fanaticism, sadism, persecution, regimentation, terror, brutality, suppression, militarism, and preparation for war has hung over all our lives, like a dark, brooding cloud that never clears.'

By the time war broke out, there was little space for dissenting voices, as the country was completely militarised. People lived in fear of hearing the squeaking leather coats and heavy boots of the feared military police, *Schutzstaffel* (SS). Up to 800,000 Germans were imprisoned for resisting, including communists and social democrats. But Otto Jung, who founded the Hot Club of Frankfurt, said, 'Generally the German people were for the Nazis. They turned against them only when they began to fail.'

The uniform and pageantry of the National Socialist regime had, in the early 1930s, impressed people who were desperate following the devastating economic crash. Hitler brought colour to drab lives and restored a sense of patriotic pride when he defied the Versailles Treaty by building up army divisions and weaponry.

Youth lay at the heart of the Hitler movement. The loyal *Sturmabteilung*, known as the SA, and translated as the 'Storm Detachment', fought and punched to defend their Führer, dressed in brown shirts, Sam Browne belts and brown breeches tucked into boots. This early thuggery was shut down by the black-shirted SS in 1934, but they went on to be given top jobs in Hitler's cabinet when he swept to power.

The SS were modelled after the shape of the classic Greek statue, tall and strong, with broad shoulders, and their uniform was designed to create the sense of one whole mass – a ripple of force and power, that everyone would want to be part of. The infantry soldier, in grey/green, wore trousers like those of horse-riding sportsmen. They were decorated with arm and cuff bands, swords and daggers, and belt buckles with the Nazi emblem, which would be much sought after by American troops as souvenirs.

Heinrich Himmler, leader of the SS, was said to have been inspired by the Jesuits to create the fearsome black uniform with white skulls, and there was something about Cromwell's Ironsides that was an inspiration for their intimidation and evil deeds. The leather, worn on motorbikes and used for their gloves and trench coats, also suggested sadomasochism. As described in George Orwell's *1984*, they were 'solid men in black uniforms, with iron-shod boots on their feet and truncheons in their hands'.

When the Third Reich came into power in 1933, the *Wandervogel*, a peaceful organisation that encouraged hiking and camping, became the basis for the National Socialist ideology. Boys and girls between the ages of 10 and 14 enrolled in the *Jungvolk* ('Young Folk') and *Jungmädel* ('Young Maidens');

from the age of 14 to 18 years, boys enrolled in the Hitler Youth and girls joined the *Bund der Deutschen Mädchen* ('League of German Girls'), or BDM. When groups like the Boy Scouts were banned, the Hitler Youth rose to almost 4 million by 1935. Jews, of course, were excluded.

Hitler said:

> Weakness must be stamped out. The world will shrink in terror from the youngsters who grow up in my fortresses. A violent, masterful, dauntless and cruel younger generation – that is my goal. There must be nothing weak and soft about them. Their eyes must glow once more with the freedom and splendour of the beast of prey.

The year 1936 was designated 'The Year of the German *Jungvolk*' the age was lowered for those born in 1926 to now be eligible to join. By the end of the year, membership in the Hitler Youth was compulsory, and as young people became more and more indoctrinated, liberal parents worried that their own children might turn them in for speaking out against the government. On 20 April 1940, Hitler's birthday, it became compulsory for all German youths between the ages of 10 and 18 to join the Hitler Youth.

As in Paris, on the first night of war, the cafés, restaurants and beer halls of Berlin were crowded with people who hoped for normality, but were nervous about the expected air raids. Life seemed normal for those who weren't in fear of being arrested, with operas such as *Madame Butterfly* and revues at Hitler's favoured venue, The Metropol, continuing as usual.

One of the most popular books to read at the time was the German-translated *Gone with the Wind* and *Beyond Sing the Woods*, an international wartime bestseller by Norwegian Trygve Gulbranssen. American movies were selling more tickets in cinemas than the German ones, with Clark Gable in *China Seas* top of the box office in October 1939.

As the Germans pushed into France and the BEF were making a desperate retreat in Dunkirk, the people of Berlin continued to stroll on the *Kurfürstendamm*, one of the most elegant streets in the city. The city remained untouched by air raids and on the avenue pavement cafés were serving up coffees and ice creams to the smartly dressed crowds who were enjoying the good weather.

The expectation in Germany, following the fall of France, was that the swastika would be flying over Trafalgar Square by mid-August 1940. There was food rationing and clothes shortages in Germany, but the artful use of propaganda created a deception to fool both its citizens and enemies.

It was a serious offence to listen to a foreign radio station, particularly BBC London, which broadcast a weekly list of German prisoners. One mother of a missing airman received letters from friends who told her they had heard on the BBC that her son was alive but captured, and in return she denounced all these friends to the police.

There were harsh penalties for anyone who spoke out against the war in Germany and in the countries it now occupied. In November 1939, nine students from the University of Prague were shot by firing squad for staging anti-German demonstrations, and in Germany two youths were sentenced to death for a theft from the home of a soldier. No race mixing was permitted, and Himmler announced that a Polish farmworker was hanged for sleeping with a German woman. Poles working in Germany were forced to wear an armband containing a purple letter 'P' on a yellow background on their coat.

According to Shirer, there were secret jokes in Germany doing the rounds: 'An airplane carrying Hitler, Goering and Goebbels crashes. All three are killed. Who is saved? Answer: The German people.' But even casual jokes or a sarcastic remark about Hitler or the war was considered anti-German, and treasonous.

Despite the attempt at the complete indoctrination of young people in Nazi Germany, not all of the youth fell into line. Between 1940 and 1945, 1,807 inmates were executed in the Brandenburg Prison alone for political reasons, some after years of forced labour – seventy-five were under 20 years of age; and twenty-two were high-school pupils or university students. In Hamburg, between 1933 and 1945, of all those sentenced for political crimes 11 per cent were youths.

The Second World War was called the Golden Age of Jazz, and for young people it acted as a way of rebelling against the German authorities, who detested American music. Jazz came to represent the anger and resentment of Occupied Europe's younger generation, who were otherwise voiceless and powerless against war and repression.

It also inspired people in other countries. Roosje Glaser was a Dutch Jewish dance instructor whose blonde looks allowed her to flout Nazi laws. Sometimes wearing the saddle shoes and bobby socks of the swing style, or completely glamorous in long gowns, she refused to wear her yellow star, and kept on dancing during occupation. Eventually betrayed and sent to a concentration camp, she used her charm and skills on the Nazi guards by teaching them to dance.

In Germany, a group of middle-class German teenagers known as *Swingjugend* or *Swing Kinder* (they referred to themselves as *Swingheinis*), wore clothing inspired by British dress – homburg hats and suits, a Union Jack pin attached to their jackets and an umbrella in hand, even when it wasn't raining.

The boys rejected the short, military haircuts that would be imposed on them in the Hitler Youth, and instead wore it long. The girls' Hollywood-inspired style – pleated skirts, silk stockings, blouses and waved hair rather than the traditional German braid – was at odds with the traditional way women were expected to dress in Nazi Germany.

Jutta Hipp joined the Leipzig Hot Club in 1940. She would sneak downstairs to listen to foreign radio, noting down the melodies. She said, 'I used to wear blue silk stockings with a red seam, red heart on the knee, and as teenagers do, wanting to be different, would walk a whole block backwards to see if anyone gets upset and then smile at them.'

Otto Jung, who discovered swing in 1938, corresponded with a Berlin jazz fan, Hans Bluthner, as they were both purists who only liked the instrumental versions. 'Jazz meant more than just music to us during the war,' Otto said. His father regularly invited Jewish musicians to their house and listened to foreign radio. The maid informed the Gestapo on him and he spent four months in prison.

In 1941, Otto and Hans formed the Hot Club of Frankfurt. They wore blue shirts and white ties, they had long hair, and chose the English style; 'to look as different from the military as possible', said Otto. Every so often, they would be ordered to get a haircut by the SS.

Their blue shirts and white ties clashed with the brown and black of the Hitler Youth, who they regularly fought on the streets. Hans Bluthner later recalled, 'I always said that had it not been for jazz, I would have died during the war. It gave me so much happiness and hope. It proved to me that I was not a German but a member of humanity.'

From its founding days, the Third Reich was threatened by jazz, as it was expressive, individual and improvised, originating in African-American culture, and in direct opposition to the regulation and strict uniformity of the Nazis. Jewish jazz composers like Benny Goodman and George Gershwin were denounced by the SS.

In the thirties the German right wing saw jazz music as dangerously sexual and corrupting to Nordic cultures. Eugenicists, who were gaining traction amongst Fascist supporters, argued that Africans had a lack of sexual control, which was evident in the music. Jazz, they thought, was the rot of society, along with communism and modern art. In the summer of 1937, Goebbels held an exhibition, '*Haus der Deutschen Kunst*' ('House of German Art') and it featured a room a room called 'degenerate art'. This attracted larger crowds than the other exhibits, as people were drawn to the jazz posters. When Hitler became Chancellor of the German Reich in January 1933, he continued their support for the banning of jazz, along with modern and abstract art. Instead, he promoted neoclassicism, including German composers like Wagner and Bach.

Swing musicians were dragged off stage by agents if they didn't have the appropriate cards. Many made the decision to flee overseas, and those who didn't escape were eventually sent to concentration camps. Here, they could perhaps extend their lives by playing in camp orchestras, providing a soundtrack to the screams in the gas chambers.

Despite attempts to repress it, swing was the musical phenomenon of 1937 and it became the cult dance among German youths. The *New York Times* reported:

> Swing is the thing in Germany. At least in Hamburg and Berlin, where there are modernistic night clubs and imported jazz bands, the fashionable young German women and men do their dancing to swing music. With the rhythm of Harlem hoofers they keep time to the band, and en masse they look like many puppets, each jerked by a separate set of wires.

By 1938 it was reported in American papers that Nazi leaders 'declared today that swing music may be fit for Negroes and Jews, but not for us Germans'. In Berlin, signs were posted up to warn that swing was forbidden, and to demonstrate the correct waltz-like dance.

A swing scene also flourished in Hamburg, made up of almost exclusively middle-class teens, with enough disposable cash to afford swing records and to wear fine, tailored suits. Rather than having come from hot jazz clubs, they met through their membership of sports clubs and exclusive dances. Their image was all-important, and they took great pride and care in what they wore. The boys were wealthy enough to afford custom-tailored suits in Glen check or pin-stripes, crepe-soled shoes, trench coats and white silk scarves. They topped it off with felt or homburg hats.

The swing kids ignored the prohibitions, putting themselves at risk during wartime, but swing was an expression of joy and freedom, in the face of restriction and complete control by the state. Swing was more than a fad, it was about survival and escapism from tyranny, and it became a matter of life and death. By 1939, there were around 100 Hamburg swings, and they used their privileged position to push boundaries. Yet, they also placed their liberal, anti-fascist parents in danger. Hans Hirschfeld's Jewish father owned a chain of clothing shops, and during *Kristallnacht*, Hans was chased and then locked up for some time because of his clothes. His father later died in a concentration camp.

The swing youth met at ice-cream parlours and dance halls, gathered at the Café Heinze or in parks with their suitcase gramophones to play the records of Duke Ellington or Artie Shaw. When they watched Hollywood movies at the Waterloo Cinema, sometimes swings like Tommy Scheel would boo during the newsreels. Scheel later proclaimed: 'We were going to tell those dumb bastards that we were different, that was all.'

In order to show off their clothing to the public, they would regularly stroll down Hamburg's fashionable *Jungfernstieg*, ensuring everyone in rush hour got a good look at their finery. They had their own codes to greet each other with, such as whistling swing tunes or saying, 'Hallo, old swing boy!' They were apolitical at first, considering themselves '*lottern*', meaning lazy, and purely occupied with their love for swing music and fashion, but as compulsory Hitler Youth conscription threatened the swing movement, their passion became more dangerous, especially if they had a Jewish family member or friend.

Demetrius Kaki Georgiadis was considered the leader of Hamburg's swing youth in the late 1930s, and he and his friend Andreas Panagopoulos, both German Cypriots, rejected the Hitler Youth, and instead chose to follow their own path. After discovering swing music, they dressed the part in order to attend dances from 1937. After the crackdown on swing dances in July 1939, they held swing parties in their families' spacious villas and traded records with one another, with Benny Goodman being a particular favourite. The strains of 'Sing, Sing, Sing' could always get a party started. The stars of these parties were Inga and Jutta Madlung, the daughters of a half-Jewish lawyer, who wowed with their perfect Andrews Sisters impressions. Inga Madlung was born in Hamburg in 1920, while Jutta was born in Hamburg in 1921.

Unfortunately, the continual flaunting of the swing youth had triggered the secret police to watch them. In February 1942, all records and performances of jazz were banned and the death penalty was implemented for those caught listening to the radio. However, sometimes Luftwaffe pilots like Wener Molders tuned into the BBC to listen to jazz as they crossed the Channel.

The Nazis were concerned about the swing youth, but it was difficult to crack down on a movement without a clear structure or leader. In 1941, the Third Reich banned dances for those under 21, which ultimately led to teenagers holding secret parties in their parents' homes. The Gestapo raided jazz concerts and terrorised swing fans by detaining them at police stations for days. The first arrests of swing youth took place in October 1940, when Tommy Scheel and Maurice Thomas were brought to the Gestapo headquarters for interrogation. After days of being handcuffed to a filing cabinet and roughed up for not revealing other names in the group, Scheel was sent to a concentration camp for hard labour.

Herr Axmann wrote to Heinrich Himmler, 'This Anglophile swing youth … their activities in the Fatherland could do damage to the German folk tradition … they should be sent to camps, made to work.' Himmler sent the report to Reinhard Heydrich, with a covering note to say, 'the whole evil must be radically eradicated', and at the beginning of 1942 the Gestapo rounded up swing members. Between 1942 and 1944 it is believed that between forty to seventy swings were sent to camps as political prisoners.

In June 1942, Demetrius Kaki Georgiadis organised a party at a country estate, with cocktails in the garden and swing dancing on the lawn. Inside the house, some of the swing youth performed their own impressions of Hitler. However, they were betrayed by a spy within the group who was a member of the Hitler Youth.

Andreas Panagopoulos was arrested in January 1943 and sent to a labour camp to break stones. On his release, he went into hiding in Berlin with his half-Jewish girlfriend. The Madlung sisters were sent to Ravensbrück Concentration Camp, where they stayed for over a year, and where they would perform swing tunes after work or after lights out. In an interview, Jutta Madlung recalled, 'Sometimes at night, after lights out, we were quite precocious and would cover the windows with our bed sheets and then we would sing.'

Inga developed sores from a lack of nutrition and was forced to look at the sun for days at a time, which destroyed 90 per cent of her eyesight. Jutta later gave evidence in the Bergen-Belsen trials that she had been interned 'because of political jokes which I made, because I had a Jewish female friend, and because I had English gramophone records.'

After 1942, youths under the age of 18 were often sent to the youth detention camp at Moringen. Here, the boys were held together as political prisoners and supported one another by singing the popular songs like 'Jeepers, Creepers' and the 'Flat Foot Floogie'. Forced to work at a munitions factory – but outside of SS jurisdiction – they could collectively enjoy swing. Günter Discher remembered, 'The salt mine where we worked had really nice acoustics. One of us played on the cartridges – these were like wooden boxes, and he would play drums with some sticks.' Their fellow prisoners, according to Discher, 'didn't know what to do with swing music. We swings became quickly arrogant and had little contact with the others.'

One of the most powerful figures of the Resistance appeared the most unassuming. Sophie Scholl, a philosophy student at Munich University, looked folksy and innocent with her side-parted bob with a daisy tucked behind her ear, Peter Pan collars and cardigans. Sophie and her brother, Hans, had originally been members of Hitler Youth organisations. But, sickened by the regime, Hans formed the 'White Rose' with a group of Munich medical students, and Sophie joined up too, becoming one of its boldest figures.

In May 1942 Sophie Scholl, just 21 years old, had arrived in Munich to attend university. She wore a pink pullover and brown pleated skirt and no make-up. The only thing that stood out was the white daisy she wore behind her ear. Sophie wasn't too concerned about her looks, but she loved nature. She felt at peace when she was outside, and in this respect, she was very typical of young Germans like the *Wandervogel*, who found a connection with nature on hillwalking and camping trips.

She wrote in her diary of her deep concerns around the regime. 'Many people think of our times as being the last before the end of the world,' she wrote. 'Can I know whether I'll be alive tomorrow morning? A bomb could destroy all of us tonight. And then my guilt would not be one bit less than if I perished together with the earth and the stars.'

Sophie and Hans' father Robert Scholl was reported to the Gestapo by his own secretary after she heard him call Hitler a 'scourge of humanity'. He was arrested but released a short time later. Despite the concerns of his father, Hans joined the Hitler Youth, and his siblings, Sophie, Inge, Elisabeth and Werner, followed, with the girls joining the BDM. The Scholl children were enthralled by the uniform and the torchlight processions and the sense of belonging to an important movement led by young people.

Hans embraced the Hitler Youth at first, and with his charismatic good looks he stood out as a leader. But he still retained his individuality. At the Nuremberg Party Rally of 1936, Hans was selected to carry the banner of his section. However, he began to question his role in this vast machine. He decided to design his own banner for his squad, something that was different and based on myths he enjoyed studying, but this action led to him being stripped of his leadership. As part of the National Labour Service, Hans was sent to work for the compulsory six months building the autobahns. He then entered into military service and in 1940 was ordered to the front line in France as a medic.

Sophie enjoyed the camping and hikes of the Hitler Youth, but her appearance didn't fit. Sophie had a dark brown bob, yet the favoured saying was 'German girls wear braids'. It was the traditional style of the peasant, embraced by the Nazis, who rejected decadent femininity. As part of the war effort, German schoolgirls were expected to bring in the hair from their brushes and combs in order to make felt. Sophie refused to contribute her hair, or sweaters and gloves to the Winter Relief fund for men at the front. She said, 'We have to lose this war. If we donate woollens now, we only contribute to extending it.'

Sophie studied to be a *Kindergarten* teacher in the hope that it would help her to avoid compulsory work in the National Labour Service, but she was still sent for the required six months heavy labour, under the instruction of fanatical Nazi women leaders who tried to strip the women of their identity. She wrote, 'We live like prisoners; not only work but leisure time is turned into duty-hours. Sometimes I want to scream, "My name is Sophie Scholl! Don't you forget it!"'

Hans met Alexander Schmorell, known as 'Shurik' to his friends, when both were training as army medics. They bonded over their hatred of the Nazis and military uniform. Alex was a Russian German from an affluent Munich family, and felt torn between his two backgrounds. He spoke fluent Russian and read Dostoevsky, Gogol and Pushkin, played Russian folk songs on the piano and the *balalaika*. Rather than dressing as the Hitler Youth, Alex preferred an English aristocratic style of riding breeches, boots and turtlenecks, and when caught wearing civilian clothes while serving as a medic in the *Wehrmacht*, he was lucky that his father was influential enough to get him out of trouble.

In the spring of 1942, Alex introduced Hans to Christoph Probst, Traute Lafrenz and Willi Graf and the group made the decision to move from inner resistance to full-out opposition of the Nazi regime. Christoph, a medic with the Luftwaffe, was tall, good looking, clean cut and fashionably smoked a pipe.

Philosophy teacher Dr Kurt Huber was another key player in the White Rose movement and helped to write their leaflets, when Sophie joined the resistance group after arriving at Munich University, and together the group pooled money to buy a second-hand duplication machine and a typewriter. The leaflets of the White Rose began appearing in Munich in June 1942. They were angry literary-cited pamphlets that called for passive resistance, for citizens:

> [to] block the functioning of this atheistic war machine before it is too late, before the last city is a heap of rubble like Cologne, and before the last youth of our nation bleeds to death because of the hubris of a subhuman. Don't forget that each people gets the government it deserves!

The name White Rose was chosen by Hans to represent innocence amongst evil, although Hans would tell the Gestapo that it came from a Spanish novel.

The fourth and last leaflet in 1942, before the group split for summer break, called out, 'We will not be silent. We are your bad conscience. The White Rose will not leave you in peace!' Sophie was sent to a munitions factory over the summer of 1942, working with forced labourers from Russia, while Alex, Hans and Willi were sent to the Russian front as medics. They were horrified at the atrocities they saw being carried out by the German Army, and the hopelessness of the Russia campaign. Hans recounted to his sister Inge that on his return to Germany, he saw a young girl being forced to work on the railway line with the Star of David on her top. She looked terrified, and he tried to give her some of his food rations, but on sight of his uniform, she threw the food on the ground. Instead, he placed a daisy on the packet and placed it at her feet. When he re-boarded the train, he looked back to see the flower tucked in her hair.

Morale was dropping throughout the country as Allied air raids destroyed German cities. Troops didn't have adequate clothing for the winter, and were exhausted from endless fighting on the Russian front. In January 1943, the White Rose reassembled, and distributed 10,000 leaflets in cities across Germany. The group travelled on trains with the leaflets in suitcases, and they would then mail these from different locations in order to cause confusion.

The journeys were dangerous, as they could be pulled up by the military police at any time, so they tried to look unobtrusive and calm in clothes that would draw no attention. Willi Graf took the biggest risk, travelling in his uniform without the right permit and looking conspicuous with his large suitcase.

On 3 February 1943, Germany was defeated by the Russians at Stalingrad. Hans, Alex and Willi marked the occasion by painting red slogans like 'Freedom' and 'Down with Hitler' onto the walls around Munich University under the cloak of darkness. However, the Gestapo was getting closer to the group, and on 18 February 1943, Hans and Sophie carried a large suitcase of leaflets to the university. They placed their flyers on the doors and windowsills of lecture theatres and in the stairways leading to classrooms, but a final decision to scatter them from the upper stairs onto the floor below cost them their lives. They were spotted by a university worker who summoned the Gestapo. At first the interrogators couldn't believe that innocent-looking Sophie was responsible.

Christoph Probst, who had written a draft of an unpublished leaflet, found the Gestapo at his house, and they ordered him to swap his air force uniform for civilian clothes, so that he could not be protected by the military. Willi

Graf was also picked up. Alex tried to escape to Switzerland but had to turn back where he was turned in by a former friend.

Sophie, Hans and Christoph were charged with high treason, but they remained as strong and calm as they could. The trial was set for Monday, 22 February at Munich's Palace of Justice. As Sophie was taken from her cell, she left in her cell her indictment, on which she had scrawled 'Freedom'.

In the packed courtroom, their guilt had already been determined and the judgement handed down. Sophie, in her unobtrusive jacket, blouse and skirt, courageously interrupted proceedings. 'Somebody had to make a start,' she said. 'What we said and wrote are what many people are thinking. They just don't dare say it out loud!'

As soon as they were found guilty, they were led away and taken to a court-yard one by one. It all happened so quickly, and while their parents had been able to see Hans and Sophie, they weren't informed that they would shortly be guillotined. They were led out to a courtyard and executed in turn. As Hans was led away, he called out, 'Long live freedom!' The next day, new graf-fiti appeared on the walls of the university, 'Scholl lives! You can break the body, but never the spirit!'

On 18 April 1943 Americans awoke to the *New York Times* article, 'Nazi Slur Stirred Students' Revolt – Woman, Brother and Another Soldier Beheaded for Issuing Anti-Nazi Tracts'. Americans were now aware that there were dis-senting voices in the Nazi regime. Sophie was named as a philosophy student called Maria Scholl, and the article added, 'When Sergeant Scholl was accused of Communist activities he replied, "I am not a Communist; I am a German".'

Huber and Schmorell were guillotined on 13 July 1943. Willi was kept in solitary confinement for seven months and on 12 October 1943, he was also executed. Falk Harnack, another member of the White Rose, was arrested but later released, as the Gestapo hoped he would lead them to other resistance groups, and after being transferred to the Greece front line, Himmler ordered his arrest. Harnack escaped and joined a partisan fighting group, where he survived the war and became a director.

Hans Leipel, another member of the White Rose in Hamburg and also a swing music fan, had taken up a collection for Kurt Huber's wife and children. As punishment he was beheaded on 29 January 1945, despite never having met Sophie and Hans.

In 1943, Thorsten Muller, a 15-year-old Hamburg swing fan, became involved in the White Rose resistance movement. He was due to be trans-ported to Moringen Concentration Camp, but made his escape during an air raid. He went on the run through Germany and Poland, until he was eventu-ally caught by the Gestapo. He was put on trial for treason, where he proudly confessed his love for the BBC and for jazz. Just as he was about to be sentenced to death, Hamburg was liberated, and his life was saved. Thorsten said:

> The swing music was the first step on my way to resistance. So, later a Gestapo man said to me, when he saw me for the second time: 'Agh, this I could have promised you. Your kind of high treason began with a tune by Duke Ellington and ends with a plot against the Führer.' I think he was right, I think he was right. The swing music was my first step on this way. And finally, I got involved with a resistance group called the White Rose.

There were also 'good' Nazis who spoke the language of jazz. In the winter of 1944, Luftwaffe Oberleutnant Dietrich Schulz-Koehn was one of the 100,000 soldiers cut off in Brittany by the Americans. As they encountered one another, they began to converse, and an African-American officer who admired Schulz-Koehn's Rolleiflex camera asked how much it would cost. Schulz-Koehn was offered three cartons of Luckies and four pairs of nylons for it, but instead he asked hopefully, 'Do you have any Count Basie records?'

Described in an April 1945 article as 'Oberleutnant Schulz-Koehn, greatcoat flapping at his ankles, the enemy jazz fiend', it was reported that in a conversation with the American lieutenant, he said, 'You know, I asked an American officer a week ago what "latch on" meant, and he didn't know. I thought you were all jazz fans.' Dietrich Schulz-Koehn had worked in marketing for Telefunken Records before the war broke out. During the war, he published an illegal jazz newsletter praising African-American jazz musicians, and he went by the name the 'Swing Doc' and later 'Dr Jazz'.

Hans Bluthner was nicknamed 'Herr Hitman' because he knew all the latest releases coming from America and the UK. He said, 'We always said that anybody who liked jazz could never be a Nazi.' Hans said of Schulz-Koehn:

> He was the only one in our small circle of jazz people who did not want to acknowledge what was happening in Germany. He behaved like an anti-Nazi but when you talked to him … well, it was schizophrenic. He wrote articles in our secret newsletter; the first issue had his photograph in uniform on the first page. If some official had bothered to notice, he would have gone to jail.

In 1936, when membership in the Hitler Youth was compulsory, it encouraged a rise in these urban groups of rebellious young men who refused to join, and instead disrupted meetings and targeted those in uniform. They were the children of liberal parents and communists and, refusing to be consumed by the Hitler Youth, they met in pubs, drank, smoked and played cards. They were the punks of their era, wearing their hair long and dressing in tattered clothes to symbolise their rejection of uniform. They chose checked shirts, old hats, signet rings with skull and crossbones, and called themselves the Navajos, the Black Gang, or the Edelweiss Pirates, after their Edelweiss badge, which was hidden under their coat lapels.

Throughout the war the gangs continued their hostility to the Hitler Youth, dressing in the swing fashion and painting slogans like 'Down with Hitler'. They teamed up with communist groups to resist and sabotage the government.

Cologne was heavily bombed and, from the city's ruins, disillusioned young people joined up in gangs, joined together to form a new division of the Edelweiss Pirates. They stole and looted to survive in the destroyed city. Fritz Theilen, born in Cologne in 1927, was a leading member of the Edelweiss Pirates and narrowly escaped public execution. Fritz had been a member of the Hitler Youth but was expelled in 1940 for insubordination. He left school at 14 to work as an apprentice toolmaker with Ford Motors, where he was horrified to see slave labour being used in the factory.

In 1943 Fritz was arrested by the Gestapo, and he was held and tortured at the Cologne headquarters. After being released, he became more active in his group, now with 128 members. Their resistance involved painting anti-regime slogans around the city, listening to the BBC and helping escaped prisoners of war. They also attacked Hitler Youth and Nazi officials.

Like others in his group, Fritz was arrested once more in 1944 and sent to Dachau, where he managed to escape and went into hiding for the duration of the war. Others weren't so lucky. In November 1944, thirteen Edelweiss Pirates, some as young as 16, were publicly hanged in the city centre of Cologne.

Children were forced into fighting as part of the *Volkssturm* (People's Army), established in October 1944. It was Germany's last desperate effort to win, and 16 to 60-year-old males were called up. With a shortage of uniforms, they wore an identifying armband with their own dyed civilian clothes in army grey or antique brown, their tram conductor uniforms, university blazers or pieces from the Great War. They looked ragtag and terrified. Untrained, many took the first opportunity to surrender, or were destroyed by machine-gun fire.

The Swing Youth, the Edelweiss Pirates and the White Rose demonstrated that some young people in Germany were dissenting, and that they had not all been brainwashed by the Hitler Youth. On 2 August 1943, an editorial appeared in the *New York Times* under the title 'Young German Martyrs', re-publishing the words of the White Rose's last pamphlet, to bring hope to young people around the world.

Ilse Aichinger, a half-Jewish poet living in Vienna, felt hope when she read of the White Rose. She said it 'made it possible for us to go on living ... It was like a secret light that expanded over the land: it was joy.'

22

Women in the Resistance

During the occupation of France, despite the Vichy Government's plans to make women's roles more traditional, women fought alongside men as part of the Resistance. Simone Segouin was an 18-year-old French woman who helped capture twenty-five German soldiers, and she was photographed in shorts, shirt and a khaki cap with a Schmeisser MP-40 gun.

By 1943 resistance groups had grown across France, as more people saw the cruelty of the regime playing out in Paris. Women delivered messages, handled guns or hid uniforms and food in the baskets of their bicycles for downed airmen. They wore outfits that helped them blend in so that they could avoid attracting attention as they cycled along country roads.

After France fell, American actress Drue Tartière wanted to do what she could to resist the Nazis, and in autumn 1940 carried out radio broadcasts to oppose the Vichy Government. As an American, she realised that with one false move she could land in jail. She was almost arrested in September 1940, when cycling to the Bois de Boulogne to go shopping with her maid, Nadine. Stopping in a café with their baskets full, she decided to call a friend, Mary Walker, who was working with British Intelligence. When she overheard the waiter on the telephone referencing her, she and Nadine quickly collected their bicycles. She stuffed her beret and raincoat into Nadine's basket, and they went in separate directions to avoid detection. She saw the waiter coming into the market area with three policemen but, 'without my raincoat, and with my blonde hair hanging down instead of tucked under my beret, I looked different, and he didn't recognise me'.

Girls were recruited by partisan groups because they could get into places that men couldn't. A *Life* journalist, Jack Belden, spoke to a 17-year-old

French girl called Nicole, in Chartres, standing apart from the crowds who were cheering as the heads of collaborators were shaved. Belden wrote:

> When I first saw her, she was standing in the courtyard of the prefecture munching on two large chunks of bread smeared with a thick, unsavoury looking jam. She neither cheered the hair-shearing nor flirted with the swarms of American correspondents. She was clad in a light-brown jacket and a cheap flowered skirt of many hues which ended just above her knees. Her legs were bare and brown. About her arm went a ribband bearing the legend FTPF. In the waistband of her skirt was stuck a small revolver.

The Francs-tireurs et Partisans Français (FTPF) was a resistance group originally created by the French Communist Party, who engaged in sabotage of the Germans and assistance to the Allied forces. They dressed in civilian clothing, with the only constant feature being the beret.

Nicole had at first been assigned small tasks such as carrying messages by bicycle between different resistance groups. She graduated to helping to blow up a bridge on a main railway line by keeping watch with her sub-machine gun. Belden said:

> I could find no traces of what is conventionally called toughness in Nicole. After routine farm life, she finds her present job thrilling and exhilarating. Now that the war is passing beyond her own home district she does not think of going back to the farm. She wants to go on with the Partisans and help free the rest of France.

Many women also worked as spies as part of the Special Operations Executive (SOE), an organisation which gathered intelligence and co-ordinated resistance overseas. The SOE was created in July 1940, when it seemed like Hitler was likely to take Britain. The SOE was led by Maurice Buckmaster, who was assisted by Vera Atkins, a severe but elegant recruiter in her thirties, who was fluent in French and preferred to keep her Romanian and Jewish background repressed. But she knew everything about the recruits and her job was to look after her agents, especially her 'girls'. Vera's tweed suit and poised appearance didn't give away a clue as to what rank she was. Later, she wore the trim blue tailoring of the WAAF after securing a commission as a flight officer.

Under the Geneva Convention, women were forbidden from combatant roles, but in 1942 the War Cabinet decided to recruit women as operational agents as it was deemed easier for them to blend into civilian life in occupied France. However, if word of the recruiting of women got out, it would have to be denied. (SOE was closed down in January 1946, and all papers filed away.)

By June 1943 there were 480 active agents in the French section. Thirty-nine women were part of the group, and thirteen of these were ultimately killed. 'Bravery was what they had in common,' Vera said, many years later:

> You might find it in anyone. You just don't know where to look. Their motivations were all different. Many women made good couriers or had worked in coding and had fingers like pianists – they made good radio operators. They might be artists or fashion designers. Why not? They had to be self-reliant, of course. Physical appearance was important. They were all attractive women. It gave them self-confidence.

Virginia Hall was an American agent based in Lyon, working undercover as a journalist for the *New York Post* while putting agents in touch with resistance groups. Tall and red-haired, she had an artificial foot she called 'Cuthbert', leading to the Germans nicknaming her 'the limping lady'. She was on the Gestapo's most wanted list, but escaped across the Pyrenees by foot to Spain, hoping Cuthbert would get her through the journey.

Nancy Wake was a Sydney journalist who married a Marseille businessman. She drove an ambulance and helped British prisoners of war to escape in France. When she was arrested and questioned by French police, she also managed to escape to Spain over the border. After SOE training in Britain, she parachuted back into the Auvergne in 1944, carrying with her two revolvers and a pair of high-heeled shoes.

A young Muslim woman, Noor Inayat Khan, was one of only three female SOE agents, along with Violette Szabo and Odette Sansom, to receive the George Cross. As the descendant of Tipu Sultan, she was an Indian princess, and had been raised in France under the peaceful Sufi religion. On the outbreak of war, she and her family moved to Britain, and Noor became a writer of children's folklore tales. But she wanted to do what she could for the war effort, despite her belief in non-violence. She signed up to the WAAF in November 1940 and was sent to RAF Balloon Command in Edinburgh, training for six months as a wireless telegraphist.

Jean Overton Fuller, who knew Noor and wrote her biography after the war, described her as small, with brown hair and eyes, and a slight voice that had a mix of Indian, English, French and American. She wore the Free French emblem of a double-barred silver cross on her clothing to show her commitment to France. After applying for a commission, on 28 August 1942 Noor came to the attention of the SOE for being fluent in French – a vital skill for those working undercover as spies.

In February 1943 she swapped air force blue for stiff khaki as she was integrated into the FANY. Women in the SOE were enrolled as FANYs and sent to Lilywhites to be measured for their serge uniforms, as it offered an excuse to train in firearms and provided a cover for being away from home for longer periods of time. It also provided protection under the armed forces if captured, and at least gave them the chance to be considered prisoners of war.

At the Special Training School (STS) at Wanborough Manor, new recruits were put through their paces, taught to shoot pistols and sub-machine guns and to use hand grenades and explosives. They were also encouraged to drink at the well-stocked bar, to see what they would reveal under the influence. Noor was sent for signals instruction, so that she could be trained up to become the first female radio operator sent to France. As agents tapped out Morse code on the move, with an aerial strung up on a rooftop or in trees, they ran the dangerous risk of their signal being picked up by Germans patrolling for any transmissions.

The final stage for agents was finishing school at Beaulieu in Hampshire, where they learnt the secrets to surviving in occupied France. For example, answering the phone in the wrong way, or calling a waiter for a *café noir* (black coffee) when milk shortages meant there was only one type of coffee anyway, could immediately arouse suspicion. Instructors were conflicted in their assessment of Noor. Some thought her too beautiful and exotic looking, others thought her too gentle and meek to handle the stress. She was clumsy, scared of weapons and found it almost impossible to lie. But Vera Atkins and Maurice Buckmaster believed in her, and when they gave her the opportunity to drop out of the mission if she felt she wasn't equipped, she refused to do so.

Noor's new identity was as a nurse called Nora Baker, and her code name was 'Madeleine'. SOE operations consisted of circuits, covering different areas of France. At the head of each circuit was the organiser, who recruited and armed local French people. They would also identify targets such as bridges and factories that would be sabotaged. Once in France, Noor was instructed to link up with the leader of a 'Prosper' sub-circuit named 'Cinema'. The Prosper circuit, established in October 1942, had expanded rapidly, and included Gilbert Norman and Jack Agazarian, code name Marcel, brother of the downed RAF pilot, Noel. Both he and his wife would eventually be killed by the Gestapo after being captured.

SOE agents spent their final days before being sent out at Orchard Court, a comfortable residence with walls covered with detailed maps of France to memorise. They were also given a wardrobe that would match their story. Clothes were tailored by Claudia Pulver, a Viennese refugee who was expert in creating European clothing by researching the threads worn by refugees. Vera Atkins would do a last check of their pockets for anything English such as cigarettes, bus tickets or money, and making little adjustments to their clothing such as stitching on the correct button or clothing label, and to ensure the hairstyle looked suitably French. It was the little details that could make a disguise a success or a disaster. They were also given a cyanide pill, in case of capture.

Noor prepared to be flown into France, dressed in her green oilskin coat. She carried with her a French identity card, ration card and her Webley pistol. Her clothing, consisting of simple dresses to suit her cover story of a nurse, and her personal effects were parachuted after. Noor was transported by plane over the Channel with Diana Rowden, Cecily Lefort and Charles Skepper, who would all be killed.

The authorities hadn't realised that the Prosper circuit had been jeopardised, and despite plenty of warnings to headquarters that it was no longer safe, they carried on communicating and ignoring the clues that something wasn't right. This carelessness led to the deaths of more agents.

While others had been arrested, Noor surprised everyone by continuing to work as she tried to rebuild the Prosper circuit. However, she was also careless in her transmissions. While active, Noor arranged the escape of thirty Allied airmen who had been shot down in France, organised arms and money for the Resistance and false papers for four agents. She was nervous that she was being watched and altered her disguise with dark glasses and by dying her hair, first red and then blonde. She carried the heavy radio equipment in a suitcase, transmitting from different locations.

As the Gestapo set traps using agents who had been arrested, she had several narrow escapes. Pierre Vienot, the Free French Ambassador to Britain, realised that the Gestapo had seen Noor, and he took her to a good Paris hairdresser to dye her hair back to brunette. He instructed her to get rid of her English mackintosh and grey dress, and gave her a blue suit, a grey polo-necked jumper and a navy-blue hat to blend in.

Buckmaster had arranged a Lysander to take her home in October 1943, but Noor was betrayed by someone named 'Renée', who gave her up for a cash reward. Noor was arrested in her apartment, and taken to the Gestapo headquarters at Avenue Foch, where other agents were also imprisoned in relatively comfortable surrounds. Noor, who refused to give up any details, joined an escape plan by removing the bars from the cell windows, and used face cream and powder to create a plaster to disguise the holes in the wall. However, when an air-raid alert sounded just as they were escaping onto the roof, they were captured, and Noor was sent to Germany at the end of November 1943.

She was held in brutal conditions at Pforzheim Prison, singled out for special treatment, almost starved, beaten, and held with chains binding her hands and feet. She was sometimes seen walking in the courtyard dressed only in a sackcloth, as her clothes had been taken away.

Following the liberation of Paris, and as American troops were almost reaching the German border, Himmler ordered all agents to be killed so that they could not reveal what they knew about the horrors the Nazis had inflicted. On 12 September 1944, Noor and three other spies, Eliane Plewman, Madeleine Damerment and Yolande Beekman, were placed on the express train to Dachau, 200 miles away. They were allowed to sit together and speak to each other, passing around English cigarettes to smoke. In the early hours of the morning at Dachau, the SS guards dragged Madeleine Damerment, Eliane Plewman and Yolande Beekman from their cells, marched them to the crematorium and shot them through the back of their necks.

Noor, who was considered a highly dangerous prisoner, was stripped and kicked with their leather boots. At dawn, as she lay on the floor, broken and bruised, an SS soldier ordered her to kneel and stuck a gun against her head. She had just enough time to shout out '*Liberté!*' before he pulled the trigger.

SOE agent Yvonne Baseden was released from Ravensbrück Concentration Camp, one of fifty women who were liberated by the Swedish Red Cross, in April 1945. She arrived back at Euston wearing a baggy woollen coat and carrying her belongings in a brown paper bag. Alone and unsure what to do, she called the Air Ministry. 'I'm sorry, but I am a WAAF officer and I have just come from Germany and I am at Euston and I don't know what to do.'

Yvonne had first flown into France in March 1944. At 21, she was one of the youngest SOE women. 'I remember being told how much money to put in my jumping suit so I didn't have anything to carry in my hands,' she later said of her moments at the airfield with Vera Atkins.

Yvonne Baseden had met Violette Szabo in a prison in Dijon after they had both been captured:

I remember Violette was sitting quite casually and she had obviously made an effort to get whatever clothes she was wearing clean. She had taken her shirt off and had washed it. She had lost none of her vivacity – or else she had been in prison longer than the others and had got used to the atmosphere.

Violette Szabo, born in Paris, was the daughter of a British First World War veteran who met her mother in France. Violette's husband, a French Foreign Legionnaire, had been killed in the war, and when Vera Atkins met her she was a 23-year-old widow with a small child. In June 1944, Violette was parachuted into France to help stop German Panzer divisions from advancing to the beaches at Normandy. 'She was an entrancing creature, to men and women alike. Everyone had wanted to see Violette off; she had bewitched the whole of Baker Street,' said Vera.

Violette waited for three days as the first two attempts to fly her out were aborted because of poor weather. Vera remembered her waiting on the lawn with a young Polish man, who was being sent over to France too:

They were laughing and chatting and Violette was playing a gramophone record over and over and over again. I can still hear it: 'I want to buy a paper doll I can call my own …' I can see her now. She was wearing a pretty summery dress with blue and white flowers and shoes she said she had bought in Paris, and she had a rose in her hair. I can still hear that damn song going round and round in my head.

In mid-June Violette, disguised as a seamstress, was reported to have been arrested. She had bravely fought off the SS with a Sten gun before she was eventually captured and was executed.

Vera looked after the possessions of the agents left behind – gramophone records, vanity cases, a camel-hair coat belonging to Violette Szabo, Diana Rowden's pair of plimsolls. She also came to personally rescue an agent when she could. Lise de Baissac, waiting in a Normandy village for orders after the Allied landings, was greeted in September 1944 by Vera, arriving with a new FANY uniform to give her and whisking her home.

Drue Tartière moved to a large house in Barbizon with her assistant Nadine in October 1940, where she continued to work with the Resistance. When Drue heard that her husband had been killed in Syria, she was encouraged to destroy any letters from him while working for the British and Free French as it could be dangerous. Resistance in France was being built up slowly, with sabotage in factories and on railroads, and connecting to England via short-wave radios.

By March 1942 Drue moved into a new property with six acres of land where they received cargoes of arms and ammunition from planes coming from England. She began cultivating the farmland to grow her own food, swapping four of her husband's shirts for a cart of manure from a farmer.

Like almost everyone else in occupied France, Nadine and Drue both read *Gone with the Wind* in the spring of 1943. 'When the American Army arrives,' Nadine said, 'I am going to pick out a Rhett Butler.' They felt they were doing many of the things Scarlett O'Hara did, like make their own clothes from curtains and bed sheets. A summer dress came from 'my rose-linen bath curtains'. They saved every piece of paper, wire, leather and string.

In September 1942 Drue was picked up by the Gestapo. She had been tending to the garden and was in 'my dirty overalls, had dirt between my toes and on my hands; had on a pair of patched sandals, and wore a big, old straw hat'. While being kept overnight in the commandant's acquisitioned house, she demonstrated that her period had started, lifting up the trouser legs to show a trickle of blood, and shocking him into sending for cosmetics, clothes and food.

After she was interned with other American prisoners of war, she used a fake doctor's certificate to be sent back home to be treated for cancer and haemorrhaging.

When her connections in the Resistance asked if she would assist in hiding English and American airmen, she felt it was one of the most important jobs she could do. In a house in the Avenue D'Orléans, she met the first young airman, Bob Giles, who greeted her with tears and hugs when he discovered she was an American too. The other two were fetched from their safe houses.

Bob Giles was 21, from Detroit, and dressed in a red turtleneck sweater and an old pair of pants belonging to one of their rescuers. Carroll Harrup, from Iowa, was wearing a beret and a tight little coat 'that made him look very French'. The third was Tom Mezynski, a Pole from Pittsburgh. After their bomber crash-landed, they hid in the French countryside, keeping out of sight as they were still in their uniforms. After three days sleeping outside and surviving on raw potatoes, they decided to approach a farmhouse, and the woman and daughter, terrified at first of their uniform, took them in, made them soup and gave them a 'pair of ragged old pants, old shirts and sweaters, and told them to go as far away as possible,' wrote Drue.

They managed to link up with the Resistance, who found them a safe place to stay in Paris. Drue helped find them clothing by bartering and swapping her possessions, such as clothes belonging to her husband. It was dangerous work, and like other members of the Resistance, she had a cyanide capsule sewn into her clothing in case she was captured.

To entertain the boys kept locked up in safe houses, Drue would bring friends like Sylvia Beach to visit, or take them on walks around Paris, disguised in French clothes or sometimes with their hair dyed to make them look less English or American, particularly if they were ginger. Occasionally, they could go to the cinema, but the Nazis were known to turn on the lights to do spot checks of the audience looking for draft dodgers.

There were 196 RAF and American boys who were successfully hidden in apartments around Paris. New clothing in France was scarce, and one woman who wished to help, but couldn't hide them in her home because she had a Jewish husband, ripped up her daughter's blue velvet hat, a first communion present, to make scarves for two aviators.

Allied planes dropped silver coils of paper to interfere with the German radar system, and villagers and peasants collected them as decorations or created rosettes for their horses as a little symbol of resistance. On 4 July 1944, an RAF bomber flew over Barbizon, dropping the coils of silver, when Drue witnessed one of the planes being hit and falling out of the sky. The Germans searched for survivors, but local farmers discovered the five men from the Royal Canadian Air Force first, providing them with civilian clothing and hiding their uniforms. Drue kept the five flyers in her home for six weeks, despite the local commandant living nearby. Drue, who was in her thirties, seemed like a mother figure to the boys in their early twenties.

One of the survivors, Lorne Frame, later remembered:

> The outstanding feature of my experience was seeing the incredible bravery of the French people who helped Allied flyers. If caught, they faced severe punishment, including death, from the German occupying forces. At incredible personal risk for themselves, their families and friends, they hid and clothed and fed air crew like myself until liberation arrived. And when it did, hundreds of Allied Air Forces personnel emerged from all over France, especially in Paris, and were returned to England. It all left indelible impressions on young twenty year old minds.

Hannah Senesh was one of thirty-two Jewish parachutists from Palestine recruited by the SOE to jump into occupied Hungary and organise resistance. Becoming a committed Zionist as a teenager, Hannah had travelled from her native Hungary to live in Palestine in 1939, but she proudly wore the uniform of the WAAFs when she volunteered for the British forces.

Hannah, as a teenager, had felt strongly the injustice and repression of Jewish people and she began exploring her identity. No one in her family was a Zionist, yet she was determined to study Hebrew to be accepted into Palestine, which she believed was the only place that could offer safety for Jews.

Arriving in British Palestine, she found the work tough, and wondered, 'Is this my purpose in life? This is not just my personal worry. It is also that of tens of thousands of young Jews. But each must fight his own battle.' She was happier when she was given the chance to do farm work, and she described her life on the Kibbutz in a letter to her mother, where she was up at 5.30 a.m., washed and dressed in 'slacks, boots, blouse, a headscarf' for working in the fruit orchard or washing the cows.

She described the way they dressed:

… certainly not what I can call the 'old style', i.e. the way I used to dress at home. Here the most usual outfit consists of boots, slacks, and leather jacket for men, and the same for women. I must confess at times it's very funny to see an old, fat lady in slacks and boots … I can't say this way of dressing is exactly an esthetic sight, though on the young with good figures slacks look smart, of course. And as far as the men are concerned, they always bring Hungarian peasants to mind, as they wear the same kind of boots and leather jackets.

She seriously considered joining the army, first as a Home Guard and then as a parachutist in the British Army. She joined the Haganah Defence Force, and then in 1943 enlisted in the WAAF. After being recruited by the SOE she took parachute training in Egypt.

Yoel Palgi met Hannah in Tel Aviv on his way to parachute training school, when she was a WAAF:

She was a soldier in the British Air Force, and the blue-gray of her uniform matched her blue eyes. Her light brown hair flowed in soft curls around her refined, elongated face; there was something delightfully harmonious about her. I liked her at once, without being able to determine exactly what it was about her that had charmed me, or why she was so completely pleasing to the eye.

Reuven Dafne, a Yugoslavian soldier, also served with Hannah when he was brought in to offer advice on how to traverse through the country:

> During my sessions with the group, a girl – the only girl in it – attracted my attention by her alert participation. It didn't occur to me at first that she was one of the paratroopers; I assumed that she, too, had been called in to give information about one of the countries the mission was heading for.
>
> The British boys working in the large parachute storeroom where we were taken to put on our harnesses couldn't take their eyes off Hannah, nor hide their amazement. The Scottish sergeant who helped me into my parachute said simply, and with considerable emotion, 'I can't believe it. I've been working here a long time, and I've fitted hundreds of parachutists, but never a woman among them.' And he added, 'If I told it to my Jewish friends in England they wouldn't believe me.'
>
> A group of paratroopers, evidently Americans, were equally surprised but assumed she was a paratrooper's wife who had come to see him off. When they met us again, just before we took off, they were shocked to see her, and one of them, extremely moved, walked over to her and wordlessly shook her hand. Hannah didn't understand the handshake, but her charming and simple reaction threw the astounded American completely off balance.

Hannah seemed relaxed and cheerful during the flight, loaded up with parachute equipment and winter clothing. Before jumping out of the plane, she gave a thumbs up – 'her favorite victory sign', and after hurtling through the air, they landed in Yugoslavia.

They spent months going through the Yugoslavian countryside to the border, and Hannah was a fascinating sight as a British officer, with pistol at her waist. She was arrested at the Hungarian border, and after her British military transmitter was discovered, she was taken to Gestapo headquarters in Budapest and beaten and tortured. Yet she refused to give up information.

Yoel Palgi said:

> Having been taught for years that Jews never fight back, that they will accept the vilest treatment, they were taken aback by her courage. The warden of the prison, a notorious sadist who was credited with the death of many he had tortured with his own hands, considered it a privilege to visit her cell daily to argue with her fearless criticism of German rule and her prophecies of an allied victory.

When she found that Hungarian Jews must wear the yellow star, she was told by one of the other prisoners, 'You're lucky not to be branded'. But in solidarity, she instead drew a large Star of David in the dust of the window. She would also make dolls in prison, including ballet dancers, Madame Butterfly, and most popular, her Palestine dolls, with boys and girls in Kibbutz clothes, with picks and shovels.

On 28 October 1944, Hannah was brought before a military court in Budapest. The Nazis were taken aback by this courageous young woman, but she was executed by firing squad on 7 November 1944. Hannah was a talented writer and poet and a poem was found on the wall of her cells, ending with the words, 'I could have been twenty-three next July; I gambled on what mattered most; the dice was cast. I lost.'

23

Victory in Europe

In June 1944, journalists raced to be the first back into Paris as the D-Day invasion pushed back the Germans and the Allies descended on Paris. Ernest Hemingway, Colonel David Bruce and Archie 'Red' Pelkey drove a jeep into the city, witnessing German officers being arrested by the French marines. Stopping for a drink in Montparnasse, they saw pretty girls in thin summer dresses offering up kisses to their liberators.

When Hemingway arrived in Place Vendôme, he was described by Lucienne as entering the Ritz:

> ... like a king, and he chased out all the British people who had arrived an hour earlier. He was dressed in khaki, but his shirt was open on his bare chest. He had a leather belt under his big stomach, with his gun beating against his thigh ... He had presence, the way people know Hemingway, but no chic.

Photographer Lee Miller made her way to Paris to witness the liberation for herself. 'I won't be the first woman journalist in Paris ... but I'll be the first dame photographer, I think, unless someone parachutes in.'

Arriving in the city, she was struck by the girls riding bicycles, with flowers in their hair. At first, she had not been too excited with an assignment on couture and style in liberated Paris, but when she saw the women, she was impressed. They were defiant in their short skirts, padded shoulders, turbans and hats balancing on their heads, with vibrant colours and high wooden or cork shoes. Miller said:

> Their silhouette was very queer and fascinating to me after utility and austerity England. Full floating skirts, tiny waistlines. They were top heavy

with built up, pompadour front hairdos and waving tresses; weighted to the ground with clumsy, fancy thick-soled wedge shoes. The entire gait of the Frenchwoman has changed with her footwear. Instead of the bouncing buttocks and mincing steps of 'pre-war' there is a hot-foot long stride, picking up the whole foot at once.

On 26 August 1944, celebrations broke out across Paris as the city was freed. Crowds cheered, threw flowers at tanks and kissed soldiers. 'The city had gone crazy with rejoicing,' said journalist Mary Welsh. 'Everybody was eighteen years old, free of shackles, bursting with joy.'

The winter of 1944 in liberated Paris was freezing, and Bettina Ballard arrived in her Red Cross uniform, amazed at the way women had continued to dress while she had been serving in North Africa and Italy:

> The Métro was the best place to see what women were wearing, as it was the only means of transportation other than a bicycle. I remember seeing one day a very elegant woman in a towering pink felt hat in which little birds nestled and over which there was a beautiful haze of tulle – something even beyond Cecil Beaton's dreams. She was being crushed to a pulp in the subway rush.

Despite not wishing to work for *Vogue* while still in her Red Cross uniform, Bettina was thrilled by the 'enormous incongruous hats of tulle or lace with roses, unbelievably Mad Hatterish in his own elegant way'. Bettina wrote of how her Red Cross uniform provided a certain degree of protection, when in American-occupied Paris in 1945:

> Taking off your Red Cross uniform and getting back into civilian clothes in Paris is exchanging thrift for extravagance, security for complications. Suddenly you are a civilian – without a taxi nearer than London, no more hitchhiking in jeeps, no more free transportation by air, no convenient Army or Red Cross messes, no cigarettes or candy from the PX, no liquor rations, no sympathetic dispensary, no efficient finance office, no quick post, and no more respectful 'Hello's' from friendly GIs. To the GI you are just another 'ooh-la-la' target with maybe a 'Gee, she smells good' thrown at you if your perfume rises above the smelly Metro. You are cut off from army protection, from the exaggerated appreciation you have enjoyed for the last two and a half years.

Fanny Gore Browne, a Wren, was stationed near Paris, and when she visited the city for fun and relaxation she recalled:

[We] noticed the women immediately. We'd all got dowdy by that stage of the war but they were beautifully dressed and coiffed, thin as rakes because there wasn't much food except for the appalling black market – and of course Paris, unlike London, hadn't been bombed.

The first thing we did was window-shopping. We went down the Faubourg St Honoré, into all the wonderful parfumiers, being sprayed as they do – to smell scent was wonderful, after Britain. I was taken to Maxim's, a senior officers' restaurant, where I had pâté de foie gras for the first time in my life.

While Parisians celebrated, there were acute food shortages in the city; many residents mourned the loss of their loved ones, their homes and possessions. Women who had been friendly to the German soldiers when occupied were now accused of collaborating. They were stripped, shaved, beaten, tattooed, raped and even executed. The 'horizontal collaborators' sometimes received the worst treatment for having slept with a German.

Photo reporter Robert Capa witnessed frightened women in torn clothes lined up against the walls as their heads were shaved and the clumps of hair piled up to be burnt. Sometimes women were found guilty of collaboration for something as simple as exchanging favours for silk stockings. It's believed that there were 20,000 women punished for collaboration, and were known as '*les tondues*', or 'shaven ones'.

Concentration camp survivors also returned with shaved heads, and were so emaciated their families couldn't recognise them. Some were mistaken for *tondues* and further traumatised.

After Belgium was freed, QAs arrived in Brussels to be stationed at hospitals treating injured soldiers and civilians. Brussels was a city of celebration, where there was unlimited champagne to pop, calvados to knock back, and where luxury hotels were commandeered as the officers' mess. QAs were able to get out of their battledress and put on their dresses once more. They also found the city a shopping paradise.

Meta Kelly recalled, 'We saw things we hadn't seen since before the war back home – perfume, make-up, Paris-type fashions. My sister was married with two small daughters and I bought them lovely party dresses. I bought make-up, too.'

Mary Morris was also posted to Brussels, where she and her friends bought lipstick and Chanel No. 5. She was also struck by the ingenuity of the fashions worn by the women:

> Some were very attractive. I noticed that two girls were wearing wigs and another had a headscarf worn turban fashion. I wondered if these girls had also attended the glittering dinner dances of the *Wehrmacht* when they were here. I once saw a girl being chased through the streets of Brussels by a crowd of women.

A particular craze in Brussels was stylish coats and capes made from the hospital blankets. Mary was 'amazed to see many Belgian girls wearing coats made from blue hospital blankets. Felt rather irritated as we are short of blankets for the patients. They are obviously being sold on the black market by ex-patients or orderlies.'

Diana Barnato was recruited by her new husband Derek Walker to ferry a photo-reconnaissance plane to the Continent. At this point, women in the ATA were not allowed to cross the Channel, even though they were desperate to do so. However, because she was officially on leave, Diana could fly the plane under the command of the RAF. Husband and wife enjoyed seeing Brussels as a city in celebration, now that it was free:

> The Belgians had sugar, sweets, wine – all sorts of things that we in Britain hadn't seen for years. They had leather shoes and handbags in the shops, and no clothes rationing coupons anymore – their war was over! So was their blackout, it seemed. Everywhere the lights were on again.

Diana was the first woman in the ATA to fly over the Channel. Not long after that, women in the ATA were allowed to fly to the Continent. By early 1945, ATA women were flying there regularly. After VE Day, Suzanne Irwin made it to Berlin, and Rosemary Rees went to Prague, carrying gifts for refugees.

After getting a taste of continental travel, Diana organised her own little racket in cocoa, as there was a plentiful supply in Britain but shortage in Belgium, and she could fit forty tins into her parachute bag:

Flying without the silken, life-saving parachute was a bit of a risk, I suppose, not to mention a surprise if one had to bail out, having forgotten one had tins not silk. Nevertheless, it was a risk I was quite prepared to take, because the cocoa cash was enough for a good night out in Brussels, plus a bit left over for shopping for unrationed sweets and leather goods.

The American Red Cross set up social clubs for the GIs in liberated Paris. As one writer noted, 'To see these boys for 48 hours and still dressed in their heavy mud-incrusted field boots and combat helmets lounging in these lush surroundings is quite a thing.'

Stanley Weinberg of the 82nd Airborne wrote to his sister, on 16 February 1945:

The people don't look like they were bad off. They are better dressed than any place on the continent or England. Prices are getting very high. If you go to a good restaurant, it costs about $15 to $20 for a meal. All the French people seem to have plenty of money. It hurts the soldiers though because they get paid in French francs.

He stayed at the Red Cross Independence Club with his own room and bath, where GI food was prepared by French chefs. After a visit to the Folies Bergère, which he found disappointing, he and his buddies went to a night-club to drink champagne, but 'I'd still rather have Pepsi-Cola'. As victory was declared in Europe, the American culture of Coca-Cola signs and jazz would soon replace the swastika and the Nazi marching songs.

The 506th Infantry Regiment arrived in Berchtesgaden and raced to Hitler's bombed-out chalet, der Berghof, to see what they could loot, despite other paratroopers and French soldiers having arrived first. Three thousand feet above was the Eagle's Nest, where Hitler had entertained Unity Mitford all those years before. (There was still a bullet lodged in her skull after a failed attempt to kill herself on the outbreak of war, and brain damage had resulted in her switching from fanatical fascism to fanatical religion.)

By 7 May 1945, the rumour that Germany was surrendering was con-firmed. The French tankers in GI overcoats and dark blue berets with bright red pompons asked the Americans if it was true, that the war really was over. '*La guerre est finie!*' they shouted, and everyone joined in, danced, shook hands, and cracked open the champagne they had liberated from Hitler's wine cellar.

They larked around with their scavenged German goods, and Sergeant Mercier even took to dressing up in a complete German officer's uniform, with a monocle in his right eye. For fun, someone marched him by rifle point to Captain Speirs, who had been tipped off. Playing along, and without looking up he ordered that the captured German be shot. Mercier, panicking that he might really be executed, called out that it was only him in disguise. 'Mercier, get out of that silly uniform,' Speirs replied.

Any sense of orderly appearance had now gone, and the scruffy and unshaven appearance of the GIs contrasted with the captured Germans, still clipped and neat and proud. 'I was twenty-seven years old,' officer Dick Winters said:

> … and like all the troops, I was wearing a dirty, well-worn combat fatigue jacket and pants, and had that bucket on my head for a helmet. I felt a little ridiculous giving orders to a professional German colonel about twenty years my senior, who was dressed in a clean field uniform with his medals all over his chest.

A mile-long convoy of German soldiers made their way along the highway north of Berchtesgaden, and having lost their purpose, they no longer carried weapons or wore their helmets. Included in the convoy were women who had been part of the German WAC and displaced refugees who had found a soldier to cling to for food and a bed. The SS mountain troops were dressed, according to David Webster, in 'beautiful, moss-green uniforms with hob-nailed ski boots and carried full battle gear and loaded weapons', wishing to surrender to the 506th.

The American GIs moved into the town of Kaprun, in the Austrian Alps. As the occupiers, they passed their time drinking, exploring the mountains and swimming in the beautiful lake at Zell am See. David Webster asked his mother to send him a pair of colourful Abercrombie & Fitch swimming trunks, and they sunbathed or played softball, their scars visible on their skin. 'What a shame all those guys who were killed couldn't have lived for this,' thought Webster. 'They would have liked it.'

The Americans in Zell am See took to wearing SS tracksuits with the silver lightning insignia on a large chest patch and formed into athletic teams to pass the time. It was forbidden for the Americans to fraternise with German and Austrian women, but for a celebration with local musicians and flowing booze, they handed out displaced person armbands to any girls they liked. As Lieutenant Foley remembered it, 'There wasn't one Displaced Person at the celebration.'

Their only duty was to guard the roads, dressed in their woollen uniforms and helmet liners, checking every car that came through. They relieved the surrendering German soldiers and SS of their fur-lined coats, camouflaged jump jackets, and watches. On 13 May, Webster wrote to his family:

> Most of these soldiers have taken it in pretty good spirit, but once in a while we get an individual who does not like to lose his watch. A pistol flashed in his face, however, can persuade anybody. I now have a Luger, two P-38s (similar to Lugers), a Schmeisser machine pistol, two jump smocks, one camouflaged winter jacket, several flags about three feet by two, and a watch. If they ever let us, I'll mail some of this back.

Stanley Weinberg arrived in Germany in April 1945. 'Finally, after all those years in the Army, I've been issued a GI watch. We got two for officers. It's an ugly Elgin but it keeps time. I still have the Bulova I bought from the PX last October. It keeps perfect time.'

Stanley Weinberg was also enjoying life in Germany, growing a moustache and relaxing his uniform by wearing his own sweater with his pants and boots. 'This is really the life,' he wrote from Germany in April 1945:

> Can't tell you what it's all about but I get up about 9. We have two meals a day. 11 and 5. Had canned chicken for dinner and steak for supper. I have a Jerry motorcycle for my use. The weather is beautiful. I was sitting in our backyard doing some paperwork for a few hours this afternoon stripped to the waist.

But with the lack of discipline, as soldiers got drunk on German booze and sped along Alpine roads in newly acquired Mercedes, a handful of soldiers tragically died in preventable accidents. Discipline was reinstated and they were ordered to dress in their Class A uniform for parade, and to smarten up from being unshaven, wearing their old fatigues and muddy boots. As the US Army collected up some of the equipment that wasn't required, the para-troopers were asked to hand in their silk escape maps. However, these maps were now treasured property and they refused, instead opting to pay the fine for keeping them.

Back in France, awaiting mobilisation orders, David Webster was given his notice of leave, and he reported to the supply room for an equipment check. The supply sergeant tried to take away his new pair of jump boots, and after an argument, Webster managed to hold on to them – instead handing in a pair of old combat boots. The sergeant also came back with a supply of new fatigues and jumpsuits and dumped them on the counter. 'We have a lot of extras. Good work clothes for civilian life':

'A uniform in civilian life? Jesus Christ!' Lifting the bundle of clothes high overhead, I smashed them down on the counter. 'Shove these rags up the Army's ass. I'll never wear another uniform as long as I live.' I hoisted my duffel bag on my shoulder and went out the door, with the supply sergeant shaking his head behind me.

As soon as the war in Europe was over in 1945, most British servicewomen were demobilised. Kathleen Godfrey discovered that after being discharged from the WAAF:

I was totally unqualified for anything, and was going to have to think seriously about what to do next. But it was here in the last months of my spell in the Air Force that for the first time I fell in love and six months later we were married.

After victory in Europe, Sheila Mills was posted to Hamburg to work with the Allied Control Council for the de-Nazification of Germany. Life in Hamburg involved tennis and sailing, socialising with the navy, the RAF and the army. At one navy party, there was an extravagant buffet with every luxury food, including lobster, caviar, smoked salmon, champagne liqueurs. 'I cannot think that it's right to have such sumptuous feasts while the rest of Europe starves, but what can one do about it,' she wrote.

When Jackie Sorour heard the war was over, her thoughts were of disappointment, 'No more Tempests and Spits and Lanes. No more Wings and stripes, excitement and fun. No more of not caring or knowing what day it is.' Jackie also discovered she was pregnant and was determined to cover it up as much as possible so that she could stay with the ATA until the final flight. Her fellow flyers 'winced whenever I slung a heavy parachute over my shoulder and climbed in and out of fighters and bombers'.

After giving birth to her daughter and receiving a King's Commendation for ferrying more planes than any woman or man in the ATA, Jackie struggled to find work as a female pilot after the war. She posted an advert, and received one reply, 'from a company marketing a new type of flying overall who hoped I would be interested in the enclosed brochure. "So this is what I flew in the war for," I said bitterly. "To make the world free … if you're a man".'

Ray Ellis, the last survivor of his regiment during the Battle of Knightsbridge in North Africa, was captured and sent to a prisoner-of-war camp in Italy. He described those days as the worst of his life, but after a daring escape from the camp he found himself in the Italian countryside, where he was hidden by a peasant family until the country was liberated. His was just one remarkable story of survival.

As the world adjusted to peacetime, military uniform was carried into civilian life. In America the Ike jacket became popular among civilians as well as returning GIs. American airmen continued to wear their leather bomber jackets when they integrated back into normal life, with some choosing to roam the United States in motorcycle gangs. GIs were given assistance to go to college, and they married their sweethearts and started families.

In Britain, the 'brothel creepers' worn by troops in North Africa soon caught on with teenage Teddy Boys, and a new generation in the sixties took on the military symbols of their parents' war and subverted them. The RAF target symbol was adopted by the Mods, while German Army jackets from surplus stores were worn by the hippies who protested vehemently against the Vietnam War.

Joan Bawden, the mother of composer Tim Rice, wrote prophetically in her wartime diary, as she reflected on her generation; those young people who lived life as if there was no tomorrow:

> This is our world: war and death and dreadfulness. We are a generation without a tomorrow, alive and beautiful in our lovely today … But we can do whatever we please because we are without a tomorrow – and our payment for our selfish present is death.

Selected Bibliography

Books

Adie, Kate, *Corsets to Camouflage: Women and War*, in association with the Imperial War Museum (Hodder & Stoughton, 2004).

Ambrose, Stephen E., *Band of Brothers* (Simon & Schuster, 2012).

Ballard, Bettina, *In My Fashion* (Séguier Editions, 2016).

Barnato, Diana, *Spreading My Wings* (Grub Street Publishing, 2008).

Bartley, Anthony, *Smoke Trails in the Sky: From the Journals of a Fighter Pilot* (William Kimber, 1984).

Basu, Shrabani and M.R.D. Foot, *Spy Princess: The Life of Noor Inayat Khan* (The History Press, 2008).

Batstone, Stephanie, *Wren's Eye View: Adventures of a Visual Signaller* (Parapress Limited, 1994).

Bishop, Patrick, *Air Force Blue: The RAF in World War 2 – Spearhead of Victory* (William Collins, 2017).

Brayley, Martin and Richard Ingram, *Khaki Drill & Jungle Green: British Tropical Uniforms 1939–45 in Colour Photographs* (The Crowood Press, 2000).

Brayley, Martin and Richard Ingram, *The World War 2 Tommy: British Army Uniforms European Theatre 1939–1945* (The Crowood Press, 1998).

De Courcy, Anne, *Debs at War: 1939–1945* (Weidenfeld & Nicolson, 2006).

Delaforce, Patrick, *Monty's Highlanders: 51st Highland Division in the Second World War* (Pen & Sword Military, 2016).

Dorril, Stephen, *Blackshirt: Sir Oswald Mosley and British Fascism* (Thistle Publishing, 2017).

Dumbach, Annette and Jud Newborn, *Sophie Scholl and the White Rose* (One World Publications, 2018).

Ellis, Ray, *Once a Hussar: A Memoir of Battle, Capture and Escape in the Second World War* (Skyhorse Publishing, 2014).

Erenberg, Lewis A., *Swingin' the Dream: Big Band Jazz and the Rebirth of American Culture* (University of Chicago Press, 1999).

Forman-Brunell, Miriam, *Girlhood in America: An Encyclopaedia, Volume 1* (ABC-CLIO, 2001).

Francis, Martin, *The Flyer: British Culture and the Royal Air Force, 1939–1945* (Oxford University Press, 2011).

Fussell, Paul, *Uniforms: Why We Are What We Wear* (Houghton Mifflin Company, 2002).

Gardiner, Juliet, *Over Here: The GIs in Wartime Britain* (Collins & Brown, 1992).

Gellhorn, Martha, *Travels with Myself and Another* (Eland, 2011).

Gibson, Guy, *Enemy Coast Ahead* (Spitfire Publishers, 2019).

Glass, Charles, *Americans in Paris: Life and Death under Nazi Occupation 1940–44* (Harper Press, 2009).

Harris, Carol, *Women at War: In Uniforms 1939–1945* (Sutton Publishing, 2003).

Hegarty, Marilyn E., *Victory Girls, Khaki-Wackies, and Patriotutes: The Regulation of Female Sexuality During World War II* (NYU Press, 2010).

Helm, Sarah, *A Life in Secrets: Vera Atkins and the Lost Agents of SOE* (Abacus, 2009).

Hillary, Richard, *The Last Enemy* (Penguin, 2018).

Hillier, Mark, *The RAF Battle of Britain Fighter Pilot's Kitbag* (Frontline Books, 2018).

Hobart, Malcolm C., *Badges and Uniforms of the Royal Air Force* (Pen & Sword Aviation, 2012).

Hyams, Jacky, *Bomb Girls: Britain's Secret Army: The Munitions Women of World War II* (John Blake Publishing, 2014).

Jewell, Brian, *British Battledress 1937–1962* (Osprey Publishing, 1981).

Jordan, Matthew F., *Le Jazz: Jazz and French Cultural Identity* (University of Illinois Press, 2010).

Kater, Michael H., *Different Drummers: Jazz in the Culture of Nazi Germany* (Oxford University Press, 1992).

Kennedy, David, *The American People in the Great Depression: Freedom from Fear* (Oxford University Press, 2003).

Knight, Eric, *A Short Guide to Great Britain* (US Government Printing Office, 1943).

Leckie, Robert, *Helmet for My Pillow* (Ebury Press, 2011).

Lestrange, W.F., *Wasted Lives* (George Routledge & Sons Ltd, 1936).

Levine, Joshua, *Forgotten Voices of Dunkirk* (Ebury Press, 2011).

Litoff, Judy Barrett, *We're in this War Too: World War 2 Letters from American Women* (Oxford University Press, 1994).

McMurray, Matthew, *WVS Uniform 1939–1945* (WRVS, 2009).

Madge, Charles and Tom Harrison, *Mass Observation, First Year's Work, 1937–1938* (Lindsay Drummond, 1938).

Meyer, Leisa, *Creating GI Jane: Sexuality and Power in the Women's Army Corps During World War II* (Columbia University Press, 1998).

Mitford, Jessica, *Hons and Rebels* (Weidenfeld & Nicolson, 2016).

Moggridge, Jackie, *Spitfire Girl: My Life in the Sky* (Head of Zeus, 2014).

Morris, Mary and Carol Acton, *A Very Private Diary: A Nurse in Wartime* (Thistle Publishing, 2015).

Mortimer, Barbara, *Sisters: Heroic True-Life Stories from the Nurses of World War 2* (Arrow, 2013).

Mosley, Charlotte, *The Mitfords: Love Letters Between Six Sisters* (Harper Perennial, 2008).

Orwell, George, *The Road to Wigan Pier* (Penguin Modern Classics, 2001).

Partridge, Eric, *A Dictionary of RAF Slang* (Michael Joseph Limited, 1990).

Rice, Joan, *Sand in My Shoes: Coming of Age in the Second World War* (Harper Perennial, 2009).

Ross, David, *Richard Hillary: The Authorised Biography of a Second World War Fighter Pilot and Author of* The Last Enemy (Grub Street Publishing, 2008).

Ryan, Kathleen M., *When Flags Flew High: Propaganda, Memory and Oral History for World War II Female Veterans* (University of Oregon, 2008).

Sadler, John, *Desert Rats: The Desert War 1940–5 in the Words of Those Who Fought There* (Amberley Publishing, 2012).

Savage, Jon, *Teenage: The Creation of Youth 1875–1945* (Pimlico, 2008).

Sebba, Anne, *Les Parisiennes: How the Women of Paris Lived, Loved and Died in the 1940s* (Weidenfeld & Nicolson, 2016).

Senesh, Hannah, Senesh, Eitan and Roberta Grossman, *Hannah Senesh: Her Life and Diary* (Jewish Lights, 2011).

Shirer, William L., *Berlin Diary: The Journal of a Foreign Correspondent, 1934–1941* (Ishi Press, 2010).

Skimming, Sylvia, *Sand in My Shoes: The Tale of a Red Cross Welfare Officer with British Officers Overseas in the Second World War* (Oliver and Boyd, 1948).

Tartière, Drue, *The House Near Paris: An American Woman's Story of Traffic in Patriots* (Victor Gollancz Ltd, 1947).

Tebbutt, Melanie, *Making Youth: A History of Youth in Modern Britain* (Palgrave, 2016).

Thomas, Donald, *An Underworld at War: Spivs, Deserters, Racketeers and Civilians in the Second World War* (The Murder Room, 2014).

Thompson, Julian, *Forgotten Voices: Desert Victory* (Ebury Press, 2012).

Toynbee, Philip, *Friends Apart: A Memoir of Esmond Romilly and Jasper Ridley in the Thirties* (Sidgwick & Jackson Limited, 1980).

Tyrer, Nicole, *Sisters in Arms: British Army Nurses Tell Their Story* (Weidenfeld & Nicolson, 2008).

Unwin, Vicky, *Love and War in the WRNS: Letters Home* (The History Press, 2015).

Vaughan, Hal, *Sleeping with the Enemy: Coco Chanel's Secret War* (Penguin Random House, 2012).

Ware, Vron and Les Back, *Out of Whiteness: Color, Politics and Culture* (The University of Chicago Press, 1992).

Watkins, Diane (ed.), *Hello, Janice: The Wartime Letters of Henry Giles* (The University Press of Kentucky, 1992).

Wauters, Arthur, *Eve in Overalls: Women at Work in the Second World War* (Imperial War Museum, 2017).

Webster, David and Stephen E. Ambrose, *Parachute Infantry* (Ebury Press, 2014).

Whittell, Giles, *Spitfire Women of World War II* (Harper Perennial, 2008).

Wyndham, Joan, *Love is Blue: A Wartime Diary* (Flamingo, 1987).

Zwerin, Mike, *Swing Under the Nazis: Jazz as a Metaphor for Freedom* (Cooper Square Publishers, 2000).

Newspaper and Magazine Articles

'10,000 Sub-debs do hard useful war work as juniors in AWVS', *Life*, 15 June 1942.

'100,000 Nazi Clowns on the Zany Front' by Collie Small, *Saturday Evening Post*, 21 April 1945.

'Adventures in Bobby Socks', *The New Yorker*, 18 March 1944.

'Air Raid Warden to Glamour Girl', *Picture Post*, 4 November 1939.

'All Mouth and Trousers' by Simon Mills, *The Guardian*, 17 June 2006.

'Anzacs arrive in Egypt to join growing Allied forces in the Near East', *Life*, 11 March 1940.

'As I Please' by George Orwell, *Tribune*, 17 December 1943.

'Ban on "Sweater Girls" Causes War Plant Strike', *The New York Times*, 12 February 1943.

'Campus Togs' by Virginia Pope, *The New York Times*, 10 August 1941.

'Complications of a Civilian in Paris' by Bettina Wilson, *Vogue*, April 1945.

'Debutante Dead for Duration, Says Miss Aldrich, One Herself', *The New York Times*, 9 July 1942.

'England at War: Now in "Battle Dress" its peculiar people mystify visiting Americans' by Noel F. Busch, *Life*, 1 January 1940.

'Ferrying the BEF Home' by Douglas Williams, *The Scotsman*, 1 June 1940.

'Frank [Sinatra]' by James Kaplan, *The New York Times*, 31 October 2010.

'Fritz Theilen: Member of the Edelweiss Pirates, the Children who Resisted Hitler' by David Childs, *The Independent*, 3 May 2012.

'Girls in Uniform', *Life*, 6 July 1942.

'Girl Pilots', *Picture Post*, Vol. 4, 22 October 1938.

'Government and Youth', *Life*, 15 April 1940.

'How to Behave in England', *Life*, 21 September 1942.

'International Brigade Dismiss!', *Picture Post*, 12 November 1938.

'In the Heart of the Empire – Piccadilly Circus', *Picture Post*, 22 October 1938.

'Is Your Sub-Deb Slang up to Date?', *Ladies' Home Journal*, December 1944.

'Land Girls: Rally in Edinburgh', *The Scotsman*, 8 November 1940.

'Last of the Long-Haired Boys', *The Scotsman*, 11 January 1943.

'Mainbocher Adds Waves to Clients', *The New York Times*, 15 August 1942.

'Nazi Slur Stirred Students' Revolt' by George Axelsson, *The New York Times*, 18 April 1943.

'Nippy', *Picture Post*, 4 March 1939.

'Obituary: Bunny Roger' by Clive Fisher, *The Independent*, 29 April 1997.

'Olive Drab for WAAC Uniform', *The New York Times*, 23 May 1942.

'Our Kids are in Trouble' by Roger Butterfield, *Life*, 20 December 1943.

'Outside Olympia', *The Times*, 9 June 1934.

'Roosevelt on US Youth, From *Life*'s Correspondents', *Life*, 1 July 1940.

'Schools and Mothers Are Urged to Unite To Check Rise in Juvenile Delinquency', *The New York Times*, 19 November 1942.

'Shepheard's Hotel: British Base in Cairo', *Life*, 14 December 1942.

'Sinatra is Classified 4F; Has Punctured Eardrum', *The New York Times*, 10 December 1943.

'Sub-Deb Clubs: The Midwest is Full of Them', *Life*, 2 April 1945.

'"Sweater Girls" Held to Have Won Victory By Pact Giving 75% Choice of Factory Garb', *The New York Times*, 4 April 1943.

'Swing Bands Blare in Carnegie Hall', *The New York Times*, 7 October 1939.

'Swing Loses Lead Among Best-Selling Records', *Life*, 18 December 1939.

'Swing: What is it?' by Gama Gilbert, *The New York Times*, 5 September 1937.

'The American Red Cross', *Harper's Bazaar*, March 1945.

'The Call for Women', *Picture Post*, 13 May 1939.

'The Columbus Day Riot: Frank Sinatra is Pop's First Star' by Jon Savage, *The Guardian*, 11 June 2011.

'The Director of the WAAC in Uniform', *The New York Times*, 19 June 1942.

'The Girl Partisan of Chartres', *Life*, 4 September 1944.

'The Sleepwalkers', *Picture Post*, 3 December 1938.

'The WAACs' by Toni Frissell, *Vogue*, January 1943.

'Trying on a Lipstick', *Picture Post*, 7 October 1939.

'Uniform Shop Aid to Service Women', *The New York Times*, 31 October 1942.

'WAAC Uniform Cost Tops All In Service', *The New York Times*, 2 July 1942.

'WAVES Uniforms Stir Enthusiasm at "Fashion" Show in Washington' by Nona Baldwin, *The New York Times*, 29 August 1942.

'*Weymouth Journal*: It was Hershey Bars and Yanks, and then D-Day' by John Darnton, *The New York Times*, 17 March 1994.

'What is a Bobby Sock?' *The New York Times*, 5 March 1944.

'Women do Big Job in an Arms Plant' by Kathleen McLaughlin, *The New York Times*, 10 June 1941.

'Zoot Suits', *Life*, 21 September 1942.

Archive Material and Interviews

Author Interviews

Vicki McIntyre, granddaughter of May Lamont, January 2018.

Mona McLeod, December 2017.

BBC People's War Project

'A Land Girl's Lot: In Nottinghamshire', Doris Una Ball, WW2 People's War, bbc.co.uk

'Breaking the Code: "A WAAF at Bletchley"', Kathleen Kinmonth Warren, WW2 People's War, bbc.co.uk

'My Memories of the Women's Land Army', Amelia 'Mitzi' Edeson, WW2 People's War, bbc.co.uk

'NAAFI Days in Woodhouse Eve', Gladys Saunt, WW2 People's War, bbc.co.uk

'Second World War in the WRNS', Maxine Woodcock, WW2 People's War, bbc.co.uk

'The Lumberjills of Scotland', WW2 People's War, bbc.co.uk

'The Swing of a Lantern', Kay Riddell, WW2 People's War, bbc.co.uk

'Women's Land Army', Emily Braidwood, WW2 People's War, bbc.co.uk

'War Years in the Timber Corps', Barbara Beddow, WW2 People's War, bbc.co.uk

Imperial War Museum

'Material Gathered: Women in Uniform', Hazel L. Williams, WAAF, September 1942–September 1945, Imperial War Museum.

Oral History, Ronald Berry, Imperial War Museum.

'Private Papers of Miss Stephanie Batstone', Imperial War Museum.

Library of Congress, USA
Alvin Dickson, Library of Congress Veterans Project.
Claude Woodring, Library of Congress Veterans Project.
Corbin B. Willis Jr, Library of Congress Veterans Project.
Jeanne M. Holm, Library of Congress Veterans Project.
Marie Brand Voltzke, Library of Congress Veterans Project.
Sally Hitchcock Pullman, Library of Congress Veterans Project.
Sam L. Boylston, Library of Congress Veterans Project.
Stanley Weinberg, Library of Congress Veterans Project.
Violet Hill Gordon, Library of Congress Veterans Project.

Miscellaneous Sources
Bhowani Junction, Letter from Miss Jean Dodd, Bombay, to George Cukor, 26 October 1954, The Margaret Herrick Library, Special Collections.
'Cap Comforters' (NAM. 1983-01-116-10), National Army Museum, Online Collection.
holocaustmusic.ort.org/politics-and-propaganda/third-reich/swing-kids-behind-barbed-wire/
Lorne Frame, Air Force: Veteran Stories, The Memory Project, WW2.
Transcript of interview with Mildred McAfee, August 1969, US Naval Institute.
'Wearing Lipstick to War: An American Woman in World War II England and France', James H. Madison, Autumn 2007, National Archives.
Warfare: Women's Land Army, May Lamont (later Smylie), Interviews at the Museum of Rural Life (September 2009), National Museums Scotland.
Warfare: Women's Land Army, Jean Macnaughton, Interviews at the Museum of Rural Life, National Museums Scotland.

Index